Berg Publishers Ltd
24 Binswood Avenue, Leamington Spa, CV32 5SQ, UK
Schenefelder Landstr. 14K, 2000 Hamburg 55, W. Germany
175 Fifth Avenue, New York, NY 10010, USA

First published 1986
Copyright © Berg Publishers Ltd 1986

British Library Cataloguing in Publication Data

Concepts of health, illness and disease: a
    comparative perspective.
    1. Social medicine
    I. Currer, Caroline   II. Stacey, Meg
    362.1   RA418

    ISBN 0–907582–18–4
    ISBN 0–907582–19–2 Pbk

Library of Congress Cataloging-in-Publication Data
Main entry under title:

Concepts of health, illness, and disease.

    Bibliography: p.
    Includes index.
    1. Health attitudes—Cross-cultural studies—
Addresses, essays, lectures.   2. Diseases—Public
opinion—Cross-cultural studies—Addresses, essays,
lectures.   3. Health attitudes—Addresses, essays,
lectures.   4. Diseases—Public opinion—Addresses,
essays, lectures.   I. Currer, Caroline.   II. Stacey,
Margaret.   [DNLM: 1. Cross-Cultural Comparison.
2. Disease.   3. Health.   4. Sociology, Medical.
WA 30 C744]
RA427.C619   1986   614.4   85–20759

    ISBN 0–907582–18–4
    ISBN 0–907582–19–2 (pbk.)

Printed in Great Britain by Billings of Worcester

Concepts of Health, Illness and Disease
A Comparative Perspective

Concepts of Health, Illness and Disease

A Comparative Perspective

Edited by
CAROLINE CURRER *and* MEG STACEY

BERG

Leamington Spa / Hamburg / New York

Contents

Tables and Figures

Acknowledgments

Grateful acknowledgement is made to the following authors and publishers for permission to reproduce material used in this volume:

Arthur Kleinman (1978) 'Concepts and a Model for the Comparison of Medical Systems as Cultural Systems', *Social Science and Medicine* vol. 12, pp. 85–93, © Pergamon Press Ltd; Paul U. Unschuld (1978) 'Die Konzeptuelle Überformung der Individuellen und Kollectiven Erfahrung Von Kranksein', Sonderdruck aus *Krankheit, Heilkunst, Heilung* Verlag Karl Alber, Freiburg, München; Claudine Herzlich and Janine Pierret (1984) '*Malades d'hier, malades d'aujourd'hui*', Paris, Payot; Hilary Graham and Ann Oakley (1981) 'Competing Ideologies of Reproduction: Medical and Maternal Perspectives on Pregnancy', in Helen Roberts (ed.) *Women, Health and Reproduction*, London: Routledge and Kegan Paul; Gilbert Lewis (1975) *Knowledge of Illness in a Sepik Society*, LSE Monograph on Social Anthropology no. 52, London: The Athlone Press; Gilbert Lewis (1976) 'A View of Sickness in New Guinea', in J. B. Loudon (ed.) *Social Anthropology and Medicine*, ASA Monograph no. 13, London: Academic Press; Gilbert Lewis (1980) *Day of Shining Red*, Cambridge: Cambridge University Press; Allan Young (1976) 'Internalising and Externalising Medical Belief Systems: An Ethiopian Example', *Social Science and Medicine* vol. 10, pp. 147–56, © Pergamon Press Ltd; Joan Ablon (1973) 'Reactions of Samoan Burn Patients and Families to Severe Burns', *Social Science and Medicine* vol. 7, pp. 167–78, © Pergamon Press Ltd; Jeremy Seabrook (1973) *The Unprivileged*, Harmondsworth: Penguin Books Ltd; Cecil G. Helman (1978) '"Feed a Cold, Starve a Fever": Folk Models of Infection in an English Suburban Community and Their Relation to Medical Treatment', *Culture Medicine and Psychiatry* vol. 2, pp. 107–37, © D. Reidel Publishing Company Ltd; Roisin Pill and Nigel Stott (1982) 'Concepts of Illness Causation and Responsibility: Some Preliminary Data from a Sample of Working-Class Mothers', *Social Science and Medicine* vol. 16, pp. 43–52, © Pergamon Press Ltd; Magdalena Sokolowska (1973) 'Two Basic Types of Medical Orientation' *Social Science and Medicine* vol. 7, pp. 807–15, © Pergamon Press Ltd.

In addition, we should like to thank Jennifer Lorch for her help with translation, Alan Currer for help with the bibliography, and the Arts Librarians of the University of Warwick for help in tracing French sources. The manuscript was typed by Jeanne Summers and Fiona Stone, to whom we are most grateful.

Acknowledgments

In shortening extracts, the following conventions have been used:

. . . in the text indicates that material has been omitted within an original paragraph.

. . . . between paragraphs indicates that material in excess of a paragraph has been omitted.

In reprinting the articles the conventions and spellings of the original have been brought into line with the publisher's house style.

CAROLINE CURRER
MEG STACEY

Introduction

Increasing interest has been shown over the last decade in concepts of health and illness and in what the systematic basis of the variations which are exhibited might be. This interest seems to derive from a number of sources. In health care delivery it is suggested that some at least of the manifold problems of communication between doctor and patient derive from their differing conceptualisation, or that professionals mistake alternative conceptualisation for ignorance or wilful misunderstanding, or that medical dominance eventuates in the only acceptable understandings of illness being those which are conceptualised in the mode of biomedical science.

Another source of interest has been the increasing understanding of the health problems of the 'third world' and a new awareness of the relevance and, indeed, utility of indigenous healers and healing. Any thorough-going critique of health care planning and administration requires the imaginative consideration of modes of healing based upon conceptualisations alternative to the contemporary dominant mode. Steven Feierman (1979) has described 'plural healing systems' where a variety of modes of health knowledge, practice and practitioners exist side by side in a society. Where there is such plurality, members have choices, both of which concepts to accept, to 'believe in', and of which healers to seek help from.

In much of the Western world, biomedicine is dominant and has a status in relation to the state analogous to that of the established Church of the medieval period. However, in Western societies not all sections of the population share the concepts associated with that body of knowledge and its modes of practice. Members also have access to, and possibly accept concepts derived from, other cosmologies or other modes of healing, and also from earlier formulations of biomedicine itself.

There are terminological difficulties in attempting to look at concepts of health and healing over time and space which, upon

1

inspection, turn out to conceal conceptual or philosophical problems. These are made plain when one tries to translate terms from one language to another and yet convey the concepts correctly. Mark Field and Alphonse d'Houtaud have become aware of this in translating d'Houtaud's French work into English. Sometimes a concept does not have an English equivalent as, for example, to 'feel well in one's skin'. Such phrases can only be translated literally. Caroline Currer (Ch. 9) discusses the conceptual as well as the terminological difficulties of translating test questions from English into Pukhto. In Arthur Kleinman's and Paul Unschuld's papers the distinction between 'illness', a subjective state experienced by the sufferer and possibly recognised by others in consequence of her/his demeanour, and 'disease', a pathological condition recognised by biomedicine, is drawn out. This is an important distinction when relating medical and lay conceptualisations to each other; it is one that can be made in German as it can be in English. In Polish it is not possible (Sokolowska *et al.*, 1975).

Translating Paul Unschuld's paper drew other distinctions sharply to mind. The resolution in terms is indicated in the note on p. 51. There is a need to have clear terms for the varieties of healing systems which are found; these terms should not imply that one system is morally or empirically better than another, and yet the terms should indicate the differences. Carol MacCormack (1982: iv–ix) has discussed some of the problems involved. The most difficult problems perhaps surround the description of the healing system which dominates in advanced industrial societies and which has spread world-wide. To call it 'modern' is inappropriate, for there are other modes which not only exist but which are innovating in the contemporary world. To call it 'Western', is hardly appropriate since it is now practiced world-wide. 'Medicine' *tout court* is inadequate because there are other medical systems. There is a case for using 'scientific medicine' as Carol MacCormack decides to do, since it can be argued that what is significantly different about this healing system and its knowledge is that its basis is one of systematic science. Yet there are problems here too. There is a risk that in calling this system 'scientific' one is by inference denying any logical basis to other systems of healing knowledge, which would be patently unreasonable. Furthermore, the sharp distinction heard in English between scientific study and other forms of systematic study does not exist in all languages. It was this distinction in English which was exploited by Sir Keith Joseph when he denied the term 'science' to the social sciences and had it dropped from the title of the erstwhile Social Science Research Council. In German, for example, the word for science is *Wissenschaft*, a word which also means learning, knowledge and scholarship. Distinctions are made between 'exact' sciences, 'natural' science and the arts and humanities by the use of appropriate adjectives (*exakte-, natur-, philologische-historische-*) with *Wissenschaft* (Cassell, 1964). Other healing systems have modes which differ from that which is associated with laboratory-based sciences. Such different systems are not necessarily illogical in terms of what they set out to do.

Inevitably, there are variations of usage in the papers that are included in this volume, drawn as they are from a variety of different conventions and languages. In our writing, Caroline Currer and Meg Stacey have agreed upon a convention which seems to us to be the best solution to a difficult problem. We use 'healing system' or 'health-care system' and 'healing' and 'remedy' as the most generic terms. These encompass all modes from those which some would call magical to those which the same people would call scientific. We have been mindful of Robin Horton's (1971) analysis. Further, we have adopted the term 'biomedicine' to describe the system which developed in the West and which calls itself 'scientific'. We have not yet traced the origins of this term, but we first picked it up in Arthur Kleinman's writings. Our usage seems consistent with his (see p. 43, this volume). We have espoused it because it seems most accurately to describe the nature of what we have in mind: a healing system which is based upon a biological understanding of the human being and which stresses these aspects above others. It may perhaps be felt by some to encompass psychiatry less well. We would, however, claim that most of psychiatry rests heavily upon a biomedical model of human suffering and also upon chemotherapy. It is in this that it contrasts sharply with other modes of handling mental distress and is in this sense quite clearly a branch of biomedicine.

The Purpose of This Book

Our intention has been to draw together some of the many contributions which have gone into the debate about lay and professional concepts of health and healing. We hope thereby to present readers with some of the key issues in a relatively small compass.

In this our aim has been two-fold. Firstly, we have tried to give the reader a feel of the range of work relating to concepts of health, illness and healing, drawing upon a variety of academic traditions. In selecting papers or extracts for inclusion, we have tried to cover a diversity of foci and methodologies as well as drawing on work from a range of cultures and societies, in geographical and historical senses. We have included some work not presently available in English: Paul Unschuld, Claudine Herzlich and Janine Pierret, Alphonse d'Houtaud and Mark Field, which last has been prepared by them from an original paper of Alphonse d'Houtaud's (1981). Two pieces have been written especially for this volume: the paper by Meg Stacey (Ch. 1) and that by Caroline Currer (Ch. 9). In the case of extracts from Jeremy Seabrook and, most particularly, Gilbert Lewis, material has been juxtaposed (with the author's consent) in a new way to sharpen the themes we want to bring out.

We hope that readers may find this collection a starting point from which to follow through aspects of the debate of interest to them. We also hope that they may gain a more rounded view than is presently available in any one volume.

Our second aim flows from this last point: it is to draw attention to important themes which run through the literature and are raised in different ways by the pieces presented here. For example, the theme of responsibility for illness is a recurring one. Roisin Pill and Nigel Stott address it directly. Responsibility is also discussed in different contexts: by Gilbert Lewis writing of the Gnau, a Sepic people from Melanesia; Joan Ablon discussing Samoans living on the west coast of the USA; Cecil Helman, whose informants live on the outskirts of contemporary London; Jeremy Seabrook writing of boot workers in early-twentieth-century England; Caroline Currer recounting the understandings of Pathan women living in late-twentieth-century England; as well as by Paul Unschuld in his wide-ranging survey.

The contributions also represent a variety of methodologies, from the ethnographic, in the work of Gilbert Lewis, Joan Ablon and Caroline Currer, for example, to the highly structured and statistical approach of the work of Alphonse d'Houtaud among the population of Lorraine. But this is not all: methodology is itself an issue. Arthur Kleinman (pp. 40–1) explicitly raises the question of what is necessary methodology for cross-cultural study, an issue which Caroline Currer had to face in her work (pp. 185–9). She raises issues about the nature of scientific knowledge and of science itself, which are also discussed by Magdalena Sokolowska (Ch. 14) and Meg Stacey (Ch. 1) and are implicit in the two images of pregnancy presented by Hilary Graham and Ann Oakley (Ch. 5). Alphonse d'Houtaud's work in this volume is directly concerned with a methodological issue (Ch. 12).

We have attempted to arrange the contributions in the following way. First come those chapters — by Meg Stacey, Arthur Kleinman, Paul Unschuld and Claudine Herzlich and Janine Pierret — which take a wide view of the field and in various ways seek theoretical explanations or useful taxonomies. Then comes a paper by Hilary Graham and Ann Oakley which focuses on gender differences in conceptualisation, especially as these have been enshrined in obstetric knowledge and practice and divide the professional from the lay person. A series of contributions follow which have been chosen because of their exemplification of societies with marked differences in the nature of their division of labour overall and, in particular, of their division of health labour. The peoples focused on also range widely in the historical sources of their healing knowledge. Thus Gilbert Lewis' account of the Gnau analyses a society with little overall differentiation of labour, save between the sexes. Allan Young, in describing the Amhara of Ethiopia, is writing of a people who have had many thousands of years of contact with elaborated healing systems as well as retaining a flourishing folk sector (in Arthur Kleinman's terms). Joan Ablon's account of the behaviour of Samoan burns patients set in a highly complex society where healing is dominated by biomedicine contrasts biomedical expectations of patients' illness behaviour with how the badly burned Samoans actually did behave. Caroline Currer's account of Pathan women living in an English industrial town shows how mistaken assumptions about the health and supposed suffering of a minority migrant people can be. Jeremy Seabrook's account of the folk cosmology of the Northamptonshire bootworkers is followed by the collusion between contemporary general practitioners and their patients in the way they describe and understand illness as analysed by Cecil Helman. Alphonse d'Houtaud's study is also strongly empirically based, being about the way French people in Lorraine conceive of health and how their conceptions vary according to various socio-economic factors. Roisin Pill and Nigel Stott's empirical study is concerned with the lay concepts of mothers in part of Wales. Finally, Magdalena Sokolowska brings us back to a more abstract level in discussing the distinction, which has already emerged in a number of the studies, between the individual and the collective conception of health and illness. The book concludes with an overall critique of the collection.

Seeing it as a whole, we are conscious that the volume does not constitute a complete overview of this developing field. In particular, we are aware of having avoided the difficult issues revolving around concepts of handicap and disability. Our more empirical extracts have a bias to acute illness and trauma. However, as editors our aim has been to provide a helpful introduction to students, both undergraduate and postgraduate, who are new to the area. We hope this book will also be useful to established scholars who may already be familiar with one part of the literature but are less aware of work in disciplines other than their own. Social and cultural anthropology, sociology, history, statistics and journalism are all represented here. We hope, by the juxtaposition we have arranged, that we will whet readers' appetites and stimulate discussion. In our view the solution of many problems, both academic and practical, associated with the conceptualisation of health, healing and illness can only come about by the dissolution of some of the conventional boundaries between disciplines. The challenge which is inherent in this volume is how to relate work across cultures and academic traditions to further our understanding of the problems involved in thinking about health, illness and healing.

1

'The first of the four papers which, in differing ways, attempt an overview of the field, is by Meg Stacey. She is interested in relating concepts of health and illness to the structure of the society in which they are found, particularly to the division of labour, the position of members, their life experiences and their material and psycho-social interests. She uses numerous examples of field studies to work out her argument, seeing the propositions as ones which can be found at the micro level and related to the macro. She suggests that the dominant concepts are those of the successful and powerful, whose interests they serve.

An initial statement of assumptions enables the reader to critically consider starting points which are often not made explicit, and to question the extent to which these same assumptions might or might not underlie the work of other authors. The bulk of the paper is then taken up with a review of the empirical work of others within the suggested framework, thereby demonstrating its value as a way of approaching this complex field and of arranging findings that arise from a variety of disciplines and may be quite disparate. The work referred to includes that of other contributors to this volume, but also ranges far wider, drawing in selections that we should have liked to have included had space allowed, as well as work more tangential to our central theme but which relates to it. Thus the paper offers a fitting way into this collection overall; a framework which focuses on social rather than cultural factors influencing concepts (thereby reflecting its author's interests and background) and which indicates a fruitful way in which the increasing and varied contributions to this field might be arranged and understood.

Eds.

MEG STACEY

Concepts of Health and Illness and the Division of Labour in Health Care[1]

My interest in concepts of health and illness has to do with the way
they relate to the division of labour. The fully fledged analysis
which I would like to see would be one in which the healers, where
they exist as specialists, would be located in the structure of the
society to which they belong; located also in the conflicts within
that society which are associated with the form of the state (of
whatever type), the mode of production, the social class and gender
orders and other social relationships. These data would be related to
the health and illness concepts to which healers and their clients
subscribe, and the concepts themselves would be related to the
cosmologies and ideologies of the society.

The evidence available for such an enterprise is increasing but
remains fragmentary. In any case, it is too vast for any one person to
contemplate. Within that, what I have been trying to do is to
illustrate some parts of what such an enterprise might look like. My
work falls into three sections, each of which represent different
avenues of exploration, and for each of which there is some empirical data available. These are:

1. Dominant conceptions and the division of labour in a society.
2. Members' social position, their life experiences and the concepts they select.
3. Concepts and members' material and psycho-social interests.
In this paper I shall mainly concentrate on aspects of 2 and 3.

My analyses are predicated upon certain initial assumptions. The
first is that for the purposes of investigation I take all value, belief
and knowledge systems to be of equal importance and validity;
initially they should be judged on their own terms and within their
own logic. Such a conceptual framework is essential for systematic

---

1. An earlier version of this paper was presented at the workshop on lay concepts of
   health and illness organised by Dr Bert Tax and his colleagues at Nijmegen,
   Netherlands, in July 1984.

analysis at both theoretical and empirical levels.[2] This means that variations in concepts of health and illness cannot be viewed merely as exotica of byegone or fading societies, or curious residual remains among eccentric groups or individuals in contemporary society, left over perhaps from the witches of old.

Allan Young (1976a) has addressed the question of how to define the field of interest of medical anthropology without using a Western medical paradigm. Robin Horton (1970, 1971) showed that there were not the great differences between Western scientific thought and African thinking that Western scientists had believed. The quest for unity underlying apparent diversity, for simplicity underlying apparent disorder, for regularity underlying anomaly, is apparently universal (Horton, 1970: 342). All people at all times try to make sense of what otherwise appears as confusion around them. Theory, Horton argues, replaces common sense; so does mystical thinking replace common sense; so, we might add, does lay logic seek to replace common sense. Mystical thinking (and lay logic) are kinds of theories. Processes of abstraction, analysis and reintegration are present in all three. The differences between African mystical thought and Western scientific medicine are described by Horton as the open and closed predicaments. Mystical thinking is closed; it cannot imagine any alternative and it does not permit thinking about alternatives. Western thought is open; it is part of the scientific process that the scientist should always be looking for explanations beyond those she/he presently accepts and should be prepared to have propositions disproved. There are limitations to Horton's theory, especially with regard to the openness in practice of Western scientific thought. The point I wish to make is that Robin Horton and Allan Young both grant equal status to all bodies of knowledge, differentiating them not on criteria of their correctness or supposed efficacy but in terms of their concepts. Young (1976b) uses the terms 'systematising theory' and 'everyday thinking' to describe them where the former strives consciously for coherence and is confined to categories of culturally defined specialists who restrict their use of systematised thinking to their own professional arena and interests.

My second assumption is that all concepts of health and illness,

---

2. It is, of course, a different enterprise within any one society (one, say, in which biomedicine is accepted as the major curative cosmology) to assess the extent to which lay concepts impede or facilitate the proper use of healing services provided.

like all healing systems, are social constructions which relate to their historically specific time or period. Powerful and pervasive systems such as biomedicine I include in this just as much as more fragmentary and localised ones. My third assumption is linked with this, namely that concepts are not neutral, they are associated with actions taken and with given sets of social relations. In this I include allegedly neutral science. It follows, of course, that social scientists, like others who seek to produce knowledge, are also creatures of their time and place. They, like others, are therefore likely to find that their creations are used in the ongoing struggle of interests in their society.

Finally, I assume the unity of the human species (cf. Ginsberg, 1961: 206) such that I take all human beings to be constructing their notions of health and illness and how to handle these phenomena with reference to an essentially similar biological base. Over and above this underlying humanness there are of course great variations from one society to another in the threats to the biological organism associated with such things as climate and food supply, as well as social and economic organisation. Within any one society, individuals also have different empirical biological experiences of health and illness. What problems there are to resolve on the health and illness front therefore vary. This may well influence how members conceive them. Nevertheless, all peoples have essentially the same apparatus of mind and body with which to handle their problems.

Dominant Conceptions and the Societies in Which They are Found

Before turning to the main themes of this paper I should perhaps give some indication of my search for reasons behind the variations in dominant concepts and the societies in which they are found. In the longer work (Stacey, forthcoming) I review some examples of societies with varying modes of the division of labour, taking the Gnau (Lewis, 1975, 1976, 1980, and see extracts below, Ch. 6), the Amhara (Young, 1976b, and below, Ch. 7), and the Manus (Schwartz, 1969) as examples, using Allan Young's (1976b) notion of internalising systems and Arthur Kleinman's (1978b, and below, Ch. 3) notion of the three domains of popular, folk and professional healing systems. Here I note that the Gnau have little division of labour in their society, no specialist healers and that their notions of

11

causality and the process of illness and misfortune fit them into Young's externalising category. Kleinman's three divisions do not apply to them. However, I note also that there is a sexual division of labour, that men more often take an active healing role than women and that there is some differentiation between women's and men's health and illness experience. The Amhara, on the other hand, have what Young (1976b) calls an incomplete internalising system; healing is only partially professional and both 'physiological' and 'aetiological' explanations are found. There is no one theory of health, illness and treatment; literate and oral traditions exist side by side and have done so for two millenia. There is considerable division of labour in Amhara health care, and healers are distinguished by their healing activities. Some healers are highly trained and differentiated specialists; others are undifferentiated in their everyday lives from other workers.

The Gnau and Amhara, like many other peoples, do not distinguish sharply between illness and a wider range of misfortune. I note that the Manus (Schwartz, 1969) accept biomedicine but take it to be a low-level theory with limited explanatory powers.

I then look at the historical development of biomedicine in Europe in association with the changing division of labour in capitalist society and pay attention to the division of labour in public domain, industry, state and market-place, within the domestic domain in the patriarchal family and between the public and private domains. This historical background cannot be explored here and must be taken as understood. There are two points, however, which should perhaps be made.

The first has been made by Steven Feierman (1979) and is worth repeating. In Tudor and Stuart England there was a variety of healing systems. Within two hundred years biomedicine had become dominant. This is a somewhat remarkable history which has been explored in a variety of ways. See, for example, Ivan Waddington (1985) and Meg Stacey (forthcoming).

The second is a point which Claudine Herzlich (1973), among others, has made. As she says, there are two sets of theories dealing with health and illness: those 'based on the objective examination of physical signs of disease and theories which view health and illness as modes of relationships — equilibrium and disequilibrium — between [people] and [their] environment, involving human factors, ecological aspects and social structures' (1973: 2). This distinction is similar to Allan Young's internalising and externalising systems (see below, Ch. 7). Claudine Herzlich reminds us how, in the course of the centuries in Europe after Hippocrates, the 'body orientation' became dominant, and anatomy and physiology developed from the sixteenth century; with exploration came interest in 'strange' diseases and the development of a geography of disease. This was linked with a recognition of the connection between disease and social conditions. But when Pasteur's theories triumphed, 'although the existence of geographical factors could not be denied — there really is a geography of disease — they appeared unimportant, and research became almost wholly concerned with the study of the microbic agent itself' (1973: 3). Recently, as she points out, there has been a reaction against an exclusively ontological view of illness, and attention has been paid to psychological factors and thus to psychosomatic medicine, to cultural relativity of concepts of health and illness and to illness behaviour. In her work with Pathan women, Caroline Currer (see below, Ch. 9) found that their conceptualisation not only of what it is to be ill but how one does and should live, varied so much from the Euro-American that well-validated psychological scales could not be used in the manner intended. The ways in which these developments have taken place in Europe and America over the centuries is further developed in the work Claudine Herzlich has done with Janine Pierret — presented in *Malades d'hier, malades d'aujourdhui* (1984) — drawing upon diaries, medical writings and many other sources (an extract appears as Ch. 1, below; see also Herzlich and Pierret, 1985).

Michel Foucault (1973) has demonstrated how, within that concentration on the body that began in the sixteenth century, crucial changes in medical conceptualisation took place around the turn of the nineteenth century: there developed the new medical 'gaze', itself linked with the development of bedside medicine and the dissection of the human body, which broke old taboos and changed the way of looking and of what was seen. The developments, occurring at a particular stage of capitalism and of the class structure, changed the notion of what constitutes disease and led, not only to a new classification of disease, but also to the foundation of modern clinical biomedicine, constituted of new forms of medical knowledge, practices and institutions. David Armstrong (1983) has taken this work forward in an analysis of the changes of medical knowledge in the twentieth century. Neither Foucault nor Armstrong, however, recognise the importance of the gender order and the masculine bias, not only in the division of biomedical labour but

13

also in the biomedical knowledge itself (see Graham and Oakley, Ch. 5, below, for a contemporary example).

With regard to contemporary societies dominated by biomedicine, R. G. A. Williams (1983) has suggested that there may be resemblances of a fundamental kind across cultures and societies in the ways in which all peoples conceive of health and illness. He suggests this after comparing his findings among older people of all classes in Aberdeen with those of Claudine Herzlich's (1973) middle-class Parisians and Normans.

In the 1960s Herzlich had asked her French sample how they thought about health and illness. She was interested in their concepts in terms of Durkheim's social representations (*representations sociales*). Later Alphonse d'Houtaud (d'Houtaud and Field, 1984; and below, Ch. 12), inspired by Herzlich's study, examined the health beliefs of people in Lorraine who were presenting themselves for a health check-up. More recently again, Williams has applied these ideas to populations of the elderly in Scotland. It was a comparison of his findings with those of others, including Herzlich and d'Houtaud, that led Williams to think about similarities. This is certainly an important idea to pursue, but it is the variation in the French compared with the British concepts which interest me, bearing in mind that biomedicine is dominant in both countries and its development in France greatly influenced its development in England. The notion of health as a balance, as a state of equilibrium is much stronger in France than it is in Scotland. Nevertheless, in d'Houtaud's (d'Houtaud and Field, 1984) study the working-class French of Lorraine more often than middle-class Parisians used the notion of fit or able to work so common among the elderly Scottish and among Kristian Pollock's (1984) Nottingham respondents. A second difference relates to the way in which fatigue or weakness is conceptualised. In both samples these concepts are separated from sickness, but the French appear to make more of the upset to equilibrium associated with fatigue and to consult more for 'psychosomatic' reasons. The Scots, on the other hand, stress the inappropriateness of adopting the sick role on grounds of 'weakness'. Williams suggests that this has to do with the 'disease-centred conception of illness, and the fear of hypochondria which goes with it' (202). One could add to this the importance in that generation and nation of the Protestant work ethic.

Williams suggests also that the fee-for-service system of payment compared with the capitation fee in Britain may give comparatively more power to middle-class French patients *vis-à-vis* their doctors and so to the popular culture. Cecil Helman (1978; and below, pp. 225–7) showed differences between his older and younger patients in what was a 'cold' to be 'fed' and dealt with by self-treatment and a 'fever' to be 'starved' and reported to the doctor for treatment. Helman suggests that between his two age groups two changes had taken place. One was the introduction of antibiotics and the other the establishment of the National Health Service (NHS), with health care free at the point of delivery. I have suggested a similar explanation for the lack of moral reasons for their illness or accident offered by my third-year sociology students, compared with Irving Zola's (1975) undergraduates when asked to explain an illness or an accident to a child.

Jeremy Seabrook's (1973; and see extracts below, Ch. 10) early-twentieth-century Northamptonshire bootworkers and their families had little access to doctors. Their explanations were full of morality, and an elaborate cosmology informed their attempts to stave off illness or disaster. When access to doctors is easy and does not require immediate cash payment, such preventive systems may be less necessary. However, the authority of the doctor increases in these circumstances. My data, collected from students of varied class backgrounds, but biased to the middle class and including some mature women and men, span the past ten years. In that time the one moral injunction which was frequently referred to was 'you must go to the hospital/doctor'. This injunction has become more frequent over the decade. These changes are consistent with Jocelyn Cornwell's (1984) discussion of what she calls 'medicalisation' of concepts, to which I shall turn later.

Kristian Pollock (1984: 245) has drawn attention to the repeated finding that social status differences in attitudes reported from the US are not echoed in British studies (e.g. Blaxter and Patterson, 1982; Wadsworth *et al.*, 1971). This discrepancy may also be associated with the existence of a universal health service free at the point of delivery. It would seem, therefore, that not only are national cultures involved in some sense but that the ordering of the professional–client relationship — specifically in this case in terms of payment to the doctor and the mode of health care delivery — also has an influence on health concepts and health behaviour. But perhaps we can understand better what happens in societies with highly elaborated divisions of labour if we turn to look at differences within those societies.

Members' Life Experiences, Social Position and Their Concepts

As part of a detailed study of the development of medical knowledge, John Gabbay (1982) has looked at the understanding and treatment of asthma. He has shown how extremely difficult it is to trace the development of medical knowledge, because of the difficulty of achieving a detached position but one in which we can be at all certain that we are talking about the same condition over time.[3] What he does make plain, however, is the symmetry between the way in which an illness is conceptualised and understood and the way in which a doctor sees the world and the political stances he takes therein. The case of Sir John Floyer is particularly instructive. Gabbay establishes upon inspection of Floyer's work that his main concern was to fit together the best of both ancient and modern doctrines. Sensible clinical observations were ones which did that. This combination of ancient and modern was also found in his religious and political thinking. Furthermore, these can arguably be seen to be the resolution adopted by a man who '*as a result of situations in which he finds himself*, has certain beliefs, concerns, interests, ambitions, passions, pressures and tensions' which inform all of his work (1982: 41, emphasis in original). Floyer was the son of a family of seventeenth-century social climbers.[4]

A conceptual symmetry which I suspect is of the same kind has recently been remarked upon by Jocelyn Cornwell (1984) in a study of the concepts of health and illness found among a sample of working-class women and men in Bethnal Green, the area of East London made famous by the studies of Michael Young and Peter Willmott; since those days much changed because of the demise of many of the London docks. It is an area in which many small

3. John Gabbay (1982: 23) argues that, however objective medical accounts of disease appear to be, they enshrine their authors' subjective cultural views; but he also argues that it is impossible to discover how inevitable the process is. An examination of the treatises on asthma over 300 years showed that physicians always claimed their theories were timeless and scientific, yet they rarely were. He argues that three points have been established: first, however convincingly physicians portray the rationality of medicine, we cannot take it on trust; second, we need to look further afield than medical writings themselves to explain medical theories and therapies: third, nevertheless, the traditional view of medical knowledge remains exceptionally successful (1982: 29).
4. As well as drawing out this conceptual symmetry between world view and medical concepts, John Gabbay notes a lack of symmetry between the concepts physicians held and the treatments they gave. Many espoused new explanations for asthma but continued to treat as before.

businesses abound and in which people do not have much control over their working lives. Yet Cornwell found that they took upon themselves the injunction to work hard and make the most of themselves regardless of the work they were doing and their lack of autonomy in it.

> There is a direct parallel in the attitude they adopt towards their health. They experience themselves as having very little control over whether or not they are healthy, and yet they take seriously the idea that having the 'right attitude' is the passport, if not to good health, at least to a life that is tolerable. The moral prescription for a healthy life is in fact a kind of cheerful stoicism, evident in the refusal to worry, or to complain, or to be morbid. [Cornwell, 1984: 129]

It was important for her respondents to prove the 'otherness' of the illness, a recognisable, separate entity which had 'happened' to them but for which they were not personally responsible. Illness must be legitimated, and the best legitimation was a medical diagnosis; this solved the moral difficulties of illness. Recognisable medical categories of illness were either 'normal' (i.e. common-place, medically successfully treatable) or 'real' illness (i.e. an unusual or severe illness on the edges or beyond successful medical treatment). Conceptual difficulties were created by health problems that were not illness. These problems medicine does not treat or its treatments are only partially successful. Such illnesses are thought to be connected in some way to the sufferer's personality, age or way of life; that is, they are problems whose 'otherness' cannot be taken for granted. Echoes of this concept emerge in Kristian Pollock's (1984) Nottingham work, to which I shall turn later.

Cornwell distinguished the 'public' from the 'private' accounts which people gave of their illnesses. Public accounts were preoccupied with moral aspects. The force of these moral accounts is being weakened by the process of medicalisation (which she uses to describe the interaction between common sense and scientific legitimation in which the dominant part is usually taken by the latter). Medicalisation in this sense is proceeding in this population. Private accounts, on the other hand, focus 'on the material concerns and practical constraints which intrude into matters of health and illness' (1984: 194). All private accounts were of illness; none were of health.

In public accounts the rules of behaviour were those applied to employment. 'Good' people are hard-working, cheerful and stoical, and if they feel ill, they prefer to 'work off' their symptoms. Malingerers are 'bad' and may also be hypochondriacal and waste valuable medical resources. In private accounts the three types of illness were only one aspect of a complex set of relationships relating to unwellness. Despite individual variations, three factors regularly occurred: employment position; position in the sexual division of labour; and past experience of health and welfare. Health hazards at work (e.g. the dust experienced by woodworkers) were experienced by men aware of the risks but proud that they had the strength, stamina and masculinity to withstand the conditions. Men might 'work it off' but at home they 'gave in' and expected their wives to cosset them. Women who were wives and mothers accommodated their symptoms to keep going, to 'carry on' and 'do what you've got to do'. They would modify their work schedules to keep the essentials going; if they could not contain their symptoms they readily consulted a doctor, hoping for treatment so that they could 'get back on their feet' and look after the children (cf. Pathan women, Currer, below, Ch. 9). These are interesting in-depth data to add to those analysed by Constance Nathanson (1975, 1977).

Consistent with the data of Cecil Helman (1978), Mildred Blaxter and Elisabeth Patterson (1982) and Mildred Blaxter (1981), the older members of Jocelyn Cornwell's sample (who grew up before the NHS) were more reluctant to use the health service. They also attached more significance to moral calibre compared with younger people, who attached more importance to external factors such as germs, viruses and social stress. Cornwell reminds us of the history of poverty experienced by these people in their youth and early adult life (cf. Seabrook, 1973) and suggests it is not only the NHS but also the welfare state more generally which is a distinguishing factor.

Health and Illness Concepts, the Biological Base and Professional and Lay Behaviour

Cornwell related health and illness concepts to the life experiences of a small subsection of British society. Pollock's (1984) work, on the other hand, focuses more upon how biological differences in perceived illness are related to respondent's conceptions. Her work also sheds further light on lay and professional differences in concepts of health and illness and related behaviours.

18

Pollock's study is based on quite intensive work with three groups of English lay people from around Nottingham: schizophrenia sufferers and their families; multiple sclerosis (MS) sufferers and their families; and a group of 'ordinary' families with no chronic patients among them.[5] As illness conditions, MS and schizophrenia share certain characteristics. Both are likely to be long term, in neither case is there a sure-fire cure, and the course of each is not altogether predictable, nor is the effectiveness of any biomedical or other treatment. Cases may resist, persist or degenerate in ways which are not always well understood.

Pollock finds interesting differences in both lay and professional responses to MS, on the one hand, and to schizophrenia, on the other. She also discusses an ambiguous category of 'nervous breakdown'. In her thesis she does not pay so much attention to class or gender differences as to the differences in concept and behaviour between her two main illness groups, for the latter was an overriding finding.

The main points of interest for this paper which came out of Pollock's study are:

1. The dominance of 'illness as occupation', an activity concept.
2. The quite different way of thinking about MS compared with schizophrenia on the part of both professional and lay persons.
3. The importance in the development of concepts of the interaction between doctors, patients and patients' relatives and interactions among the sufferers and their relatives.

One major difference in the treatment of schizophrenia and MS patients was in the information their physicians gave them. MS patients as well as their families were aware of the diagnosis and the limited ability of medical practitioners to cure or control the disease. Many schizophrenia patients, on the other hand, were unaware of their diagnosis, although more of their relatives were. Many, both patients and relatives, thought the sufferer had had a nervous breakdown from which a more or less good recovery had been made. They had great faith in their physicians' ability to cure them.

We are, therefore, faced here with two conditions which medical

---

5. Kristian Pollock's (1984) research was sparked off by her participation in the WHO (1979) international study of schizophrenia. She had medical co-operation and access to patient records for her own study. Some of the schizophrenia patients in her own study she had already met in the WHO study.

science cannot heal. One might have expected that, given this, the reaction of practitioners in both cases would be similar: lacking power to heal they would retain power by withholding information. But not so, the practitioners treated each case quite differently. The physicians of the MS patients were willing to tell, but not those of the schizophrenia patients. I shall return to this in the final section.

Many MS sufferers, like sufferers from various conditions interviewed by Blaxter and Patterson (1982) and Williams (1983), did not accept that they had lost their good health, although they were suffering from quite severely handicapping conditions. Furthermore, respondents were willing to say their health was good, despite having various illnesses. (Pollock points to similarities in the work of: Dunnell and Cartwright, 1972; Wadsworth *et al.*, 1971; Hannay, 1979). The emphasis was on 'activity', 'keeping going', getting the work done. As Pollock puts it, health was 'not so much a state or condition [as] a visible expression of qualities such as strength of character or self-control, as well as providing evidence of a moderate and upright way of living'. She comments, 'It is not surprising that people are keen to believe their health is good' (1984: 28). 'Attitude of mind' was most important for respondents in avoiding illness, in restoring or maintaining health. 'Fighting the illness' (Herzlich's illness as occupation) and adopting a positive attitude were most important for MS sufferers, being mentioned twice as often by them as by the ordinary sample. 'The mind' (connected in some way with the brain but distinct from it) was important in this enterprise. Here a difficulty was seen for those with schizophrenia. They were thought to somehow have lost their mind. The need to retain this in order to fight illness was thought to disadvantage sufferers. Furthermore, schizophrenics were not held responsible for their illness. They were not thought capable of preventing or controlling it, let alone curing it. Here is a difference from Cornwell's respondents who put mental illness into the internal/ avoidable/blame category. Pollock's respondents thought some ability to fight the illness remained in the case of 'nervous breakdown'.

Pollock had not intended to study 'nervous breakdown', which she considers to be a folk illness and not a disease category found in biomedical nosology. She investigated it because many people believed it existed, that they or people they knew had suffered or were suffering from it. This included schizophrenia sufferers and their relatives who did not know the diagnosis and believed themselves to have or have had a 'nervous breakdown'.

While Pollock may be right that 'nervous breakdown' is not a recognised medical syndrome, it is a term which doctors have in the past used and which is presumably related to a concept they then held. It may well be that some of these patients' doctors had used the term, or had not denied it as an explanation when suggested by patients or relatives, given that they were almost all concealing their real diagnosis. We do not know. Such an explanation would fit with the way in which Helman (1978) has shown his general practitioner colleagues to use folk notions in discussion with patients. He has demonstrated that the general practitioners he studied not far from London were in some ways nearer to their patients in the models they used that they were to their medical schools of origin.

To return to Pollock's sample: there was less moral opprobrium in having a nervous breakdown rather than schizophrenia because in the case of a nervous breakdown the sufferer was more likely to be able to help her/himself: 'Nervous breakdown was typically thought to result from a mind that was overwrought, exhausted, disorientated, etc. Schizophrenia was thought to involve some kind of structural damage to, or organic impairment of, the brain' (1984: 173). It was possible to recover from nervous breakdown, although the person was often seen as in some way lastingly impaired or diminished because of it. The damage experienced in schizophrenia, on the other hand, was thought to be irreparable.

Claudine Herzlich (1973) distinguished three ways in which lay people conceptualise illness: as destructive, as occupation and as liberator. All of these concepts were present among Pollock's respondents. Some of Herzlich's respondents thought of illness as destructive; they were active people who thought of themselves as indispensable. All their life was located in the social world; illness imposed a retreat from this and 'desocialised' them. When ill, such people experienced inactivity, dependence and social exclusion as intolerable and destructive; no solution could be found in illness (1973: 108). They were dead, although they remained alive (1973: 109). This led to behaviour which was unacceptable to their carers. These respondents initially took a view of omnipotence with regard to illness, such that they carried on working and denied its existence. When unable to deny it any longer, they swung to a position of total impotence. Conceptualising illness as destructive, Herzlich concludes, is characterised by social deviance, personal annihilation

21

and powerlessness over one's physical condition, all being involved together (1973: 112). Denial and passivity are both possible responses to this state of affairs.

This concept of illness contrasts with the second which Herzlich identified; namely, illness as liberator. As in the case of illness as destructive, a main characteristic is that illness is desocialising. But in this case illness is a pleasant and valuable experience simply because it takes one out of the normal social ruck: one can withdraw and there find oneself. The limitations of this conception derive from the harsh realities of society: the invalid can only enjoy solitude and desocialisation so long as her/his associates cooperate.

Herzlich's third category was that of illness as occupation, a category which keeps cropping up in British and Anglo-Saxon studies. This conceptualisation involves an admission of the state of illness, of recourse to professional advice, but also, critically, the active involvement of the patient in achieving the desired goal of recovery. There is no desocialisation: the patient sees her/himself as one among many others who have similar problems to deal with.

While all three of these concepts of illness were present among Pollock's respondents, it was consistent with their normative view of health that the dominant norm was to see illness as an occupation: the appropriate response was for the patient to struggle actively to regain health or in chronic illness to keep going. Pollock, along with professional and voluntary workers, saw a failure to take this attitude as a failure to adjust to MS. Few of her respondents used the notion of illness as liberation: some from each of her three samples saw nervous breakdown as a form of escapism, an attempt to avoid difficulties and responsibilities; some MS respondents saw the adoption of a passive and dependent attitude and the ready acceptance of help as 'giving in'. A small number of MS sufferers, who wished they did not know their diagnosis and concealed it from others, had a negative image of the illness and felt there was nothing to be done about it. These were those who saw illness as destructive and whom Pollock, herself partaking of the dominant norm, saw as 'badly adjusted' to their illness. These did not take part in self-help groups.

The evidence we have looked at so far about social situation, including illness experience, seems to suggest that one reason for the concepts and explanations which people espouse is that, from those available in the culture, they select the ones which fit their life circumstances. They select concepts which help them to understand

and cope with their health problems and those of others, and which help them to retain their essential humanity and dignity. This seems to apply to professionals as well as to lay people. There is more than one version of the biomedical model, just as there is more than one popular or folk model.

The Relationship Between Concepts and Material and Psycho-Social Interests

There are some questions to be asked about the way in which interests are involved — the vested interests of individuals or groups. How far can the notion of a link between material or other interests and concepts go to explain the differences in conceptualisation of MS and schizophrenia evidenced in Pollock's study? First of all, why did physicians tell their diagnosis to MS patients and not schizophrenics? We can only guess because the evidence is indirect. The crucial variable to my mind (Pollock does not discuss this) is that in the case of MS the physicians understand quite clearly the physiological changes which are the cause of the suffering. It made sense to them in their own biomedical terms. They had knowledge which they felt they could and should honestly convey; they were not in doubt or disagreement among themselves. They were dealing with a biomedically definable condition for which, unhappily, up to now no solution has been found, although more amelioration is possible than some of Pollock's respondents gave credit for. (After all, physicians deal with many such conditions, and they know, what lay people mostly do not appreciate, that knowledge of cause does not automatically lead to power to cure.) Schizophrenia is a different matter. The syndrome is well recognised, although perhaps there is less agreement as to whether it is one or more conditions. What gives rise to the condition remains at best in dispute and at worst mysterious. Indeed, what 'it' is probably remains unclear. Physicians in this case are in a hazardous position to speak out. They have at least one unguarded flank they might expose.

It may have been that doctors' interest as human beings were also involved; their wish, shared with other human beings, was to guard their essential humanness. I suspect that medical practitioners and scientists espouse some of the notions of the differentness of mental from physical illness expressed by Pollock's lay respondents. That hypothesis would be worth testing. In practice, withholding information left their patients vulnerable. Armed with their diagnosis, MS patients set out to find everything they could about their condition. Schizophrenia patients could not do that nor could their relatives. Furthermore, Pollock argues, the belief of many schizophrenia sufferers and their relatives that the patients' illness was a 'nervous breakdown' led them to apply a most inappropriate model to the illness and reduced the patients' and the families' coping ability. Physicians may have honestly believed that it was better not to tell schizophrenia patients or they may have acted self-interestedly. Either way, it appears to have been against the interests of the patients and their relatives.

There seem to be interests involved too in the lay conceptualisation of illness. Problems arise, for example, in the conceptualisation of illness as occupation and in the associated self-help movement. When the illness is very advanced it becomes increasingly hard to pursue that notion. Herzlich (1973) is clear that when she talks of illness as destructive, this is concept and not empirical reality. Yet in situations like this, perhaps the 'buck stops'. The conceptualisation comes up against the reality of the disintegrating body. Pollock remarks that the very disabled were less welcome at meetings; they presumably presented evidence of illness as destructive — unwelcome to those who conceived of it as occupation. Jan Brankaerts (1984) has reported that the Huntingdons Chorea Association in Belgium encountered a similar problem.

One is reminded of E. J. Miller and G. V. Gwynne's (1974) study of people in long-stay homes for the chronically sick, a study which they undertook at the request of some of the inmates. These homes adopted either what Miller and Gwynne call a 'warehousing' or a 'horticultural' model. Either way, they were depressing places; in the first case because the patients, who had undergone a social death already, were simply being serviced and stored until their physical death took place; in the second case there was a dominant notion of development, an idea that the patients should be encouraged to develop themselves and live full lives. Miller and Gwynne felt that this was inappropriate in the case of people who were facing a long, slow and continual reduction of their capacities, who were so severely affected that they had already been forced to withdraw from active social life. It would have been more appropriate to talk with and support the patient in their increasing disability and their inevitable death, as well as helping them to make the most of their present life.

It would seem that the 'development' attitude is associated with notions of health and illness as occupation such as Pollock found dominant in Nottingham. The 'shutting away' of the more severely disabled, the embarrassment that they create at self-help meetings, helps to preserve the norm. It is not in the interests of the able-bodied or of still-active sufferers to accept the destructive consequences of illness. These are not material interests in the economic sense but in the sense of preservation of the self.

Illness as occupation also closes off schizophrenia sufferers from the rest of the population. Schizophrenia patients were not thought by Pollock's lay respondents to be able to make use of the concept of illness as occupation, their mind and their whole being was affected, rendering them helpless. This was true of the ordinary and the MS samples, but also of most of the schizophrenia sample. There were a few patients who thought they had recovered from a nervous breakdown and who used a model of illness as occupation to account for this. They were a small minority of the sample. The notion of illness as occupation fits well with the dominant norms of a capitalist industrial society. It also fits well with whole facets of the imagery used by clinical medicine, where concepts of 'fight' and 'struggle' abound; with the ethics of curative clinical medicine, where the goal is to beat death or put it off as long as possible.

The contrast with the passive behaviour of Gnau sufferers reported by Gilbert Lewis is striking, although they are equally concerned to dodge death. In addition, there is no idea of malingering among the Gnau. One would therefore be surprised to find the concept there of illness as liberation.

In modern capitalist societies, and closely associated with the welfare state, the education system, helped by psychological testing, grades members of modern industrial societies for appropriate places in the elaborately ranked division of labour. This ranking sets some (e.g. the mentally handicapped) right outside the productive division of labour. In a similar way, the 'notion of illness as occupation', while proving useful to many chronic patients, has the effect of setting some beyond the pale and without dignity. This common lay conceptualisation that I have suggested, is consonant in broad outline with the normative ideas of the ruling élite and of many members of the medical profession.

These hypotheses relate to the nature of the division of labour in the public domain, to relationships with waged work and profit-making. There is also work to be done to develop the relationship between health and illness concepts and the sexual division of labour in the domestic domain, and the latter's interface with the world of paid work. The evidence remains fragmentary, although it is accumulating. Jocelyn Cornwell (1984), as we saw, offered some interesting insights. Gilbert Lewis (1975) seems to suggest that women's structural position in the Gnau patriarchal and patrilocal family leads them to think of health and illness somewhat differently from men and to behave differently. Hilary Graham and Ann Oakley (Ch. 5, below) reveal starkly the difference of interest as well as conceptualisation between obstetricians and their pregnant or parturient patients. This conflict has yielded a rich literature over the last twenty years. (See, for example, Kitzinger, 1962, 1979; Kitzinger and Davies, 1978; Oakley, 1979, 1980; Phillips and Rakusen, 1978; Rich, 1977).

There is evidence also that the medical profession differentiates what it sees as health and illness among women and men. Indeed, feminists have argued that medical manipulation of women's concepts about their bodies and their health has been a main way in which male domination has been sustained over the last 150 years (e.g. Ehrenreich and English, 1979; L'Esperance, 1977; Scully and Bart, 1972–73; Ruzek, 1978). It is reasonable to suppose, given the initially rigid gender order in the division of labour in health care (women nurses, men doctors), that health concepts vary not only by sex but also regarding the sexes in ways that are consonant with the maintenance of the ideology of a male-dominated society. The close connection between concepts of femininity and masculinity and concepts of health and appropriate ways of behaving in illness would seem to suggest this.

Underlying such divisions of physician and client, ranks of rulers and ruled, women and men, concepts of health and illness also have features relevant to the maintenance of human dignity which are pertinent to all members of society. This may be the fundamental and universal aspect of concepts of health and illness to which Williams (1983) referred. At the same time, it is important to note that our dominant norms seem to be maintained at the expense of some sufferers.

2

From a consideration of the way in which concepts are influenced by *social and political* factors, we turn now to Arthur Kleinman's emphasis on medical systems as *cultural* systems. His framework is different from that used by Meg Stacey in the last chapter, not only in his emphasis on the cultural rather than the structural but also in its scope. Kleinman's model and his agenda in this paper is at once wider and narrower than Stacey's. While Stacey is concerned to see healing systems and concepts of health and illness as part of the whole society, Kleinman's emphasis is much more on the medical systems themselves. He is concerned to explain the relationship between healers and healed in terms of their differing concepts, associated as he sees them with different 'sectors' of the medical system. A better understanding of these relationships will lead to improved therapeutic outcomes in his view. In this sense, Kleinman attempts a more detailed explanation than does Stacey. There are some points of similarity, however, particularly Kleinman's use of the 'popular' sector, an arena of the health-care system reminiscent of Stacey's 'domestic' or 'private' domain within the socio-political system, although Kleinman does not address issues of gender.

Kleinman distinguishes three sectors within the medical system which he calls professional, folk and popular. Empirical studies often focus on healing work and associated concepts within one or other of these sectors. The value of his model is that it relates these three within one framework, thus enabling comparisons and suggesting avenues for further research. Moreover, he points to the need for a new research methodology and terminology in investigations of the popular sector and of lay concepts. This is a suggestion endorsed by a variety of authors, some mentioned by Kleinman himself in support of this assertion, but see also Caroline Currer in this volume (pp. 185–9) and Hilary Graham's (1982) discussion of the key concept of 'coping' in her analysis of what it means to be a mother. Some of the points made in this paper are further developed in others which follow; Cecil Helman's paper, for example, discusses the moving together of professional and lay concepts in practice (see pp. 227–9).

A model is designed to be tested against new work and is essentially a tool. Only by using these terms and this framework, and thereby exploring their strengths and limitations, can we see how far they offer a useful way of describing interactions between the various sectors of a health care system and/or individual actors within them.

The paper was published originally in 1978.   *Eds.*

ARTHUR KLEINMAN

Concepts and a Model for the Comparison of Medical Systems as Cultural Systems

Introduction

The task assigned to me was to examine theories and concepts that can be used to compare medical systems as *cultural systems*. Review of the relevant medical anthropology literature, in preparation for writing this paper, revealed, with a few notable exceptions,[1] a paucity of well-developed theoretical positions on this subject which would be neatly summarised, compared and contrasted. Instead, most of the literature is taken up with empirical studies that usually do not specify the theoretical frameworks they employ, that unsystematically import concepts from social science or biomedicine, and that, as a result, are fragmented and difficult to relate. We possess a large array of empirical descriptions, but few cross-cultural comparisons, and hardly any attempts to test specific hypotheses. Here is evidence of the lack of a theoretical base, which is the reason for holding this Conference.[2]

Rather than to try to integrate and offer a critique of the few theoretical straws in the wind, frail things that they are, I shall, at

1. An outstanding exception is the work of Horatio Fabrega, which has been unrelentingly theoretical (*see* Fabrega, 1973a). But since most of his work is concerned with the relation of culture and illness, and only passingly with medicine as a cultural system, I have decided not to review Fabrega's ideas, although the model I describe builds upon certain of these. Similarly, I do not deal explicitly with the approaches of Alland (1970), Dunn (1976), Freidson (1970a), Kunstadter (1975) and Leslie (1974), which focus on other aspects of medical systems: their adaptive functions (Alland, Dunn and Kunstadter), their social structural arrangements (Freidson), and their changing (e.g. modernising) institutional structure (Leslie). But the theory I advance draws from these sources as well.

2. This paper was originally prepared for the Conference on 'Theory in Medical Anthropology,' National Science Foundation, Washington, DC, November 20–2, 1976.

the risk of appearing egocentric, present a model that I have been working with for the past five years. That model is itself an out-growth of my own field research and my reading of what relevant theory there is (Kleinman, 1973b, 1975a), as well as empirical studies. The model is an attempt to understand health, illness and healing in society as a cultural system, and to compare such systems cross-culturally.

A theoretical model of medicine as a cultural system, if it is to be useful, should specify what that system is and how it functions. It should provide a method for describing individual systems and for making cross-cultural comparisons between different medical sys-tems. It also should produce a more systematic analysis of the impact of culture on sickness and healing than is possible without such a framework.

Furthermore, a model of medicine as a cultural system will be valuable if it can (1) operationalise the concept of culture in the health domain in more precise and potentially quantifiable ways; (2) relate directly to clinical questions; (3) specify hypotheses which could be falsified against existing data or confirmed in prospective field studies; (4) provide systematic interdisciplinary translation between anthropology and the health sciences; and (5) provide a terminology that is not limited to biomedicine, but through which biomedicine can be related to other professional, as well as popular and folk, healing traditions within a broader comparative cross-cultural science of sickness and health care.

My interest here is not to convince you that this is *the* solution-framework for our field, but rather to place before you *one* type of problem-framework that we can react to, criticise and hopefully move beyond. Provisional though it be, this model does suggest at least a few of the advantages to be gained by developing a theory of medicine as a cultural system. It doubtless will also illuminate limitations, but these relate to the specific characteristics of the model, not to models for this field generically. Thus, this presenta-tion is intended to provoke participants at the Conference and readers of the proceedings to take this model apart in order to build others that will perhaps eventually provide us with a unified framework. Even if it simply provides a common set of terms useful for talking about medicine in different societies that would be an advance over the chaotic situation that now prevails. The model has been found helpful in the study of medicine in Chinese cultures and in making comparisons with medicine in the US (Kleinman, 1975a,

1975b).

A word of caution is indicated. No matter how they are construed, medical systems are *both* social and cultural systems. That is,
they are not simply systems of meaning and behavioural norms, but
those meanings and norms are attached to particular social relationships and institutional settings. To divorce the cultural system from
the social system aspects of health care in society is clearly unten-
able. The title of this paper merely reflects an emphasis on the
cultural dimension. I am sure that other participants at the Conference will make the alternate emphasis. The model described below,
which has been construed in other papers as an ecological model
relating 'external' (social, political, economic, historical, epidemiological and technological) factors to 'internal' (psycho-physiological, behavioural and communicative) processes, grounds medical
beliefs and activities in socio-political structures and in particular
local environmental settings. Again for reasons of emphasis, I shall
not focus on this aspect of the model, only note that it is consistent
with the view of medical systems as *cultural systems*. Our concern
will be to understand how *culture*, here defined as a system of
symbolic meanings that shapes both social reality and personal
experience, mediates between the 'external' and 'internal' parameters of medical systems, and thereby is a major determinant of their
content, effects and the changes they undergo.

Health, Illness and Care as a Cultural System

*Health, illness, and health-care-related aspects of societies are arti-
culated as cultural systems.* Much field research supports this thesis,
which marks a divide between the older and the newer approaches
to medical anthropology (Kleinman, 1975a; Leslie, 1976; Lewis,
1975). Such cultural systems, which I shall call *health care systems*,[3]
are, like other cultural systems (e.g. kinship and religious systems),
symbolic systems built out of meanings, values, behavioural norms
and the like. The health care system articulates illness as a cultural
idiom, linking beliefs about disease causation, the experience of
symptoms, specific patterns of illness behaviour, decisions con-

3. I use the term 'health care system' simply to underscore the health care activities
at the centre of these systems. I recognise that health system may be a better term
for general use, since it is more inclusive, indicating the preventive as well as the
healing functions these systems perform, while it is not medico-centric like the
term 'medical system'.

cerning treatment alternatives, actual therapeutic practices and evaluations of therapeutic outcomes. Thus it establishes systematic relationships between these components.

Because they are part of a cultural system, health, illness, and health care need to be understood in *relation* to each other. Health beliefs and behaviour, illness beliefs and behaviour, and health-care activities are governed by the same set of socially sanctioned rules. To examine one in isolation from the others distorts our knowledge of the nature of each and how they function in the context of specific health care systems; it also leads to errors in cross-cultural comparisons. Semantic network analysis (Good, 1977) is one method of demonstrating these linkages and their important implications for health care. Symbolic analyses have also disclosed the organisation of the health care aspects of society as a cultural system (Ahern, 1975; Gould-Martin, 1975; Harwood, 1971; Ingham, 1970; Obeyesekere, 1976; Turner, 1967a). However, it is to be expected that full appreciation of the structure and functions of this cultural system will only follow upon ethnographic studies that test specific hypotheses generated by theoretical models of the system and that use those models to focus their phenomenological descriptions.[4] We can already see this happening in field studies of medicine in Chinese culture (Kleinman, 1975a), which have become more sophisticated, in part, in response to better medical, anthropological and cross-cultural medical models. Cross-cultural comparisons either must wait for the emergence of this new kind of medical ethnography or incorporate that approach simultaneously in several different field settings. Studies of *change* in health beliefs and practices must examine changes in health-care systems.

The Structure of Health Care Systems

Most health-care systems contain *three* social arenas within which

4. Allan Young (1976a), for example, presents some researchable concepts about traditional medical systems, such as the notion that the efficacy of their healing approaches has an important 'ontological consequence', in which episodes of sickness 'communicate and confirm ideas about the real world'. This must be appreciated, he argues, if the efficacy of traditional healing is to be properly studied. This concept can be used by the medical ethnographer either to inform his phenomenological descriptions or to generate specific hypotheses about the efficacy of traditional healing which he can then set out to test. The same holds for Young's statement that withdrawal is characteristic of all sickness episodes, which is refuted by evidence from a number of societies, including our own.

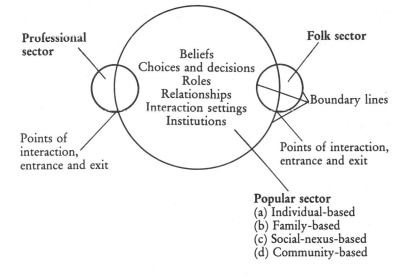

Professional sector

Folk sector

Beliefs
Choices and decisions
Roles
Relationships
Interaction settings
Institutions

Boundary lines

Points of
interaction,
entrance and exit

Points of interaction,
entrance and exit

Popular sector
(a) Individual-based
(b) Family-based
(c) Social-nexus-based
(d) Community-based

Figure 1. Health care system: internal structure

sickness is experienced and reacted to (Fig. 1). These are the *popular*, *professional* and *folk* arenas. The popular arena comprises principally the family context of sickness and care, but also includes social network and community activities. In both Western and non-Western societies somewhere between 70 and 90 per cent of sickness is managed solely within this domain (Hulka *et al.*, 1972; Kleinman, 1975b; Zola, 1972b). Moreover, most decisions regarding when to seek aid in the other arenas, whom to consult and whether to comply, along with most lay evaluations of the efficacy of treatment, are made in the popular domain. Until very recently, medical anthropology tended to de-emphasise studies of this domain, while at the same time it overemphasised studies of the folk arena. The latter consists of non-professional healing specialists, sometimes classified by ethnographers into sacred and secular groups. The professional arena consists of professional scientific ('Western' or 'cosmopolitan') medicine and professionalised indigenous healing traditions (e.g. Chinese, Ayurvedic, Yunani and chiropractic).

These arenas contain and help construct distinct forms of social reality. That is, they organise particular subsystems of socially legitimated beliefs, expectations, roles, relationships, transaction

33

settings, and the like (Freidson, 1970a). These socially legitimated contexts of sickness and care, I shall refer to as separate *clinical realities* (Kleinman, 1978a). From the standpoint of our model, these clinical realities are culturally constructed. They differ not only for different societies but also for the different sectors or arenas of the same health care system, and often for different agencies and agents of care in the same sector. Furthermore, they accurately reflect major *changes* in the underlying sociopolitical sectors of care and their ideological (cultural) structures.

The Core Adaptive Tasks of Health Care Systems

From a functional perspective, health care systems perform certain culturally (and frequently psychosocially) adaptive tasks in the face of sickness.[5] For analytic and comparative purposes, *six* core adaptive tasks can be distinguished:

1. The cultural construction of illness as a socially learned and sanctioned experience (see section on disease/illness below).
2. The cultural construction of strategies and evaluative criteria to guide choices amongst alternative health care practices and practitioners, and to evaluate the process and, most importantly, the outcome (efficacy) of clinical care.
3. The cognitive and communicative processes involved in the management of sickness, including labelling, classifying and providing personally and socially meaningful explanations.
4. Healing activities *per se*, including all types of therapeutic inverventions, from diet, drugs and surgery to psychotherapy, supportive care and healing rituals.
5. Deliberate and non-deliberate health-enhancing (largely preventive) and health-lowering (sickness producing) behaviour.[6]
6. The management of a range of therapeutic outcomes, including cure, treatment failure, recurrence, chronic illness, impairment and death.

These functions are what health care or healing is all about. Although each function can be identified in systems of health care in

---

5. A fuller treatment of the core adaptive tasks of health care systems is to be found in Kleinman, 1975a and 1975c.
6. I follow Fred Dunn on this important function, which admittedly I have neglected in previous elaborations of the model (*see* Dunn 1976).

virtually all societies for which we possess adequate ethnographic data (Kleinman, 1974, 1975a), the cross-cultural variation in the mechanisms used to fulfil these core clinical tasks is considerable. There also are obvious differences in the way certain of the tasks are performed by the entire health care system, while others are carried out by particular sectors or subsectors. Major discrepancies in the performance of specific tasks also reflect substantial differences in clinical realities.

Healing, in one sense, is the sum of the core clinical tasks of the health care system. This implies that it is the cultural system as a whole which heals. This type of healing we shall refer to as *cultural healing*. Although the healing process usually involves two related activities — the provision of effective control of the disease and of personal and social meaning for the experience of illness — cultural healing principally involves the latter. From this perspective, then, we recognise the paradox that the cultural shaping of illness as a psychosocial experience, under the influence of cultural rules which govern the perception, valuation and expression of symptoms and which determine the particular characteristics of the sick role, is itself part of the healing process. Similarly, the socially sanctioned criteria for evaluating therapeutic efficacy, another ingredient of cultural healing, can produce the additional paradox that healing is evaluated as successful because the sickness and its treatment have received meaningful explanations, and related social tensions and threatened cultural principles have been dealt with appropriately, in spite of the fate of the sick person and his sickness, as has been suggested by Turner (1967a), Douglas (1970b), Kleinman and Sung (1976) and Young (1976a). From the standpoint of the health care system model, cultural healing occurs so long as the core clinical tasks are adequately performed. When that happens, healing *must* take place; there is a 'fit' between expectations, beliefs, behaviour and evaluations of outcome. Cultural healing clearly raises basic questions about how sickness and therapeutic efficacy are to be construed, and how the core clinical tasks of health care systems are to be evaluated and compared; questions which we shall return to later in the paper. Healing, then, needs to be evaluated on different analytic levels: physiological, psychological, social and cultural.

Just as the cultural construction of the illness experience and of the criteria for evaluating therapeutic outcome are built into health care systems, so too are institutionalised conflicts between lay and practitioner views of clinical reality and evaluations of therapeutic success. These conflicts, which are heightened by increasing differentiation (specialisation of knowledge and social role) and which therefore are greatest in more modern societies and in illness episodes which cross different sectors and subsectors of the health care system, systematically produce problems for clinical care. I shall refer to this process as *cultural iatrogenesis*.[7] In other words, on the level of the cultural system, certain obstacles to effective health care, such as major discrepancies between the therapeutic goals of practitioners and patients (Cay *et al.*, 1975; Kane *et al.*, 1974), are built into the workings of the health care systems, as the next section will illustrate.

Explanatory Model Transactions in Health-Care Relationships

In each sector of the health care system, explanatory models (EMs) can be elicited from practitioners, patients and family members for particular sickness episodes (Eisenberg, 1976; Englehardt, 1974; Kleinman, 1975c).

EMs contain explanations of any or all of five issues: aetiology, onset of symptoms, pathophysiology, course of sickness (severity and type of sick role) and treatment. EMs are tied to specific systems of knowledge and values centered in the different social sectors and subsectors of the health care system. Thus they are historical and socio-political products. Health care relationships (e.g. patient–family or patient–practitioner relationships) can be studied and compared as transactions between different EMs and the cognitive systems and social structural positions to which they are attached. On the cultural level, we can view these transactions as translations between the different idioms into which the separate health care system sectors articulate illness as psychocultural networks of beliefs and experiences. Not infrequently, EMs conflict. When they do, recent evidence suggests that these conflicts impede health care (Kleinman, 1975c; Lazare *et al.*, 1975). Here

---

7. I am indebted to Charles Leslie for this term. Of course, literally 'cultural iatrogenesis' means that culture produces sickness. Although there is considerable evidence to support this notion, I use the term here in a broader sense to refer to problems in general in health care that are systematically derived from cultural factors.

communication has been shown itself to be a major determinant of patient compliance, satisfaction and appropriate use of health facilities, while cultural influences on clinical communication, when unappreciated and not responded to, have been shown to lead to substantial problems in patient care (Harwood, 1971; Snow, 1974). In terms of our model, EMs contruct different clinical realities for the same sickness episode, which in turn are reflected in discrepant expectations and miscommunication, and ultimately in poor clinical care. These conflicts reveal the underlying discrepancies in status and power between the key participants in health care relationships.

Since much of clinical communication takes place in the context of the family and lay referral system, and since, even when it occurs with practitioners, it often involves the family as well as the patient, the traditional dyadic model we employ to understand this process is inadequate and almost certainly a serious distortion of the more complex, multi-person transactions that actually occur in most of health care. For example, though the EMs of biomedicine may structure a view of clinical reality in which the sickness is located within the body of the sick person, and care is viewed as treatment of the diseased organ by the doctor, those of the popular culture may locate the problem in the family and may label the entire family as sick. The target of treatment, then, will be seen as involving considerably more than the patient's body. The doctor will be viewed as only one, and perhaps not the most important, agent of treatment. And the family–patient relationship or family–doctor relationship will be regarded as the 'real' therapeutic relationship. Similarly, patient and family EMs will lead to treatment interventions and evaluations of therapeutic outcome that most of the time have nothing to do with biomedicine, and that therefore require other than biomedical concepts for their explication.

The explanatory model concept illuminates how problems in clinical communication frequently represent conflicts in the way clinical reality is conceived in the popular, folk and professional arenas of the health care system; and, therefore, it points to the systematic entailment of these problems within that cultural system. An illustration of this process is the usually tacit but often significant conflicts between professional medical (especially biomedical) EMs that construe sickness as *disease* and lay (popular culture) EMs that construe sickness as *illness* (Eisenberg, 1976).

Disease and Illness EMs of Clinical Reality

A valuable, if still incompletely worked out, theoretical distinction in medical anthropological writings (Fabrega, 1973a) is that between *disease* and *illness* aspects of sickness. In the language of our model, disease denotes a malfunctioning in, or maladaptation of, biological and/or psychological processes. Illness, on the other hand, signifies the *experience* of disease (or perceived disease) and the societal reaction to disease. Illness is the way the sick person, his family and his social network perceive, label, explain, valuate and respond to disease.

Neither disease nor illness is a thing, an entity; instead, they are different ways of explaining sickness, different social constructions of reality. Disease is most commonly associated with the EMs of professional practitioners (modern or indigenous), where it relates to special theories of disease causation and nosology that are stated in an abstract, highly technical, usually impersonal idiom (e.g. the disease models of biomedicine or Chinese and Ayurvedic medicine). Although these EMs are frequently segregated from the general public and have traditionally involved limited access for an élite group, more and more in modern societies this knowledge has been made available to, and is used by, the laity. Illness is principally associated with the EMs of the popular culture arena of health care, where sickness is most frequently articulated in a highly personal, non-technical, concrete idiom concerned with the life problems that result from sickness. Besides the family, illness EMs are sometimes used by practitioners who employ a psychosomatic or family therapy framework, and especially by folk practitioners, who, even if they employ a technical theoretical EM, tend to couch it in the popular cultural idiom (Horton, 1967; Kleinman, 1975c; McCorkle, 1961). Support for the last category comes from the frequently documented finding that folk healers who work with cosmological explanations often proffer them in association with strikingly sensitive sociological and psychological explanations (Douglas, 1970b; Kleinman, 1978a; Turner 1967a).

Viewed from the perspective of the cultural system, health care relationships frequently are transactions between disease and illness models of sickness. Here we find the culturally construed conflict, previously mentioned, in which professional practitioners see sickness only as disease and proffer explanations that transmit technical information and treatments that are technical 'fixes', whereas patients seek not only symptom relief but also personally and socially meaningful explanations and psychosocial treatments for illness (Eisenberg, 1976). Put somewhat differently, professional practitioners talk about sickness in a sector-specific language of biological functions and behaviour, whereas patients and families, even when they incorporate terms from the former, talk about sickness in a culture-wide language of experience.[8] One reason why indigenous folk healers do not disappear when modernisation creates modern professional medical systems is that they often are skilled at treating illness (Kleinman and Sung, 1976). Indeed, we can look upon the legitimated role of social workers, psychiatrists, pastoral counselors and patient advocates, as well as folk healers, in fully modern societies such as the US as using a language of experience and treatment for illness, which would otherwise go untalked about and untreated when sickness extends beyond the context of the family into the professional biomedical domain.

Future comparative cross-cultural studies of health care systems may be able to test the intriguing hypothesis generated by this discussion that cultural healing should be a regular feature of small-scale, preliterate societies, a less regular feature of modernising societies and significantly weakened in fully modern societies, whereas cultural iatrogenesis should relate inversely to this predicted correlation. A related hypothesis is that the symbolic meanings attributed to the experience of illness are the cultural medium for the placebo effect as well as the basis for clinical management problems, and that the former is lessened and the latter heightened by social change and cultural pluralism. Other interesting hypotheses, spun off from our model, will be taken up in the final section of the paper.

Another researchable issue is whether in fully modern societies the spread of the biomedical disease model in the popular culture (Zola, 1972a) is transforming the health-care-related beliefs and expectations of that sector, so that lay people, especially in the educated middle class, are operating with a more mechanistic and less psychosocial model of clinical reality, and are accordingly more interested in technical information and interventions, and less interested in socially meaningful explanations and psychosocial interventions. To answer this question we will have to learn much

8. I owe the distinction between languages of behaviour and languages of experience to my colleague, Professor David Raskin, Department of Psychiatry, University of Washington School of Medicine.

more about the structure of popular medical rationality in developing and fully developed societies, not just amongst minority groups but also in the mainstream culture. And we will need to be able to compare and contrast popular medical rationality with both biomedical rationality and its transforms in actual clinical practice. That will obviously require a new research terminology since biomedical rationality cannot be used to study these other cognitive domains on their own terms. For example, Zola (1972a) argues that to appreciate the nature of popular medical thought, we must begin with the concept of 'trouble'. This is a broad popular category containing, amongst a range of troubles, troubles due to sickness, and linking to a broader set of management options than simply medical treatments. It also will require a new research methodology for analysing and comparing clinical realities, including biomedical versions of clinical reality. Here an autonomous anthropology of suffering and human services would offer distinct advantages not to be gained from a medical anthropology dominated by biomedical paradigms.

The EM model, unlike the research strategies found in most medical ethnographies, focuses on actual transactions between patients (and their families) *and* practitioners. It suggests that merely eliciting the ideas of the one or the other, without studying how those ideas interact, is insufficient. It is the process of interaction which discloses the real structures of knowledge, logic and relevance that operate in different health care sectors and systems, and which reveals how they are *used* in the healing process. Ethnomedical taxonomies do not provide this data, and therefore are a serious distortion of the nature and function of medical cognition. On the other hand, the EM model, because it is a model of *cognitive transactions* in health care, promises to grant us a deeper appreciation of the mechanisms through which culture influences decisions about the evaluations of treatment.

Models of communication and cognitive change, like the EM model, can be used to study pluralism in medical beliefs, choices and treatments, whose extent and significance we are only now beginning to appreciate (Kunstadter, 1975); indeed, the EM model is based on an understanding of health care systems as pluralistic systems. Such models also can be applied in studies of how medical modernisation and indigenisation affect cognition and behaviour as well as institutions (Obeyesekere, 1976). These are the kinds of questions that new conceptual models in medical anthropology need to study. Such models, like the EM framework, must be able to examine both individual as well as social dimensions of health care beliefs and actions. Neither alone gives a satisfactory analysis of sickness and healing.

But the study of explanatory model transactions in health care is only one component of the larger comparative study of clinical realities. That larger study, which almost certainly will extend and change our knowledge of the cultural context of sickness and care, requires methods which are not yet available. Those methods, given the nature of the problem, must be interdisciplinary; they must draw from ethnographic, clinical, epidemiological and social psychological sources. They must relate sociopolitical and environmental determinants to biological and cognitive processes through the medium of cultural systems of meaning. Clearly, they will require models and concepts which consider health and sickness to be the results of complex multi-factor interactions on biological, psychological and social levels, not the results of single determinants operating on only one level of analysis. Notwithstanding this early stage of development in research methods, the evolution of a more precise and complex problem-framework is an indication of the advance of theory, and also a sign that our present theories are still inadequate.

All of which suggests that this area of medical anthropology is undergoing a shift in paradigms. The old research paradigm, built by Rivers, Sigerist, Ackerknecht, Clements and other 'founding fathers' of our discipline to conceptualise medicine in 'primitive' societies, is simply no longer sufficient for integrating the more complex and sophisticated findings that are the result of an extension of our interest towards the full range of social contexts and medical systems, and towards a much wider set of concerns than the traditional biomedical issues in 'medicine' (Kleinman, 1975a). The new paradigm, whatever it be, will probably not only help us to rethink aspects of our own discipline but also to rethink medicine as well, since the medical enterprise is similarly suffering from antiquated conceptual models and the absence of new meta-theoretical exploration, especially with respect to its social involvements. For example, now that family medicine and primary care see social science as one of their basic sciences, it is appropriate to use medical anthropological ideas to help them construct a new paradigm for clinical practice. Another example would be reformulating the 'medical model', which, as it presently stands in biomedicine, is notoriously inadequate. A reformulation of the medical model ought to include medical anthropology's understanding of medicine as a cultural system, as well as our appreciation of the mechanisms by which culture systematically influences disease/illness and healing. These are illustrations of the importance of systematic translation of medical anthropological concepts into the medical field; and the reverse is equally important. New models for our field should facilitate this process of translation (Kleinman, Eisenberg and Good, 1978).

The Biocultural Context of Health Care Systems, and Its Relation to Socio-Psycho-somatic Interrelationships in Sickness and Healing

Of many other issues about health care systems which could be elaborated, their biocultural context is of special interest. Although this subject is far too large to be reviewed in this space, certain points, relevant to our model, are worth noting. Stated baldly, the cultural construction of illness as a psychosocial experience entails complex psycho- and socio-somatic processes that both feed back to affect disease and play a role in the process of healing disease and illness (Kagan and Levi, 1974; Kiritz and Moos, 1974; Mauss, 1950; Teichner, 1968). The fact that these processes are involved in the organisation of health, illness and healing as a cultural system means that the health care system helps to mediate the impact of social environmental and psychological factors on physiological processes. Various models have been advanced to explain how this occurs, including operant conditioning, social learning, information theory and others (Lipowski, 1973; Platonov, 1959; Schmale *et al.*, 1970; Werner and Kaplan, 1967). However it is accomplished, it is clear that these processes are actively involved in the relation of stress to disease (Holmes and Rahe, 1967) and the effects of psychotherapy and other symbolic therapies on physiological pathology (Frank, 1974). Incomplete as our knowledge still is, it is nonetheless essential that future studies of health care systems focus on this biosocial bridge and employ appropriate methods for assaying its significance in health, illness and health care. This argues for a strong biological anthropology component in medical anthropology (Damon, 1975), one which is concerned with the relation of culture and stress; and it also argues for the need to add a biological dimension to the cultural dimension of medical anthropological theories (Dunn, 1976; Kleinman, Eisenberg and Good, 1978; Young, 1971: 499–553). It adds further support to the view of medical anthropology as an interdisciplinary bridge between biomedical and social sciences, a bridge often acknowledged but rarely studied.

Hypotheses for Ethnographic and Comparative Cross-Cultural Studies of Health Care Systems

A comprehensive model such as this is best evaluated with respect to its applications. I have used this model to study cultural patterning of the phenomenology of depression amongst Chinese patients (Kleinman, 1977), to analyse clinical communication, to compare it for a range of types of practitioner–patient transactions (Kleinman, 1975c) and to study the efficacy (and mechanisms of efficacy) of shamans and other indigenous healers in Taiwan (Kleinman and Sung, 1976). In each instance I found the biomedical paradigm to be inadequate, and the model I have discussed more useful as a research framework. The *raison d'être* for the model is precisely to provide an alternative social and cultural model to challenge the egregiously distorting biological reductionism of the biomedical model in research and teaching (Eisenberg, 1976). Unfortunately, it is not feasible in this space to both describe *and* demonstrate the model. But the hypotheses which follow should enable the reader to assess certain of its uses.

These hypotheses, which fluctuate widely in degree of specificity and feasibility for being tested in the field, flow directly from the model and concepts that I have outlined. Some can be applied in ethnographic and comparative cross-cultural studies, and some are directly relevant to clinical and public health issues. Others are simply open-ended questions, an invitation to readers to ask specific questions about the model and concepts, or to raise more general issues about the study of medicine as a cultural system. Not surprisingly, the hypotheses reflect the interdisciplinary tug between anthropological and medical interests in our field: a source of difficulty but also of great opportunity. That tension is responsible for much of what is unique about our discipline. Rather than try to reduce or ignore it, we ought to exploit it as a basic dialectic running through our work.

Hypotheses

1. Except for those relatively few societies which lack professional (indigenous or Western) and/or folk practitioners, the health care systems of contemporary and historical societies can be described by the tripartite typology outlined above. All health care agencies, agents and functions can fit within the model. Both pluralism and change can be mapped on the model.

2. By specifying the differences in clinical realities and explanatory models for the sectors and subsectors of a given health care system, we can predict conflicts which result from their interaction. Recognition of such differences, and attempts to negotiate between the discrepant EMs of patients, families, and practitioners, should prevent major conflicts in health care transactions. Prevention of major conflicts between EMs, and the clinical realities they represent, should exert a positive influence upon patient adherence to the medical regimen, satisfaction and appropriate use of health facilities, and potentially might speed ejection from the sick role and return to normal social role and function.

3. Inter-system comparisons of clinical realities should disclose the chief mechanisms by which culture influences health care systems. Both inter- and intra-system comparisons of clinical realities should also reveal the nature and extent of historical, political, economic, technological and epidemiological influences on health care. That is, the health care system can be looked upon as a micro-record of these effects.

4. Such comparisons will demonstrate particular patterns of conflicts and dominance between sector and subsector clinical realities which are characteristic of each system, but which also show a clear pattern of influence resulting from modernisation and Westernisation. Recognition of such typical patterns may help predict (and thereby prevent) problems for health care produced by the processes of modernisation and Westernisation.

5. All clinical realities and the EMs they entail can be shown to be culture-specific, including those of biomedicine. Conversely, biomedicine does not contain culture-free clinical realities and EMs. Furthermore, clinical realities and EMs also are specific for their social structural position within the health care system. Thus, in our own health care system, for example, the conflict between medical and social deviance models with regard to mental illness, in part, must be viewed as due to their social structural specificity as

44

biomedical and sociological models, and to the underlying professional and political struggles for power that conflict implies. Resolution of this conflict cannot occur within either subsector but requires incorporation of these models into an overarching scientific framework for studying sickness and treatment across cultural system and social structural boundaries. That resolution will require major social and political change. Any candidate for that overarching framework must view medicine as cultural system, and biomedicine (or medical sociology) as only part of that system.

6. Most, and perhaps all, of the so-called culture-bound disorders can be construed as extreme examples of the general function of health care systems to culturally pattern universal diseases into culturally-specific illnesses.

7. When the EMs of patients, families and practitioners are alike, there will be improved clinical communication, fewer problems in clinical management and better patient adherence and satisfaction. Conversely, when their EMs are substantially dissimilar, clinical communication and patient adherence and satisfaction will be worse, and there will be an increase of significant problems in clinical management. Cultural healing will be more likely to occur in the former case than in the latter. Indigenous folk healers should do better than professional practitioners in clinical communication and the treatment of illness, while professional practitioners do better at the treatment of disease. When the latter are trained to systematically negotiate with patient and family EMs, and to recognise and treat illness, clinical communication and patient adherence and satisfaction should improve, and problems in clinical management should be reduced.

8. The six core clinical tasks of health care systems can be shown to produce culturally, psychosocially and biologically adaptive effects. Health care systems can be evaluated by analysing how successful they are in producing these adaptive effects. Along with this measure of their efficacy, health care systems can be compared with respect to the nature and extent of the problems for health care that they create. Their efficacy in the treatment of specific disease/illness can also be determined.

9. Evaluations of the efficacy of health care must take into account the two-fold nature of healing: provision of control for the disease and of meaning for the illness. The healing of disease and the healing of illness must be evaluated separately, if cross-cultural comparisons of the efficacy of health care are to hold any significance.

10. For ethnographic description and cross-cultural comparison, health care systems need to be treated as *local* systems. Specific types of local health care resources and the patterns of utilisation dependent on them, for example, may account for significant variation between localities. Political, economic and social determinants can produce similar local variation. Local settings are useful for field studies because they allow investigators to relate health care systems to particular environmental influences, and thereby to reconstruct the ecology of those systems. Because they are local systems, health care systems cannot be equated with an entire society. Each society possesses distinct local systems of health care. In Chinese cultural settings, for example, we find many health care systems in the same society (e.g. Taiwan or Hong Kong), and these differ from each other as well as from health care systems in other Chinese societies and in non-Chinese societies with substantial Chinese populations (Kleinman, 1975a). Thus one can make intra-societal, inter-societal but still intra-cultural, and inter-cultural comparisons of those health care systems.

11. Comparison between health care systems in different cultures will reveal significant differences in the relative size and salience of particular systems and their sectors. For example, there are differences in the kinds of problems legitimated as belonging to systems of health care or their sectors; and these differences may increase or decrease the social space they occupy. There also are differences in the extent to which health care systems perform important non-medical functions, such as social control. Comparison of health care systems in traditional, developing and fully developed societies should enable us to test the medical sociological thesis that there is a progressive medicalisation of modern societies, such that problems previously labelled moral or political are increasingly legitimated as part of the health care system, especially its professional sector (Kunstadter, 1975). This thesis runs counter to the anthropological argument that in small-scale, preliterate societies medical systems tend to serve more general (non-medical) functions than in more developed and differentiated societies (Cawte, 1974). These hypotheses are of special comparative interest because they can be examined in historical as well as in cross-cultural studies.

12. Kunstadter (1975) has hypothesised that pluralism of medical beliefs, choices and therapeutic strategies offers adaptive advantages to health care systems. Instead of producing negative effects, as some proponents of the symbolic unity of cultural systems have led

us to believe, cognitive dissonance (multiple and competing health care strategies), at least in the health care system, may well have distinct advantages for biological survival, the resolution of psycho-social tensions and the evolution of adaptive cultural strategies. The EM framework can be used to articulate this hypothesis in a more precise and quantifiable form that then can be either confirmed or disconfirmed in field studies.

13. Finally, the very fact that it has been recognised and studied as a cultural system has placed a particular bias on the anthropological study of medicine in society. This happened because most earlier interest in this subject grew out of an anthropological study of religious systems. As a result, the non-sacred aspects of sickness and treatment received little attention until fairly recently (Seijas, 1973). Ethnographers looking for a strategic focus for studying medicine as an ethnographic category tended to centre on ritual activities. That has produced considerable distortion in many ethnographies since *sickness* must be centered on in order to grasp the scope and activities of health care systems. This bias, I predict, will not be found in most future medical ethnographies (see Lewis, 1975, for an example of what is to be gained from correcting this bias). Those ethnographies, and comparative studies along with them, should rewrite the story of medicine in society: in part, because they are biomedically sophisticated; but in larger part, because they represent an advance in conceptualising and investigating medicine as a cultural system, and in so doing challenge the traditional biomedical paradigms with anthropological concepts and methods which achieve a broader and more inclusive understanding of sickness and healing in society.

3

In the preceding chapter Arthur Kleinman proposed a model which could be used in the cross-cultural study of healing systems. That model concentrated on cultural aspects and was concerned principally with the interrelationships of the explanations for illness episodes which occur in the popular, folk and professional domains of any society.

In the paper which follows, Paul Unschuld is also interested in the way in which illness is conceived, but he situates his search for explanation not only at the symbolic level but also in the nature of the society of which the ideas are a part. Like Arthur Kleinman, he is interested in the co-existence of mutually incompatible concepts, but seeks a dynamic explanation of them, tracing their development over time. He seeks to show that this plurality of conceptualisation, of systems which are mutually incompatible, is associated with the presence in the society of groups which have different ideologies. Any fundamental social change in a society will, he argues, be accompanied by fundamental change in predominant concepts of illness, since these are part of the world-view of that society, which will itself have undergone change. Older views may be sustained by a minority and new views developed by opponents of a regime.

Paul Unschuld develops these arguments by reference to ancient and modern China and Sri Lanka, and in greater detail to the Ojibwa and the Ndembu, as well as to the Occident, which he examines historically from the earliest days of Christianity. He concludes with interesting speculations about contemporary changes in the structure of biomedical knowledge and their relationship to changes in the social, economic and political structure of advanced capitalist societies, particularly with regard to where the responsibility for illness is thought to lie: in the individual, the collectivity or in particular groups.

The paper was published originally in 1978.   *Eds.*

PAUL U. UNSCHULD

The Conceptual Determination (Überformung) of Individual and Collective Experiences of Illness

Preface

Illness is to all appearances an individual and collective human experience.[1] Reactions to illness by one or more individuals have been recorded in all past or present societies that are known to us. Such reactions, as we know in certain tribal communities, may have amounted to no more than relieving minor illnesses with simple natural remedies, while those afflicted by serious illness are abandoned because they are a burden on the group since they can no longer fulfil their obligations to the community and so prevent others exercising their own duties. It is not possible to prove whether this behavioural pattern is culturally more ancient than the provision of comprehensive aid. The important point is that in most past and present-day civilisations whose history is documented, illnesses of individual members or groups were, or are, considered conditions which require help.

In this connection people have for many thousands of years looked for explanations which give a *raison d'être* for illness in its various disquieting forms. Time and again, and in many places, systems of ideas were gradually developed which tried to system-

Translated by Volker Berghahn.

1. In this article *Kranksein* has been translated as 'illness' and *Krankheit* as 'disease'. 'Medicine' has only been used for the German *Medizine* and 'medical' for *medizinische*. Otherwise 'remedies' has been used for such terms as *Arzneitmitteln* or *Heilmittel*. *Heilkunde* has been translated as 'healing' rather than 'medicine', the aim being to reserve the latter English term for 'biomedicine'. *Überformung* constituted a considerable difficulty and has therefore been left in brackets, the somewhat unsatisfactory English term 'determination' being the best solution found. The literal translation 'super-formation' does not convey the German meaning and 'over-determination' has a technical Marxist meaning not intended here. We have also preferred to use the gender-neuter term 'humanity' rather than 'mankind' [*Trans. and eds.*].

51

atise existing knowledge about the causes, the nature, the prevention and the treatment of all those conditions experienced as 'illness'. It was on this basis that both afflicted and healthy members were exhorted to do, or to avoid doing, certain things.

Subsequently, we shall explore some of the underlying reasons for the fact that humanity has adopted quite divergent conceptual systems to provide explanations of illness. In stating this, we are not merely thinking of concepts of illness which, being mutually exclusive, followed one another in history and which tried to enquire either into the ultimate causes of an individual's illness or that of a group of people. The point is that such mutually exclusive and contradictory systems often co-existed, not merely in divergent cultures but even within one and the same culture. We are therefore particularly interested in those peculiarities of medical thought which gave rise to such differences. Thus we shall ask ourselves why we encounter this conceptual pluralism in every civilisation. We also raise the question of what factors were responsible for the acceptance and predominance of concepts of healing knowledge in the course of historical development. It should be self-evident that lack of space does not permit us to do more than draw attention to a few selected explanations and factors.

The traditional explanation, particularly of the problem of the historical sequence of fundamentally divergent models concerning the nature of illness, is that surrounded by a sea of ignorance and irrationality, some scholars, working over centuries, have brought together more and more precise knowledge of how the human body is structured and how it functions under normal conditions or under conditions of illness. Progress of this kind, it is argued, has led unerringly from the early beginnings of medicine among primitive tribes, and later among the Greeks, to the astonishing results of the present. There can be no doubt that the sum total of all successful medical interventions has grown enormously since antiquity. However, it is an open question as to how far 'outdated' and 'mistaken' concepts live side-by-side with those of 'scientific truth', not only among the uneducated strata of society but also among those which may be regarded as educated. There is also the unresolved question of why modern medical concepts are convincing and acceptable for some parts of society while those same concepts are rejected or even bitterly opposed by some other social groupings. There are many examples of this in the history of several civilisations.

The nature of systems of medical ideas is interpreted differently from that of traditional history of medicine by a strand in Anglo-American cultural anthropology which has developed further some of E. Ackerknecht's work dating from the early 1940s. Ackerknecht applied Ruth Benedict's ideas to the medical systems of non-Western societies. He discovered that the medical concepts of the peoples he investigated harmonised strikingly with the broader life experiences and social arenas of these ethnic groups, and were hence culturally specific. What appeared to legitimate this view was the fact that it was based on the observation of rather undifferentiated civilisations within which each member shared the worldview of all the others. However, it remains questionable how far it is possible to transpose this notion of culturally specific conceptualisations of illness onto complex societies, as is done even today. We mean by this a notion which treats the concepts of illness of the Chinese, the Indians or the Occident as if there were medical conceptualisations which were culturally specific to China, India or the West. Certainly, this approach is unable to explain why there are at one and the same time several independently conceptualised and mutually exclusive medical systems in all complex societies in which two or more social groups adhere to divergent world-views. Historical change is totally ignored by an approach which emphasises cultural specificity.

The quest for explaining the phenomena of plurality and of changes in medical thought has resulted in a new approach in recent years. This approach believes that the conceptualisation of the experience of illness is more likely to be moulded by social structures and ideas about society than by the respective civilisation in general. In line with this perspective, innumerable studies have meanwhile been produced which are devoted to studying the theoretical superstructure of the medical systems existing in different tribal communities and societies. Kleinman (1973a, 1973b), Fabrega (1976) and Janzen (1978) can be mentioned here as authors who reflect the latest stage in the development of this perspective and who shed light on the research of earlier scholars. All these studies reach the conclusion that systems of ideas which have been developed around the experience and treatment of illness are not simply objective descriptions of phenomena of illness and of man's reaction to it; rather, they are to be regarded in large part as one of several manifestations of the symbolic reality which has penetrated the entire societal structure and the ideological orientation of those people who consider those medical ideas correct. This means that medicine can hardly be understood by describing its practice and its concepts. Rather, its has to be understood within the context of the total cultural scene in which this kind of medicine is recognised and practised. Conceptualised medicine has gone far beyond the individual doctor–patient relationship as far as its significance and effectiveness are concerned.

Further arguments will be presented on the following pages in support of the view that it is questionable to see changes in the conceptualisation of illness as part of an abstract process which leads humanity closer and closer to the ultimate truth. The notion that medical thought, as a manifestation of a symbolic reality, is specific to a particular world-view (with all the implications which stem from this) provides a satisfactory explanation both of the phenomenon of conceptual pluralism and of fundamental historical change. Wherever, within a particular society, groups of different ideological persuasion co-exist, we shall also encounter mutually exclusive systems of medical conceptualisation. The question of which of these is predominant is resolved by the predominance of a particular world-view. Such world-views are comprehensive; not only do they contain insights into certain causal connections of all sorts of phenomena, they also provide, as a rule, specific instructions as to how conflicts of an individual or collective nature may be avoided. We start from the assumption that protagonists of a particular world-view who believe they know about an ideal — that is, the harmonious or at least 'ordered' organisation of society (however 'harmony' and 'order' may be defined!) — will try to promote their ideas and even to put them into practice. It is from such strivings that ideologically motivated claims to domination are derived. Of course, such claims may be supplemented by the simple power-aspirations on the part of individuals or groups. Anthropological notions of human nature and man's position in the universe are hence just as much an integral part of world-views as ideas about the co-existence of people in communities or societies. In view of the organic character of ideologically based knowledge, it is not surprising that there exists, within one and the same world-view, an intimate connection between medico-anthropological concepts concerning the causation, peculiarities, prevention and treatment of organic illnesses, on the one hand, and of socio-political ideas concerning the causation, peculiarities, prevention and resolution of societal (or communal) crises, on the other. From this follows:

1. A fundamental change of the predominant concepts of illness is unavoidable in all those societies which undergo fundamental social change; a reorientation on the level of medico-anthropological ideas goes hand in hand with societal reorganisation.
2. Older medical ideas which predominated in earlier periods will survive in marginal groups which support a world-view subsequently squeezed out by the ideological notions of other groups.
3. A group which, on the basis of a particular world-view (or merely under the guise of one) and on the basis of specific socio-political ideas, endeavours to establish an effective opposition movement or even to obtain a position of predominance for its world-view will sooner or later develop or support its own conceptualised medical anthropology. This anthropology will harmonise with its social-theoretical ideas and will be opposed to the world-view of its political rivals.

These connections between medical and social-theoretical anthropology are of great importance to those few people in any society who are conscious of the above-mentioned congruence. Systems of medical ideas invariably also have repercussions for the individual and collective behaviour of all the members of the community or society. Contradictions appear whenever the individual or collective behaviour prescribed by a particular medical system clashes with the conduct which a ruling group considers indispensable for the maintenance of the 'correct' social order. As examples from the past and present of our own and of other civilisations demonstrate, there are only three ways in which these contradictions can be resolved.

The first way is by replacing the system of medical ideas which is called into question by another which accords better with societal norms. Chinese Marxists are an example in the present century, when they tried to import concepts of modern Occidental medicine to replace those influenced by Confucian thinking which were incompatible with their social philosophy. Croizier (1968) has demonstrated by reference to the political arguments which pervaded this debate how much some Chinese Marxists were aware of the conceptual affinity between traditional medical ideology and the old Chinese social order which they were trying to overcome.

The second alternative is to replace the social order in question by one which does not contradict the prescriptions followed by a particular group in the avoidance of illness. This solution is advocated by those social-reformist circles in present-day Western societies which believe that the socio-economic system should be changed; they argue that the current social environment makes it more difficult to be and remain healthy, if it does not even make it completely impossible.

A conceptual syncretism would offer itself as a third solution. It would leave scope for all participating world-views to exist independently and yet to interact more or less peacefully within a multi-layered system of ideas. This kind of situation appears to have existed in ancient India before the intrusion of Islam (Basham, 1978: 169).

In this connection we must draw attention again to the well-known phenomenon that divergent medical systems have not only developed different ways of dealing with one and the same organic illness, they frequently also define as illness different physiological phenomena. They thus combine clusters of symptoms in a way which diverges from other systems and call them illness. Obeyese-kere (1976) has provided an impressive example of this in his study of the influence of Ayurvedic ideas upon culture and individuals in Sri Lanka. It is a consequence of the Ayurveda concepts that a number of symptoms, which appear to be without connecting links and more or less without significance to Western-trained physicians, have been combined to constitute the illness of *prameha*. Patients who, while displaying the symptoms of *prameha*, consulted a Western doctor, would be classified as healthy and hence would not normally be given any treatment. An Ayurveda physician, on the other hand, would be forced, when confronted with this cluster of symptoms, to adopt a particular therapeutic course. He knows that ignoring these symptoms at an early stage will lead to growths and inflammations and, later still, to incurable diabetes.

We shall therefore have to differentiate in our subsequent analysis between illness and disease. Following Coe (1970) and his distinction between illness and disease, we define illness (*Kranksein*) as feeling unwell in a subjective sense. It is a feeling which may prevent the sufferer from going about his daily activities (Coe, 1970: 92). Disease (*Krankheit*), on the other hand, is a deviation, objectively conceptualised within a particular system of medical ideas, from a health norm (with whatever defining characteristics). Through being ill a primordial human experience expresses itself which depends on individual or collective perceptions. Disease, on the other hand, is the conceptual determination (*Überformung*) of this experience and thus a cultural product which is ideologically specific.

Subsequently, we shall provide evidence for what has been said so far by reference to a number of examples. One of these is the Ojibwa tribe, which is ideologically undifferentiated; the second example is taken from the Ndembu tribe which is going through an ideological upheaval. The final example will be the ideologically complex civilisation of the Christian Occident and the recent development of medicine in the highly industrialised West. In line with our hypothesis concerning medical conceptualisation as being a manifestation of an overarching symbolic reality, we shall also have to incorporate in our four examples a brief discussion of the societal context in which the systems under review are rooted.

Medical Ideas and Social Structure

World-View and Illness among the Ojibwa

The Ojibwa are a Red Indian nation in North America. They were still in existence in the 1950s when their medical system was first analysed. They lived in an existentialist community of the dead and the living. In this respect their case resembles that of the Chinese of the Chang period or of similarly numerous tribes and peoples of our time. Notwithstanding the enormous variety of medical detail which is revealed by a transcultural comparison, their medical ideas may be considered to represent communities organised in a similar way and holding a comparable world-view.

As far as the Ojibwa were concerned, the permanent existence of the dead was just as much a certainty as the existence of their living neighbours. The former played an important role both in the daily life of the living individuals and in the functioning of the community as a whole. They appeared in people's dreams and gave instructions which had to be followed if illnesses were to be avoided. Any serious illness was related by the Ojibwa to earlier behaviour which represented a violation of existing norms and morals. Falling ill was seen as a consequence of actions which deviated from the expected behavioural pattern among the living or from that relating to their ancestors. Public confessions of earlier misdemeanors were a prerequisite of recovery. They also had a 'preventive' function: the adolescents were invariably witnesses of such violations of the moral codes. In this way they gradually came to understand the differences between socially acceptable and socially unacceptable behaviour.

The relatively simple form of social organisation of the Ojibwa was based on the independence and status equality of the individual member of the tribe. Measures to prevent and treat illness were directed against such deviations and against any innovations which undermined the foundations of the tribal organisation. Values which in the course of treatment were invariably seen as threatened and as being ignored were therefore the following:

1. *The maintenance of equality.* I.e., the need to avoid an accumulation of material goods in the permanent possession of individual members of the community; greed, the refusal to share things with others and the denial of hospitality or the refusal to lend goods. All these endangered the principle of the equal distribution of available goods and were thus seen as a violation of norms and as a cause of a person feeling ill.

2. *Social behaviour.* Hostile, offensive, threatening or aggressive behaviour was likewise diagnosed as a cause of illness and was treated by means of a public confession accompanied by a promise to better oneself.

3. *Recognised forms of sexual activity.* Under the rubric it was not merely sexual practices classified as deviant which led to a person's being ill; above all it was the selection of a sexual partner who was not socially accepted. The survival of Ojibwa social structure was decisively dependent upon the strict maintenance of kinship ties between individual clans and hence upon marriage taking place among people who came from specific groups of persons (Hallowell, 1963).

The conceptualisation of individual and collective experiences of illness among the Ojibwa therefore had a social function, whether conscious or unconscious. It was designed to maintain an ancient social structure. Ojibwa medicine was rooted in anxieties which were unleashed by illnesses considered serious; it was also based on guilt feelings, generated in the person affected, by the establishment of a connection between their medical condition and their misdemeanor. Confronted with the introduction of modern medical concepts, which mitigated the relationship between feeling ill and prior 'immoral' behaviour, the social system of the Ojibwa lost one of its main props within a very short period of time and collapsed.

Illness and Social Conflict among the Ndembu

The Ndembu, a people in the region of the former Belgian Congo, like the Ojibwa, share their living space with their ancestors; they believe that all long-term or serious illnesses represent either the punitive intervention of a deceased ancestor or can be reduced to the secret malevolence of wizards and sorcerers. They also know that punishment by the ancestors is unleashed by a neglect of sacrifices; that is, by the exclusion of the dead from the exchange of available goods. Further instances are the violation of ritual taboos and the failure on the part of relatives to live together in a well-ordered and harmonious fashion. Such misdemeanors, it must be emphasised, do not merely cause a person to fall ill, but it may also produce other forms of mishap, such as unsuccessful hunting expeditions.

A conceptualisation of individual and collective experiences of illness as unspecific as this one is by no means limited to the Ndembu. Many societies in all parts of the world do not know medical activity in the Western sense. This applies in particular to those societies which connect medicine with a belief in the powers of non-human authorities (ancestors, a god, several gods). For them medicine is merely an integral part of crisis resolution. The Ndembu are familiar with many illnesses (headache, stomach ache, toothache, etc.), but they do not know disease in our sense. In the place of 'illness', the Ndembu, like many other communities and societies, created the more comprehensive concept of 'mishap'. It explains individual and collective illness just as it does many other individually or collectively experienced discomforts, such as bad harvests, unsuccessful hunting expeditions, bad weather or military defeat. As a result, it was unnecessary to have a medical doctrine that was independently conceptualised. That is why it was unknown. The Ndembu and other comparable peoples did, however, possess a far-reaching system to cope with individual and collective crisis situations. These situations provoked anxieties because they threatened the continued existence of the individual or the collective.

The Ndembu underwent a period of profound social change and restructuring in the 1950s and 1960s. This change, which was the result of changing economic conditions among the Ndembu (see below), became reflected in a novel conceptualisation of the experience of illness. It manifested itself in the practice of the *ihamba* cult which was adopted by the Ndembu at the time. The premises of this cult require brief description so as to enable us to point up the connections which have been indicated.

Ihamba is the Ndembu word for the upper incisor teeth of the hunters. The hunter's power over the animal kingdom is contained in these teeth. If a hunter dies, the incisor teeth will normally be removed and kept as a charm to ensure successful hunting. The Ndembu know that the *ihamba* of deceased hunters can penetrate the body of living people and cause pain. In order to restore the well-being of the person concerned the *ihamba* must be removed from the body through a ritual. The Ndembu hold the view that general mishap, including illness, and all deaths have their actual cause in tensions between different members of the tribe. It is only these social conflicts, resulting from the anti-normative behaviour of individuals or whole groups, that induce the ancestors to sink their incisor teeth into the culprit as a punishment. In this way the person falls ill.

It is the task of soothsayers, who are consulted and who normally come from other tribes, to ask questions of the afflicted person relating to the deeper causes of the tensions and conflicts. The treatment, which represents in the final analaysis a very remarkable reconciliation between the parties in conflict, is designed to do away with the cause of the illness and of the physical discomforts of the afflicted person by removing the *ihamba* in front of everybody. The soothsayer is therefore less concerned to cure the afflicted individual than to mitigate the troubles of the society. After all, the illness of the individual patient is merely a symptom of the suffering of the community as a whole. It is not to be expected that the patient's situation will improve before the aggressions and tensions in the relations of individual clans have been mollified.

Like all other systems of medical concepts, the *ihamba* cult aims to promote certain norms and values of human cohabitation. Until just before the emergence of *ihamba* ideas, hunting was the main male occupation of the Ndembu and hence the basis of communal life. But by the beginning of the second half of our century, game had become less plentiful. At the same time the population increased. There were growing opportunities for the men to find employment in the copper industry of Northern Rhodesia. As a result, a modern money economy had been introduced into the Ndembu economic system. In the course of this development, new demands were created on the part of those who had contacts with the outside world. The traditional forms of life and organisation could no longer fulfil these demands. Tensions arose between the increasingly divergent world-views of individual groups within Ndembu society. The old norms and values, which were derived primarily from the attempts to secure a collective existence through hunting expeditions, clashed with new social norms and values, which resulted from commercial and contractual relations. The *ihamba* cult, in this situation of rapid change which threatened the old order, may be interpreted as an expression of the community's collective guilt feelings that it was digressing more and more from the traditional norms and values of a society of hunters. It was thought that deceased hunters would follow these changes with growing attention and it seemed plausible that they would sink their teeth precisely into those people who had opened themselves up to the innovations most willingly (Turner, 1964).

Healing and World-View in the Christian Occident

Let us now turn to the essence of medical systems in differentiated societies in which there co-exist different groups with divergent world-views. The organic connection which was made at the start of this article between conceptualisations of the experience of illness and ideas about society and which can be discovered in a world-view that spans both spheres, may be tested by reference to how the basic ingredients of medico-anthropological thought developed in the West.

The history of Western medicine is probably the best documented and most intensively researched field of medical tradition. There are the attempts of medical historians, which have been going on for many decades, to illuminate the advances of medical science during the past two thousand years; there are also extensive works by historians of religion who have with similar thoroughness analysed the conceptual origins and the practice of Christian medicine and put their findings before the reader of the present day. There are finally the studies by philologists and historians of Occidental civilisation in general which have introduced us to the political and cultural environment within which conceptualisations of illness occurred. All this research allows us to evaluate synoptically the relevant primary and secondary literature in a manner which is hardly possible in any other civilisation.

The system of medical ideas that has emerged in the West would seem to be suitable in many ways to illuminate the background to the plurality of systems of medical concepts in complex civilisations; it also enables us to examine some of the causes for the rejection or acceptance of such systems by social groups and individuals in a civilisation of this type. There are parallels with the history of medical thought in China and these cause us to conjecture that we are not dealing, in these two developments in the Far East and in Europe, with accidental or isolated cases; rather, they represent a basic anthropological pattern in the conceptualisation of illness which, if properly undertaken, can also be brought out with reference to other civilisations. But, inasmuch as the sources permit, further research will be necessary in the fields indicated in order to confirm or contradict the general validity of our results.

We shall put at the centre of our subsequent analysis the conceptualisation of the experience of illness which might be called the healing practice of the Christians. The early history of Christian healing is particularly instructive because it faced a twofold antagonism. On the one hand, it was trying to demarcate itself from the ideologies of the heathens of the Middle East, of Greece, Rome and later of northern Europe, and in particular from a special form of demonology. On the other hand, there were the tensions and contradictions resulting from the relationship of Christian healing with the secular medicine of the Hippocratic–Galenic tradition. Let us turn to the first of these two problem areas.

Starting from notions of a future 'kingdom of God' on earth and from a dualism between demonic evil (as manifested in Satan) and an absolutely benign and just God in the heavens above, the New Testament mentions three causes of illness, with the dualism of course persisting until the eschatological promise has been fulfilled in the world. These are the demons of possession (e.g. St Mark 9: 17–28), the sinning of those involved or of their ancestors against God's commandments (St John 5: 14) and, third, acts of God stemming from his omnipotence (St John 9: 3). The therapeutic ideas of the New Testament become plausible if we look at this aetiology and the knowledge that salvation can be found alone in God. Apart from exorcism, Jesus recommended prayer, fasting and the laying on of hands as healing procedures which would give the faithful the benefit of God's powers.

At the beginning of the new Christian community, but also in later centuries, Christians were confronted with a problem, however, which resulted from this particular conceptualisation of illness and healing: they had to set apart the belief in the existence and activities of evil spirits, which they shared with non-Christians, to such a degree that it became clear that Christians exclusively served their God and not, as in the case of other religions, God and the demons. For the early Christians the most appropriate reaction to the incidence of suffering was therefore charismatic healing procedures through prayer or the laying on of hands in line with the directions given by Jesus. Apart from the charismatic procedures, early Christians also practised exorcism as described by the New Testament in order to treat patients. Exorcism was at first practised informally. But it became institutionalised in the office of the exorcist, which is documented for Rome for the first time in the third century. Exorcism is part of the sacramentals which proliferated once the differentiation of the liturgy had begun. Apart from representing a refinement of the cult, exorcism was designed to ward off demonic influences and to effect the physical and spiritual well-being of the faithful (Franz, 1909: 14).

The conversion of the Emperor Constantine (c.285 to 337) brought about a decisive change in the character of Christian healing knowledge. Large numbers of people now flocked into the Christian Church. But their understanding of the faith to which they professed to adhere remained largely superficial. It was in this way that 'superstitious' ideas came to be infused and continued by the faithful. The Church leadership fought throughout the Middle Ages, but with no more than limited success, against those beliefs in demons which viewed evil spirits as partners in a direct dialogue. Numerous edicts against soothsayers, astrologers and magicians, as well as the use of magic formulas by the population, proved that such concepts and practices continued to exist without interruption. They could not be removed by official pronouncements and became particularly virulent in times of crisis.

The other problem with which early Christian theology was confronted was the need to define its position on the widespread use of herbal, mineral or animal-based remedies which were founded on magic or empirical knowledge or sometimes even on a theory of essences. The Church's position had to avoid a clash between this knowledge and the belief that God, acting through his Son, was the source of all salvation. The discussion of this problem, too, extended through the Middle Ages down to the modern period. It was conducted not merely between Christians and non-Christians but also among the Christian community itself, where it led to different views.

These debates, which determined to a considerable extent the development of theology and dogma, resulted in several processes of a complex historical nature. To begin with, many of the most important medical customs of late antiquity and the Germanic period were taken over by Christianity. These included the wearing of charms, the sacrifice of food and valuables or the use of remedies. Christian teaching and theology integrated these customs, separated from the concepts which originally accompanied them, into biblical ideas of the nature of illness and of salvation. In the twelfth century one distinction played a not insignificant part in this respect. This was the distinction of the *sacramenta maiora* from those sacramentals in which pre-Christian concepts survived from late antiquity and from the Germanic period. Secondly, already in the early communities a rapprochement occurred between one Christian sect and the Galenic concept. However, it was only from the tenth century onwards and after the excommunication of the members of this sect that ideas that illness had natural causes became slowly more widely accepted in Europe. This development was also due to the work of non-Christian (Jewish) scholars in the schools at Salerno and Montpellier and to the promotion of these ideas by secular authorities.

We can deduce from the statements by various Christian authors who opposed the use of medicines based on the Hippocratic–Galenic essence theories, that they were aware of the threat posed by concepts of natural science to the spread of the Christian faith. Knowledge of the causes of illness as a result of pathogenic, climatic, emotional or dietary conditions contradicted biblical tradition concerning the links between sinful behaviour and being ill. It therefore called into question the need to follow the Christian ethic in order to prevent illness. This was a motive force that must not be underestimated.

What, finally, is likely to have retarded the breakthrough to the adoption of secular-scientific concepts concerning the origins and nature of illness was that these concepts also endangered certain economic interests. Thus many ecclesiastical, but also secular, organisations (town governments, monasteries etc.) had increasingly invested in relics, at least since the eleventh century. They often made enormous profits from the pilgrimages to see these relics or from the sale of remedies which were supposed to have gained a special healing power through contact with the relics (Franz, 1909: 450–9). It is not too far-fetched to assume that the representatives of such organisations felt no incentive to be won over by the new knowledge concerning the origins and the appropriate treatment of illness; they were even less interested in furthering such knowledge, which removed the theoretical justification from these sources of income. The history of medicine of other societies also shows that the survival of old concepts or the introduction of new ideas is enhanced, if economic interests are bound up with them.

The Church and Christian theology were furthermore faced with a special problem when confronting medicine based on the natural sciences. This was the fact that Jewish medical scholars not only had a decisive influence on Salerno and Montpellier — the two places which were later regarded as the centres of the revival of medical science — but they also gained more general recognition in the practice of this type of medicine. That Jews should be doctors was bound to go against the grain of the Christian notion that there existed a connection between healing and salvation. Certain parallels with China cannot be overlooked. There the Confucians saw the all-embracing validity of their world-view threatened by the healing theories and practice of Taoism and Buddhism. The reactions of Christianity to Jewish physicians was therefore similar to that of the Confucians to free-lance Taoist and Buddhist practitioners. We know of numerous sermons against the activities of Jews who had concluded a pact with the Devil, among them the sermon by Johann Geiler von Kaysersberg (1445–1510) and Johann Herolt (1462) (White, 1897: 42). The *Index Sanitatis* by Philipp Begardi, written in the sixteenth century, is a good example of the arguments and motives with which secular and Christian physicians then proceeded against their Jewish competitors (Sudhoff, 1907–8).

The path which finally led to the predominance of a medicine based on the natural sciences was a long and complicated one. In accordance with the power of the Christian message and with the underlying societal changes in Western history, the balance shifted away from pagan concepts of earlier times towards a predominance of Christian ideas of healing. And from the eighteenth century, secular-scientific concepts gained the upper hand. However, none of the earlier concepts has passed into oblivion. Magical healing is still effectively being practised in this century, such as the 'marrying of warts'. By the same token, Christian ideas still pervade the daily experience of illness of large sections of the population in Europe and in the United States. They range from prayer and the adoration of relics to the laying on of hands, and they do so partly by adopting scientific biomedical methods, partly by totally rejecting them.

Conceptual Stratification as an Historical Compromise

However, with the adoption of Galenic medicine from its Arab 'exile', the debate on the 'correct' conceptualisation of illness was no longer conducted strictly in terms of alternatives. Thus Abbess Hildegard von Bingen (1098–1179), in her description of remedies, combined concepts concerning the knowledge of the healing power of God and of the dangerous powers of Satan with insights into the natural empirical healing qualities of plants (Riethe, 1974: 28, 81–83). This example demonstrates that there were forces in Christianity which tried to combine scientific concepts of healing with the theological notions of the Church. In this way the foundations were laid for a situation in Europe in which there exist many layers of concepts, largely similar to that examined by Basham (1978: 169ff.) in his discussion of ancient Indian medicine. This development made possible a harmonious co-existence of science with Christian dogma because of the reconciliation of two previously incompatible alternatives. The successful scientist of today may be an atheist or he may be a practising Christian. There is, of course, no doubt that the erosion of the authority of the Church in the public and private lives of the population in the modern period has facilitated the adoption of a compromise formula of this kind. However, it should not be overlooked that there are in existence today, both in orthodox Judaism and in orthodox Christianity, groups with a large membership which resist adaptation to a changing socio-political environment. They continue to practise healing on their own, dogmatically based on ideas which are contained in the literature on the Old and New Testaments.

It is no coincidence that the development of a harmonious plurality of Christian and non-Christian world-views, starting in the nineteenth century first in England and France and, from 1850, also in Germany, have favoured the unique historical situation of medical advances. Over one hundred years up to the mid-twentieth century all the advances were derived from very intensive and wide-ranging basic research which elevated modern Western medicine, irrespective of all its weaknesses, to a position where it represents the most effective system for the treatment of physical ailments that has been known. Occidental healing knowledge was devoid of ideological contradictions for about a hundred years. The compromise of a multi-layered pluralism that had been struck permitted a fruitful exchange of ideas among all those sections of the population which were interested in the solution of acute medical problems and the augmentation of scientific knowledge.

There emerged a medical practice based on concepts which faithfully reflected the societal developments of the time. The liberal economic system, with its emphasis on the individual and on achievement (shared by all relevant groups) and in which the creative person rises in free competition with others, while the unfit occupy a lower social rank, made it possible for Darwin's ideas on the survival of the fittest to become acceptable; but this intellectual climate also furthered the theory of germs according to which physical fitness of the individual and interest in personal hygiene are deemed to be crucial for health.

The importance of this latter theory has been reduced and modified in the last two decades. Concepts of immunology have gained ground instead as explanations of the causes of illness. This development has been parallelled by a growing influence of 'welfare-statism' upon the societies which conduct medical research. The political notion that need, poverty and even criminality are caused by the failure not of the individual but of social systems accords with the notion of the immunity of the organism to certain disorders; it has in turn led to the search not for intra-organic but for extra-organic, extra-personal and environmental causes of obvious failure.

Healing Knowledge and Ideological Polarisation in the Contemporary Period: Sociogenesis of Illness or of Disease?

In particular, the search for extra-personal and environmental disturbances of immunological systems is one aspect of a renewed polarisation of world-views whose repercussions are noticeable in contemporary medical theory and practice. The beginnings of this can be traced back for example to the mercantilist views of the seventeenth-century physician William Petty (Rosen, 1977a: 29–30) or to the writings of the French philanthropist Claude Humbert Piarrou de Chamousset (1717–73) (Rosen, 1977b: 82). They found expression increasingly in the view that the statistically verifiable membership in a particular social group can be correlated with proneness to particular diseases. One of the earliest German studies of this type was Max van Pettenkofer's analysis of health status in the city of Munich, which appeared in 1873 and was widely noticed. Indeed, his sensational report marked a turning-point in two respects. To begin with, Pettenkofer, taking up the ideas of Petty and Chamousset, pointed to the economic significance of illness. Christianity had motivated its adherents to provide aid to sick fellow human beings by holding out the promise of the 'mercy of suffering' and, after death, heavenly rewards. Since Pettenkofer, however, the criterion for the introduction of health programmes was almost exclusively the economic aspect (Sigerist, 1943: 61, 68). The second point of Pettenkofer's report which we would also see as a symptom of major change was that he pointed out that particular social groups are prone to particular diseases.

Pettenkofer's research possibly did more than anyone else's to bring about a fundamental conceptual reorientation in the whole history of the human healing art as conscious and theoretically determined. In 1934 R. H. Britten published his study in which he demonstrated the economic causes of ill health; that is, its correlation with a particular income group. He found that in ten states in America there existed, in the age groups twenty-five to forty-four of 100,000 inhabitants belonging to particular income groups, the following mortality rates due to tuberculosis: professionals (doctors, lawyers, etc.), 28.6; white-collar employees, 67.6; skilled workers, 69.0; unskilled workers, 193.5. A statistical survey covering the years 1928 to 1933 showed that in 1932 in families in which all members were unemployed, the rates of serious illness were 48 per cent above that of families in which all members had a job. In families who, having enjoyed average prosperity, came to depend on state welfare, a rate of serious illness was found that was 73 per cent higher than that of families who continued to live in comfortable conditions during those four years (Sigerist, 1943: 56). These early analyses may seem questionable when compared with the sophistication of this type of study today. But they led H. E. Sigerist, the well-known historian and social reformist physician, to the conclusion that 'all the available evidence points to a very close link between the economic situation of a particular population group and the extent of ill-health from which it suffers'. Since the Second World War and with the introduction of computers, innumerable studies and huge sums of money have been devoted to the discovery of this link. One of the spectacular studies which this type of research has yielded is the recent book by Harvey Brenner of Johns Hopkins University. He showed on the basis of extensive and complicated computer analyses that there is a statistically significant correlation between the ups and downs in the incidence of mental illness and the state of public finance. The *New York Times* presented this news to its readers on the title page. Radio and television stations broadcast interviews with Brenner. The extent to which this kind of knowledge concerning the causes of illness has been recognised as important, not merely by the media but also in the universities, is also reflected in the fact that new chairs have been instituted in this branch of medicine, known as sociology *in* medicine (not sociology *of* medicine). These chairs are held not in the arts faculties but in the medical schools and enjoy equality with the subjects of pathology or anatomy.

There are two reasons for the unprecedented importance which we attach to this development. Analysing the causes of illness as a dependent variable and social-group attachment as an independent variable means that we are turning away from looking at the individual who has fallen ill and towards the ill-health of groups. Accordingly, there are now in the US and in some other countries schools of medicine which are devoted to studying the former phenomenon and there are schools of hygiene and public health which study the latter problem.

There is never a perfect correlation between illness and economic situation. It is hence not applicable to individuals. The theory that social conditions have an effect on people's health is hence no more than a conceptual determination of collective experiences. The postulate of modern science that the individual experiment must, if repeated, produce the same causal connections has been abandoned. It has been replaced by the notion of a statistically recognisable correlation or, as it might also be called, a correspondence. This correspondence between income and ill-health can be statistically demonstrated. However, the chains of causality remain uncertain; even the direction in which they proceed must remain doubtful. Many theories are being offered to explain why social class has an influence on ill-health (and few authors tend to indicate that it might also be the other way round). But all these theories fail when it comes to the individual case. What is left for the time being is the belief or knowledge, as in empirically supported correspondences in the science of magic, that the manipulation of the one variable has an impact upon the second variable. There is no way of telling whether the connections which have been recognised are 'true'. The quantitative analysis, which is invariably subjective in its approach, is dependent upon the ideological positions of our period. It is possible that such studies will tell the neutral observer of later decades or centuries no more than something about the ways in which we presently group and categorise the totality of the members of a particular society and what kinds of diseases we include in such analyses. Both aspects are highly subjective and related to one's world-view: they are dependent on the socio-political tendencies of this age.

We have argued above that this development, which was pioneered by Max von Pettenkofer among others, probably reflected the most fundamental conceptual innovation in the known history of medicine. By this we mean something else in addition to what we have said so far; we mean the notion of a 'right to good health', with all its consequences. In statistical terms illness appears to be more frequent in those social groups in the industrial nations which are economically worse off. This has led reformist circles, who take up the interests of these groups, to believe that good health can be equated with work, capital and wealth. The ruling and wealthy groups, so the argument goes, withhold from the masses full employment and hence the right to work; more than that, they withhold the control over capital and hence the right to a share of the national wealth commensurate to their labour. In the same way, the argument continues, the ruling groups — that is, those that are (as can be shown statistically) healthy — withhold from the masses the right to good health. For the first time in history it is not the patient himself who is responsible for his condition, because, for example, he has committed a sin (as many religiously founded concepts maintained) or because he has violated social norms (as concepts based on secular social theories argued). Those who are healthy and privileged are the ones that are responsible and guilty! It is not the patient who has to change his life-style in order to make a recovery; it is those who are in good health who have to do so in order to help the 'underprivileged' to achieve good health.

Thus the organic connection between the conceptual determination of the experience of illness and particular socio-political ideas within an overarching world-view appears to determine medical thinking today as fundamentally as ever.

4

The piece which follows shares two features with that of Paul Unschuld: the authors are unsatisfied with analyses of health and illness concepts which do not go beyond the micro-sociological and take an historical approach in the search for explanations of change and persistence. The emphasis and the orientation are different from Paul Unschuld's, however. There is a strong focus in the constitution of ideas about illness on what lay people believe. Furthermore, while Paul Unschuld's thinking appears influenced by Marxian analyses, the work of Claudine Herzlich and Janine Pierret follows a Durkheimian tradition. Claudine Herzlich's earlier work (*Health and Illness*, 1973) discussed by Meg Stacey (pp. 12–14, this volume) was overtly in that mode.

What appears here is a shortened version of one chapter of a much larger work about patients and illness in times past and today (Herzlich and Pierret, 1984). In a discussion of the intentions of that book in English (and of concepts about epidemic disease), they say their interest was to show how lay and professional people express 'a collective discourse that draws the full and meaningful picture of biological misfortune' (Herzlich and Pierret, 1985: 146). They see these conceptions as related to the biological experience, and therefore varying over time as biological experiences change for the whole collectivity. They also see the particular conceptions of individuals as related to that individual's illness experience and to her/his position in the social order.

In the chapter which follows, the focus is on illness causation and the varying modes of explanation, both professional and lay, which have been offered over the centuries. Histories, diaries and letters are used as evidence.

Eds.

CLAUDINE HERZLICH
JANINE PIERRET

Illness: From Causes to Meaning

While physical symptoms and bodily changes are of course the means by which sick people know they are ill, they also wonder about the 'causes' of their illness and look for explanations. In so-called 'traditional' societies, illness, a crucial but incomprehensible event for both the individual and the group, has always given rise to questioning and interpretations which go beyond the body itself. The problems of the causality of biological illness is therefore at the heart of any society's system of beliefs and of the data which anthropologists must observe and theorise about. It is also at the heart of the history of medicine. 'If we wish to date the origins of a real humanity from the very moment of conscious thought' said Walter Riese, 'then at this same time rational, and thus scientific, medicine was born' (Riese, 1950: 1).

The Concept of Causal Explanation of Illness

Here, however, there are a number of pitfalls, not least the concept of 'cause'. Walter Riese's statement shows the central importance of the notion of cause in a particular conception of science, but in fact in the history of medicine this was not so clear for a very long time. Foucault, for example, shows that at the end of the eighteenth century, medical classification, the nosology, still 'involves a figure of the disease that is neither the chain of causes and effects, nor the chronological series of events nor its visible trajectory through the body' (Foucault, 1973: 4). Our understanding of illness is not based on the distinction between cause and effect; in some cases, the effect may have the same theoretical status as the cause. When dealing with madness, he makes the same analysis of the distinction, long

Based on a translation by Dorothy Parkin

prevalent in medical theory, between 'ultimate causes' and 'proximate causes': in fact, the 'proximate cause' of the illness is often difficult to distinguish from the symptom it is supposed to explain; it is simply, according to Foucault, a sort of 'causal actualisation of its qualities' (Foucault, 1961: 262). On the other hand, there are an infinite number of theories about ultimate causes, and during the seventeenth and eighteenth centuries, in the case of madness these increased to include all inner events of the soul, including, among others, passion, sadness, study and meditation, as well as external events, climate and different aspects of social life. To sum up, Foucault demonstrates a 'polyvalent and heterogeneous causal link in the origins of madness' (Foucault, 1961: 270), found not only in the medical literature but also in its effects on practice in asylums.

In addition, it is no doubt wrong to assimilate, as Riese does, the idea of cause with the beginnings of a scientific way of thinking, opposed to all the magico-religious conceptions. Here the examples from the history of medicine are like those in anthropology. The historian Sigerist (1951), for example, shows that in ancient Egyptian medicine, on the one hand, empirical and magico-religious elements are closely associated; on the other hand, magico-religious therapy is based on the idea of cause: the demon or ancestor which must be expelled from the patient is the 'cause' of the illness. Yet in empirical-rational therapy, the only symptom which counts is the one which the material remedy, a herb for example, is trying to suppress. In the same way, there is much anthropological evidence to show that it is difficult to contrast, as the anthropologist G. M. Foster (1976) has done recently, 'personalistic' theories — where the illness is attributed to positive and deliberate action by a human being, a spirit or a god — with 'naturalistic' theories, where the illness is due to natural forces or elements. It is even more difficult to discern any insurmountable opposition between wholly magical conceptions and those where we can see the beginnings of a scientific approach.

It is not our intention here to synthesise the contribution of anthropology or retrace the history of aetiological theories of medicine. However, the difficulties of the idea of cause should not lead us to underestimate the constant importance of the need to explain illness. There is therefore some merit in trying to see how people who are ill, or at least those who are not doctors, have questioned biological illness, and to discover the events and phenomena which they have related to it, whether or not this follows the model of causality. Is it possible in this way to see the part still played in our deliberations today by the questions and explanations of the past and to find in these the origins of our current explanations? Here, however, there is the problem of the autonomy of lay thinking — that of ill people and their families — *vis-à-vis* that of the doctors: is there some degree of independence or is it entirely subordinate to the doctors? This is one of the areas where, despite some side-tracking, medicine has most clearly established its dominance over the years: today the 'scientific' explanation which medicine offers us has acquired total legitimacy. The lay perception of the causality of illness is thus never independent of the development of aetiological models in medicine. It would nevertheless be incorrect to deduce from this that it is simply a question of the one being subordinate to the other: there are plenty of examples (cf. Goubert, 1977) to show that at the beginning of the nineteenth century scholarly medicine had not yet definitively asserted itself over the diverse popular bodies of knowledge. Throughout the ages, we can see not a one-way dependency but interplay and exchanges between scientific and non-scientific modes of thought.

If, as we have seen, our view of the body has become increasingly anatomical and physiological and structured through medical knowledge, we can hypothesise that questions about the origins of illness are never wholly answered by medicine. 'Why me?' 'Why now?' These questions still arise today when illness strikes. They require an explanation which transcends the individual body and the medical diagnosis. The response to these questions goes beyond a search for causes and becomes a quest for meaning. We are trying always to relate illness to the order of the world and to the social order.

Thus the explanation of illness extends beyond medical explanations because it is sought in a way which goes further than medical explanations do. It also bypasses them because at the other extreme, one might say, explaining one's illness is also a question of daily observation and perception of which any of us is capable. We all think, given the evidence and operating at the most sensory level, that we can perceive the nature of some of our illnesses. Here, to some extent, medical knowledge is known to be unnecessary. This was what Montaigne referred to when writing about the stone which was troubling him:

This other peculiar commodity I observe, that it is an infirmitie, wherein we have but little to divine. We are dispensed from the trouble, where-into other maladies cast us, by the uncertaintie of their causes, conditions and progresses. A trouble infinitly painful. We have no neede of doctorall consultations or collegiall interpretations. Our senses tell us where it is, and what it is. [Montaigne, 1603: 651–2]

Even today, when we are bombarded with scientific schemas, there is still a place for an account of sensory perceptions in explanations of illness. In 1972, for example, a young girl of seventeen in hospital with pleurisy said, 'I have caught a chill. *First I felt it*, then the doctors told me that it could be caused by a chill. The night before, I felt it: I went out and felt the cold strike'. In the same way, we often refer to the sensory qualities of our surroundings, especially the air, anticipating, with a feeling of immediate evidence, that it will be harmful to us.

Biological Illness, Natural Disorders and Divine Punishment

Medical and lay explanations of illness have long attributed import-ance to *air, climate* and *seasons*. Is it the sensory evidence of the quality of the air, the ability to observe climatic phenomenon and the immediate perception of the way they change which accounts for this? It would seem so. All these elements constitute, in different ways, one of the oldest modes of explaining biological illness, and one of which there are still traces today. Here was the genesis of a new vision, found first in the work of Hippocrates. As opposed to a conception of illness as exclusively divinely caused, this vision integrates causation into the natural order of things. The theory of 'airs', where air and climate are the major means of explaining illness, is found throughout the ages, but it is perhaps at the end of the eighteenth century that it was taken to an extreme of climatic determinism. Worried about epidemics and fatal epizootic diseases which threatened the economy, the royal administration, in the person of Turgot,[1] decided in 1776 to create the Royal Society of Medicine which it entrusted to Vicq d'Azyr.[2] For sixteen years a hundred or more doctors established links between epidemics, morbidity, climates and seasons and created a picture of health in

1. Turgot, A-R-J., Minister of State of France 1774–76 (*eds.*).
2. Vicq d'Azyr, F., *Docteur réqeut* of the Paris Faculty of Medicine, Member of the French Academy 1788 and of the Academy of Sciences (*eds.*).

France of which there was no previous equivalent (cf. Desaive *et al.*, 1972; Peter, 1971).

But these ideas making air and/or climate and seasons the major determinant of illness are widespread. Throughout several centuries non-medical writings show how deeply rooted they are in society overall. They also show us their complexity. Pierre de L'Estoile, for example, often refers to them. Usually for him humidity is seen as the essential factor; it could also, however, be the cold.

The air would be 'malignant' and 'corrupt'. 'Many prolonged fevers, even scarlet fever, a sign of great corruption' he writes in August 1609 (L'Estoile, 1958). The idea of 'corrupt' air and 'corruption' is central to medical discourse throughout several centuries, especially in relation to epidemics. Ten years earlier, in 1599, it was invoked by a doctor in Burgos, quoted by B. Benassar: 'It is not really the plague, because for plague a universal cause is needed, such as corrupt and putrifying air', he wrote of the epidemic which raged in Spain (1969: 513). But the idea was also found among lay people. In 1717, during her travels in Turkey, Lady Montagu always spoke of 'contaminated' air to explain the plague:

> I was made beleive [*sic*] that our 2nd cook who fell ill there had only a great cold . . . I am now let into the secret that he has had the Plague. There are many that 'scape of it, neither is the air ever infected. [Halsband, 1965: 338]

In *Jane Eyre*, published in 1847, Charlotte Brontë, ignorant of the role of lice, attributes the outbreak of a typhus epidemic to the miasmas and mists of the unhealthy climate:

> That forest-dell where Lowood lay, was the cradle of fog and fog-bred pestilence; which, quickening with the quickening spring, crept into the Orphan Asylum, breathed typhus through its crowded schoolroom and dormitory, and, ere May arrived, transformed the seminary into an hospital. [Brontë, 1969: 89]

As we can see, the corrupt air itself is attributed to various causes: a 'malignant' combination of heat and humidity, miasmas from the ground, the marshes in the country, putrid effluvia from the corpses of men and animals, and also emanations from living bodies and soiled clothing, stagnant air in excessively narrow town streets — all these ideas converged and intermingled.

However, at least during the eighteenth century, references of a completely different kind were added. While it was linked with the air and climate, biological illness was also related to other natural disorders: strange meteorological events such as eclipses, earthquakes, storms and tempests, conjunctions of stars, 'heavenly bodies' and comets. Daniel Defoe claimed that one of these heralded the London plague. Finally, illness is linked to a disorder of those souls which do not conform to the divine will. Both series of phenomena can be invoked simultaneously. Boccaccio, writing about the 1348 plague, used both the 'celestial bodies' explanation and reference to God: 'Some say that it descended upon the human race through the influence of the heavenly bodies, others that it was a punishment signifying God's righteous anger at our inquitous way of life' (Boccaccio, 1972). A fragment of L'Estoile's journal also shows us how phenomena of biological life, unusual and rather frightening natural events such as storms and tempests, can be combined with those of social life and customs into one syncretic vision:

> The disposition of the air was malignant, full of thunder, storms, sudden rain and tempests, symbolising the humours of the century, carried off large numbers of people of all ages, sex and condition. Diarrohea, apoplexy and all kinds of strange and sudden deaths killed many more and annoyed the people who nevertheless did not mend their ways (August 1609). [L'Estoile, 1958: 513]

Physical disorders are thus related both to corrupt air and corrupt morals. The disorder comprises natural phenomena, bodily phenomena and human behaviour. But God's will hangs over all. It is God, in the last analysis, who sends illness to mankind. This idea has been inherent in medical theory, as in the whole of society, for many centuries in Western Christendom. One may, of course, seek various different 'causes' of illness, but God alone is the 'prime cause'.

Contagion

However, as we have seen, different terms of reference can function simultaneously. The ultimate recourse to God does not prevent the slow emergence of empirical ætiological concepts; that of *contagion*, for example, is frequently associated with corrupt air. We know on this score that the man in the street observed and pondered this before the doctors and scientists. It is true that by the mid-sixteenth century, Fracastor[3] had already formulated a theory of contagion and had isolated three kinds: contagion from one person to another, indirect contagion by means of objects which could transmit the illness and, lastly, contagion at a distance, without human contact or exchange of objects. Doctors, however, did not support these ideas, which nevertheless were widespread among the people and gave rise to various practices of hygiene and isolation. In popular language, the term contagion was synonymous with plague; this is how Montaigne uses it when returning from his travels. But it also conveys the idea of transmission without contact, to do with the quality of the air. Healthy air can become 'poisoned' and transmit the 'contagion'; it will be all the more virulent because it has 'overcome' healthier air:

> Both within and round about my house, I was overtaken, in respect of all other, with a most contagious pestilence. For, as soundest bodies are subject to grievous diseases, because they onely can force them: so the aire about me being very healthy, where in no mans memory, infection (although very neere) could ever take footing: comming now to be poisoined, brought forth strange effects. [Montaigne, 1603: 624]

In August 1603 Pierre de L'Estoile also mentioned a case of indirect contagion through imported goods:

> At the end of this month, in the *rue des prêcheurs* in Paris, at the sign of the cock, the plague was discovered. It had not been heard of in Paris for a very long time. It was said that it had been brought by goods from London, where it was claimed that 2,000 people were dying each week. [L'Estoile, 1958: 113]

As for contagion passed from person to person, it is clearly indicated in a report dated 1740 about one of the miracles of the convulsionaries of Saint-Médard.[4] There was, we read 'a very simple young man who had an attack of scrofula through sleeping with a relative of his master who had the same disease'. However, in the eighteenth century, this concept was not yet accepted by all doctors and a dispute raged between contagionists and anti-

---

3. Girolamo Fracastoro, 1478–1553. Born in Verona and studied in Padua. Man of letters, musician and doctor, he wrote extensively, notably on contagion (*eds.*).
4. This report, which was passed to the authors by David Vidal, is in the Bibliothèque de l'Arsenal, fonds Bastille 6884. The convulsionaries were Jansenist fanatics who fell into convulsions at the tomb of François de Paris at St Médard (*eds.*).

contagionists. The corpuscular theory, reformulated by Phillipe Hecquet as the theory of miasmas, is a contagionist theory.[5] Others speak of the 'pestilential seed' or blame an epidemic on living creatures, such as worms or insects. However, on their own side of the argument, the anti-contagionists — who were in agreement with the political authorities in wishing to avoid the panic associated with the idea of contagion — were not short of objections. They emphasised the links between plague and famine and, above all, drew out the character of the 'popular prejudices' about contagion discerning in it, sometimes justifiably, the taint of 'superstition' (cf. Ehrard, 1957).

In medical circles, the debate about the existence of contagion and the nature of its processes lasted until the discoveries of Pasteur[6] and took many different forms; Bretonneau's[7] perceptive view at the beginning of the nineteenth century was not enough to convince people that diptheria and typhoid were contagious. In the middle of the nineteenth century, in Vienna, Semmelweis[8] fared no better with puerperal fever. Tuberculosis was not declared a contagious disease in France until 1889, although it had been recognised as such in Italy and Spain since the beginning of the century.

But with the discovery of the *microbe* and the elaboration of Pasteur's model of specific ætiology, all medical conceptions were transformed and hygienics acquired a new content. Eighteenth- and nineteenth-century hygienists had envisaged combined action, although rather imprecise in its processes, of various factors in the environment, ranging from material elements to social conditions. The new bacteriology focused on the ultimate and decisive link, the germ, in triggering off disease. From that time on, the concept of the 'specific cause' of illness being a germ has been taught in school to successive generations and now goes unchallenged. When we look at some statements made by people who are ill, today or in recent times, one might think that the germ theory is accepted as by far the

5. Phillipe Hecquet, 1661–1737. An MD of Paris, he wrote prolifically and in an animated style on medical matters, greatly influencing the medicine of his day. He did not accept the value of innoculation and opposed its use.
6. Louis Pasteur (1822–95), the well-known French scientist who proved the existence of atmospheric germs. Lister's application of this finding led to the origins of modern aseptic surgery.
7. Pierre Bretonneau (1778–1862) of Tours, a distinguished French clinician, who described diptheria (the first to use that name) and introduced tracheotomy.
8. Ignaz Phillip Semmelweis (1816–65), whose insistence that medical students wash their hands in chloride of lime reduced death rates in his maternity ward from 18 per cent to 3 per cent, but whose contemporaries did not accept his theories.

major cause of biological illness. In 1961, a young thirty-year-old engineer stated, 'Illnesses are principally caused by bacteria'. In the same year, a forty-one-year-old woman said, 'I think that nowadays illness is really *entirely to do with germs (microbes)* or viruses which take hold, multiply and become more or less resistant to antibiotics, vaccinations or any other means of protection which have been discovered'.

Nevertheless, even in 1960 — and twenty years later, this is even more true — 'germs' were not the only explanation of illness. There was, for example, if we look at cancer, the most distressing of all illnesses, a semi-magical image of infection, quite divorced from germs. In 1960 an employee, aged 53, who had a breast cancer, told how she and her family coped with mistaken notions of contagion:

> I said to myself: 'I am an object of dread now'. I asked the doctor: 'Now tell me, is it contagious?' He told me: 'You're being silly, of course not. People don't know, people are stupid . . . but by all means, share your daughter's plate, you can, it won't harm her'.

We can see the negative and positive effects on the patient: the best way for the family to reassure the patient about their continuing emotional and social support is to dispel these unfounded fears, so that he or she does not feel isolated. The patient continued

> I have had friends come and drink from my glass when I was ill, to show they still cared about me. It was marvellous, it did not seem very much but it was one of the things which helped my morale.

Some people, although acknowledging the existence of germs, think that illness 'has no cause'. Thus a young woman aged twenty-four said in 1960:

> The awful thing about illness is that there is no reason for it. It's because there is a germ, for example, in infectious diseases. In other diseases, tuberculosis, you can't say. Often people say, 'it's because he's overworked'. Has he really just caught a germ? Nobody knows, with these things.

Sometimes, almost as important as the specific cause, germ or parasite, there is a social cause. Sometimes, as in the past, it may take the baleful form of the 'stranger'.

Germs cannot then entirely explain illness. We must still find, as in the ancient schema, a 'prime cause' which explains its presence and action. Otherwise the patient is still in the dark, like the woman, aged sixty-one, interviewed in 1972, who could not explain the viral hepatitis which she had 'caught' a few years earlier.

> Viral hepatitis can be caught without you knowing how you've caught it. It's a virus . . . you can catch it in hospitals, without ever knowing, you could have brushed against someone. But why? *It doesn't just come upon you like that, does it?* But you never know, you could have touched something belonging to someone, or it could be injections . . . I had them once or twice a week . . . perhaps that's how I got it? You can't tell, it's difficult.

Thus the germ itself is too specific an explanation and therefore unsatisfactory and inadequate, lacking a concept which will allow the individual to attribute illness to a number of causes. 'There are a number of causes for a man's death', as an Ivory Coast villager told the ethnologist (quoted Auge, 1975).

Life-style as a Cause of Illness

Today we use the concept of our 'modern way of life' to integrate various factors and give the causality of illness real significance. This concept has already been applied to the germ when — like contagion in the old theories of airs — germs are associated with air. The particular factor is integrated into a wider causality, taking into account the environment and contrasting the urban and rural way of life. In 1960 an artisan's wife linked, on the one hand, life in the country with air and freedom from germs and, on the other hand, lack of air and space, germs and illness with life in the town:

> In the country there is air and the germs don't do as much harm as here . . . In Paris, cramped housing plays a part too, because when there are a lot of people in a room, there is no air and if someone is ill, there are germs.

Nevertheless, from the 1960s onwards, contaminated air is due to pollution rather than germs. Thus the concept of the contamination of nature and man's environment by urban society and way of life emerges. A link is then forged between the particular agent, pollution or germs, and the quality of the environment and society as a whole. Pollution — 'toxins', 'chemicals', as people used to say in the 1960s — is the waste product of conurbations and of our industrial society; it is the cause of illness. According to a thirty-five-year-old painter in 1960:

> The atmosphere in a city like Paris can be quite harmful. The amount of CO_2 which people breathe in Paris makes you anaemic and then the acid fumes from burning all kinds of fuel are definitely bad for the lungs and that must let the germs in and increase the likelihood of 'flu, bronchitis and so on.

An engineer mentioned more serious troubles:

> They have analysed the air in Paris and found that smoke from factories and chimneys causes a great deal of air pollution and fills the air with molecules which cause disorders of the blood, the nerves and even a particular kind of cancer.

Interviewed in 1979, a young woman working at the PTT (Post Office) took up the same themes. Atmospheric pollution is thus one of the essential symbols of the life of the city, and of the 'modern way of life' and illness is the price that has to be paid.

The 'modern way of life' is thus at the heart of our representations of the causality of biological illness (cf. Herzlich, 1973, Part One). Of course, this has its antecedents in the Rousseauesque vision of the relationship between nature and society. At the end of the eighteenth century in particular, it is expressed in medical topographies and in the work of social observers such as Louis-Sebastien Mercier[9] or Rétif de la Bretonne.[10]

Today, however, the concept 'modern way of life/cause of illness' is no longer confined to medicine or to a small group of scholars or observers of the social scene. It has become a general view (*representation collective*), which, moreover, is formulated in a complex way: at the individual level, 'way of life' is the cause of the illness; at the level of society as a whole, it shapes the type and distribution of illness; we have seen the salience of the 'illnesses of modern life' in the collective consciousness. More generally still, 'way of life'

---

9. Mercier, L-S. (1740–1814), Avocat of the Parliament, Deputy of the Convention, Member of the Council of the Five Hundred, Member of the Institute and author.
10. Restif (Rétif) de la Bretonne, N-E. (1734–1806). An extensive author, his anecdotes and character sketches provide much information about eighteenth-century Parisian life, especially among the poor.

embodies and fashions identically, while perverting, all the factors which can affect health. This shared meaning, which can be attributed to the various elements in an individual's spatio-temporal environment, to the rhythm of his life and to certain of his behaviours, is what makes 'way of life' the integrating concept, the *prime paradigm of the causality of illness*. And here, too, behind the search for the causes, behind the possibilities of combination and modulation which give the 'way of life' concept its infinitely variable content, we find yet again the quest for meaning. If illness is brought about by a way of life, then illness has some meaning: it represents objectively in a physical way, our negative relationship with what we call 'the social'.

Diet too is included in this paradigm. It would be tedious to attempt to trace, as we have done for the air-climate-contagion-germ configuration, the development of the ideas linking health and diet, especially as their relationship is long-established. Throughout centuries haunted by the spectre of famine, a good diet was thought to be more or less equivalent to good health. Moreover, for a long time it was virtually the only treatment patients could expect in hospital. F. Lebrun, for example, enumerates the elements in the regime prescribed for 'sick paupers' in the regulations of the Hotel-Dieu in Angers in 1588: each would receive a quart of wine per day and a 'village rye loaf weighing two pounds' (1975: 276). Roast or boiled meat was served every day, except on Fridays or certain days in Lent.

Today things have changed radically; for centuries, illness and especially epidemics were associated with lack of food, famine and scarcity. The Burgos doctor already quoted by Bartolomé Benassar wrote, 'The present sickness has a specific cause, lack of food for the poor' (1969: 45). At the end of the eighteenth century, the same cause was held responsible for a particularly lethal epidemic of dysentery in Anjou: 'I cannot conceal from you that scarcity of food was the cause of this disease', wrote the Intendant of Tours Du Cluzel in 1783 (quoted Lebrun, 1975: 276). A century later, undernourishment was still regarded as one of the main causes of consumption. One may recall the terrible words of a consumptive woman textile worker from Lille quoted by the Bonneff brothers in their research: 'Since I was married I have never eaten my fill', was all she said. As late as 1914, Maurice Bonneff published a novel, *Didier Homme du Peuple*, about a consumptive trade unionist in which undernourishment plays its part.

Less than fifty years later, overeating is considered by everyone, not just by those whom fortune has favoured, to be responsible for all our ills. According to a taxi driver in 1960, 'People eat too much rich food and it's well known that this is harmful'.

However, above all, our diet today is affected by the 'modern way of life' which is transforming food production. From 1960 onwards, people have drawn attention to the fact that we were eating products whose 'natural' character had been changed by the introduction of 'chemical' elements. Fertilisers, for example, came under heavy attack. Along with dozens of others, a postal worker aged forty-six claimed:

> I've begun to wonder about eggs; we eat eggs, but the hen has been pecking at seeds with chemical fertiliser; in the meadows where the hens graze, there is chemical fertiliser. Is this natural? Or is this really respecting nature's ways?

He contrasted this with the old methods of producing food, where both the content of the product and its 'natural' cycle to maturity are observed.

Twenty years later these ideas have taken root more and more, substantiated by the results of work done on epidemics. The idea that various chemicals used in food products change their 'nature' has taken shape due to additives and preservatives. The idea of a 'forced', or 'faked', 'suspect' product, interfered with for dubious purposes, expresses the individual's feeling of alienation in a society which tampers with the most vital elements and thus creates disease.

Debilitating Work

The perception of a link between illness and *work* has developed differently. Today work, like diet, constitutes an essential element in the representation of the way of life as a cause of illness. In the past, however, for centuries nothing was heard on this from the sick. Doctors in early times related disease to occupation: in the thirteenth century Arnaud de Villeneuve was interested in this, analysing the harmful elements — heat, humidity, dust, poisons, posture at work — which could cause trouble to the workers (cf. Grmek, 1961). In the sixteenth century there was interest in lead poisoning, and in the eighteenth century Tenon described mercury

poisoning (see Valentin, 1978, 23ff, 85ff). In 1701 Ramazzini published his 'Traité des maladies des artisans', a study of more than
fifty occupations (cf. Farge, 1977; Valentin, 1978, 79ff). In the
nineteenth century there was the work of Villermé and other
hygiénists.[11] Lay people, those at least whose evidence can be found
— aristocrats, bourgeois, writers, who, even if not altogether idle,
were not physically burdened with heavy work — were unable or
unwilling to observe and bear witness. Louis-Sebastien Mercier, for
example, in *Le Tableau de Paris*, gives us a good description of the
harsh conditions and work of the ordinary people in Paris: 'The
traveller, whose first glance makes him a better judge than we who
have become accustomed to it, will tell us that of all people, the
people of Paris work hardest, are the worst nourished and appear
saddest' (quoted in Roche, 1981: 150). He describes them as 'bent
under a constant burden of fatigue and work, constructing and
building, forging, deep down in quarries, on the roof-tops, wheel-
ing enormous loads' (Roche, 1981: 151). Yet, as we have seen, it is
the air and more generally 'the city' which is blamed as the cause of
disease.

As for those whose work had a direct physical effect on them —
peasants; artisans; working men; and working women, too, who
according to Madeleine Reberioux (1980) were very common from
the Middle Ages onwards — it was not until the industrialisation
and social conflicts of the nineteenth century that we begin to hear
from them. At the time of the campaign, manifestos and open letters
accompanying the political upheavals in 1830 and 1848, the theme
of work and fatigue as a source of impaired health and cause of
disease emerged in the language of the workers in a way which
today we would call militant.

In 1848 at the National Assembly's enquiry into work, a mining
worker from the Loire gave evidence; for him, if the miner's
conditions of work were not improved, 'we shall soon see the
majority of workers disabled by the age of thirty-five or forty'. He
added, 'it is recognised than on average workers only last until they
are thirty-eight or forty' (quoted in Trempé, 1981). In April 1870
the newspaper *La Marseillaise* gave an account of a worker's statement at a mass meeting of strikers in a sugar refinery:

11. The authors nevertheless emphasise that it is the more general notion of 'poverty'
rather than work and social relationships which is the focus for the work of the
hygienists.

Piece-work is killing us and ruining us. It makes us ill, then we are accused of intemperance, and when we are ill and exhausted, they keep us on our feet for two days. If we are not to succumb, it is imperative that we work a little less and earn a little more. [Quoted Cotterau, 1980, Introduction, note, pp. 23–4]

From then on, exploitation at work is an issue and its physical effects are denounced. We may recall the controversy over tuberculosis at the end of the century; was it a disease of the slums, as the doctors thought, or was it caused by being 'worn out' by work as the workers' unions claimed? Work wears one out: some occupations are killers. The Bonneff brothers called one of their enquiries into occupational disease *Les Metiers qui tuent*. In it they stated, 'The Departments where there is heavy industry have the highest mortality rate for tuberculosis. *The remedy for this state of affairs is not just the drawing up of health regulations. There is a social problem to be resolved*' (Bonneff and Bonneff, n.d., 108, emphasis in original).

Still today we sometimes find the theme of being worn out by work, especially among older workers; for example, in 1972 a man of sixty-five, hospitalised due to serious respiratory problems, who worried about his retirement and how he would manage on reduced means when he could no longer work. In the same year, a printing worker blamed his palpitations on his hours of work and especially the three-shift system:

Before I had no palpitations, I wasn't doing the same job, but now I am doing this job and I can tell you, it's hard going, not the job, but the hours. I work three shifts, so obviously it's gruelling. You have to realise that it's very hard and that your body feels it.

In an interview in 1960, a thirty-five-year-old painter also mentioned working hours, made harder in the cities because of travelling to work:

They told us it's much better now than in 1900. In fact, that's nothing wonderful, because if someone worked fourteen hours in 1900, he lived near his work and when he'd worked for ten hours, he went home to bed and to rest. Now we work eight hours, but after that there's an hour on the underground and an hour on the bus and then half an hour on the train. It's obvious that this leads to lack of rest, *nervous tension, anxiety* which is extremely harmful.

In the contrast between 'nowadays' and a perhaps mythical '1900' we once again see the concept of a 'modern way of life', marked by work subordinated to each individual's occupation and a creator of illness. This concept prevailed in 1960, but for the middle classes it was less a question of being physically worn out than of a decreased physical potential. People talked about 'disequilibrium', 'fatigue' or 'nervous tension' and 'strain', like the taxi driver who spoke not only for himself but for all his fellows:

> Obviously in the life in Paris you can't avoid nervous exhaustion, because everyone in our job has great nervous tension. I'm often tired as others are — it's not just me, it's everyone in this job: everyone complains of nervous fatigue because of the traffic and life in Paris.

This concept of the link between work and illness, like the whole idea of a harmful way of life, is not without some form. People speak less of their state of personal health, or their actual conditions of work and the social relationships which go with this and instead blame in a rather generalised and abstract way the 'agitation', 'overwork' and 'strain' of modern life, which becomes a sort of overall environmental phenomenon effecting everyone equally. In the same way, through questioning the 'social', we are expressing our relationship to it; the illness functions here as a signifier underlying our condemnation of what we call 'society'. Nevertheless, the vision which emerges is transformed: the 'social' is objectified into material environmental conditions — air pollution, processed food, and so on. Illness literally embodies the unsatisfactory relationship which we have with society, but it is only when this relationship becomes material and imprints itself upon nature and distorts it, that our bodies can be affected by it; furthermore, they are all affected in the same way.

However, there was a strong feeling of exteriority and constraint, expressed in the vision of a relationship between individual and society underlying the 'way of life cause of illness' concept. A woman translator aged fifty, for example, gave a very clear analysis of the constraints placed upon her by her way of life. It was impossible to change:

> If I go to the doctor, he says: 'Change your relationships with your family, your daughter and husband, your way of life and your work, your colleagues — then you will get better'. What do you want me to make of this sort of advice? It may be psychologically very sound, but in practice it's useless, because you can't reorganise your life. You're in a

particular situation and that's how it is. The doctor is telling me to leave my job. That's all very well: what if I tell him to leave his job? It would mean changing one's whole way of life; it's not possible.

The impression of feeling a stranger to one's way of life is often expressed in interviews. It is not, people say, 'made for them', nor even in general, for anyone at all: 'I don't believe the human body is made to live like this', said a young female teacher; 'generally speaking, towns are designed to make people ill'. This way of looking at things calls into question our definition of society and of man's very nature, not just the causality of biological illness. Many people spoke of the idea of man's very nature being changed by modern society and our way of life.

Lay Representations and the Medical Debate

Today, coupled with criticism of the limitations of modern medicine in overcoming disease and emphasising the need for preventive medicine, there is a whole literature stressing the importance of thinking about causality in terms of multiple factors. Only a systems approach, involving an analysis of the interrelationships between the different variables, enables us to advance our understanding. This broader conception of health and illness must certainly include variables in the environment, the physical and social milieu. In a polemical article which attracted a great deal of attention in English-speaking countries, John Powles shows how certain improvements in our 'way of life' (better food and hygiene) have had as much effect as medical progress on the reduction in infectious diseases. However, he does add, 'Unfortunately this new way of life, because it is so far removed from that to which man is adapted by evolution, has produced its own disease burden. These diseases of maladaptation are, in many cases increasing' (Powles, 1973: 12). However, not everyone accepts these ideas, and the medical world is divided on this issue. Dr Lewis Thomas, Director of the Cancer Research Institute of the Sloan Kettering Foundation in New York, believes in a causal mechanism for each disease:

> For every disease there is a single, central, mechanism that dominates all the rest, and if you are looking for effective treatment or prevention, you have to find that mechanism first, and start from that . . . I believe that

cancer will turn out to have a single switch gone wrong, somewhere at
the deep interior of the cell . . . I agree that there are numberless environmental carcinogens, all capable of launching cancer, and perhaps multiple
cancer viruses as well, but in the centre is that switch, common to all
forms of cancer, waiting to be found. [Thomas, 1977:25–6]

How are we to understand this relationship between lay representations and medical debate? Should we see it as a successful
dissemination of scientific ideas and theories which have been
accepted by the public at large which echoes them? Certainly, on
particular issues, such as the connection between smoking and lung
cancer, or in connection with specific pollution, information has
been widely diffused, especially in recent years. However, the idea
of our way of life generating illness is much more than just a
spillover of medical knowledge: the problem is much more complex. First we can see that in the 1960s, information on these issues
— popular books and articles, information in the serious news-
papers and the media — was already available. In addition, some
factors which were already 'discovered' — the link between tobacco
and cancer, for example — were precisely those which were treated
with scepticism and about which information was greeted largely
with incredulity. The collective representation of a harmful way of
life seems much more a self-generating phenomenon. Basic anthropological explanations — those of illness from the exterior, of a
disease entity which attacks the intrinsically healthy individual —
are expressed according to sensory perceptions of an environment
and conditions of life shaped by industrial production and urbani-
sation. We have been aware of these since the eighteenth century.
Into this framework may be fitted various kinds of information
emanating from the body of medical knowledge and debates, but it
is only because they are congruent with these already existing
socio-symbolic explanations that they can be assimilated and make
sense.

As we have already shown in the case of contagion, we must
therefore think of the two-way relationships between professional
and lay concepts. Moreover, current environmentalist and preventive trends in medicine are not new. They bring us back to the ideas
of the eighteenth and nineteenth century hygienists, and a debate,
which, although still vigorous today, has already gone on for more
than a century. This debate also shows that the fundamental schema
of medical knowledge are rooted in anthropology and that they may

well be derived from the same sources as lay knowledge. Medical debates today do, of course, originate in the sophisticated models of epidemiology, but they are also informed by observation of our common thought and schema. Furthermore, in medicine too, the problem of meaning is not wholly absent. Medical science is essentially a social science according to the nineteenth century hygienists, and few doctors today would disagree. Medicine cannot therefore, ignore the view of society which is at the heart of the concept of the way of life as a cause of illness.

The Individual and His Illness: The Hidden Meaning

All the ætiological conceptions which we have described, whether they concern air, contagion, germs or the way of life, have one thing in common: they see *illness as something which comes from the exterior*. However, anthropologists have shown us that in most human societies, conceptions of illness oscillate between two extremes: 'exogenous' conceptions, where the illness is identified with an attack by some factor from the exterior, and 'endogenous' conceptions, where in different ways, *illness is 'within the individual' and part of him*. This idea of illness coming from within is sometimes expressed in lay terms in the extreme form of the 'existence' of an illness which everyone carries within themselves and which one day manifests itself. In 1960 a thirty-one-year-old business man expressed his views on the origins of illness in the following way:

> In my opinion, everyone is ill and most people are not aware of it; that's to say, *we all carry illness within ourselves* . . . and depending on our times and circumstances and the state of our nerves, the illnesses may or may not reveal themselves.

In 1917 Franz Kafka produced the idea of 'two beings' at war within himself, one of which, the benevolent one, identified itself with the wound which is the tuberculosis while the other inflicted it and subsequently took advantage of it (Kafka, 1967, letter of 30 Sept./ 1 Oct. 1917).

In the two examples quoted, the well-known writer and the anonymous individual, the illness, albeit in very different ways, had an autonomous existence. Internal to the individual, it nevertheless had its own life and being. This 'ontological' view, however, is by

91

no means the most frequent. More often, the endogenous explanations are those such as a disorder of the body or a break in its rhythm where there is also a link with the external: in Hippocratic theory, 'temperaments' are due to a balance between natural elements (air, fire, earth and water) and 'humours' belonging to the individual (blood, phlegm, choler and melancholy). For centuries these ideas, extending beyond medical knowledge, structured the speech of the man in the street and were the basis of his perception of himself. In the seventeenth century, for example, Pierre de L'Estoile tells us of the treatment he received from his doctor, M. de Helin: 'very learned, very wise and every expert, he treated me gently and wisely according to my humour and complexion' (L'Estoile, 1958: 464).

However, in the mid-nineteenth century the notion of heredity, whose spectre, Jean-Paul Aron tells us, 'had been quietly making its way in medical thought for a century, suddenly erupted into the current vocabulary' (Aron, 1980: 15). This constituted one of the major periods for the endogenous view of illness. However, according to Jean-Paul Aron, heredity was at first and for a considerable period a social and institutional concept, a role codifying filiation and generative relationships, before it was expressed as actual biological knowledge (Aron, 1969: 187–203). Mendel's laws of cross-fertilisation were not formulated until 1865 and were forgotten for a long time until genetics was established. On the other hand, in the early nineteenth century, the best-known dictionary of natural sciences did not yet contain any mention of 'heredity'. Among lay people, moreover, the whole nature of consanguinity remained a mystery for a long time.

However, the notion of pathological heredity, transmitting disease through the generations, existed, as we see from the Bible, long before our overall understanding of the problem of heredity. Here it is a question, since the Atrides, of the lasting nature of disease and its resurgence in generation after generation. It is this theme of disease, biological disease, social disease, which comes to the fore in the mid-nineteenth century in the idea of 'bad blood' — in medical theories about degeneration but also in the work of Zola, or in the distress which permeated the whole society when faced with alcoholism or syphilis. This moralistic view of pathological heredity is a persistent one.

Nevertheless, it is questionable whether the idea of an illness entirely linked to heredity has ever been accepted. If, as we believe, there is always a search for the meaning of illness behind the enquiries into its causes, can the idea of inherited disease be accepted other than with utter despair — Oswald in Ibsen's *Ghosts* for example? Furthermore, is not pathological heredity usually seen as something concerning *other people*; for example, the bourgeoisie attributed defective children to the drunken proletariat, and the people linking the debauchery of the aristocracy with the line dying out and degenerating. For the individual himself, however, the idea of attack from the exterior is necessary to enable him to contemplate without revulsion the disorders which afflict him. The neutral character of genetic concepts in recent years has changed nothing: 'way of life' not DNA remains central to our perceptions of illness.

However, even more than in notions of heredity, situation or disposition, the recognition of the intrinsic relationship between the individual and his illness is conveyed by the frequent citing throughout history of the role of the mind, of mood — happiness or sadness — of morale, the psyche, in the development of disease. A few examples are enough to convince us that this is a fundamental insight. At the time of the great epidemics, it was widely agreed that a happy man did not catch the plague. In the sixteenth century, Montaigne attributed the good health of the inhabitants of Brazil to their calm disposition:

What we are told of the inhabitants of Brazil, that they never die but of old age, is attributed to the tranquility and serenity of their climate. I rather attribute it to the tranquility and serenity of their souls, which are free from all passion, thought or any absorbing and unpleasant labours.[1603: 486]

In 1960 a sales representative in industry expressed the same thought: 'Since I got married, I've never been ill and I feel it's because I'm happy and I have the impression it is because I am happy that I am no longer ill'.

Conversely, sadness and grief have been recognised at different times as direct causes of illness, by lay opinion as well as by doctors. Thus Pierre L'Estoile's analysis in 1608 of the death of Queen Elizabeth of England: 'The opinion of all the Queen's doctors and of those who had attended her and served her privately in her chamber is that her illness is caused by a sorrow which she has always concealed' (L'Estoile, 1958: 98). In 1972 a woman of forty-nine, a pianist without work, interpreted the incipient tuberculosis

93

which had brought her into hospital in the following way:

> I think it's a general condition following a very, very long period of
> distress and a very, very long period of suffering, with a lot of difficulties
> of all kinds. It's almost, I think, the outcome of twenty-five years of
> uninterrupted hardship.

Illness of the Self

At the present time, perhaps more than at any other, 'morale' and
the psyche are thought of in connection with organic disease. The
slightest thing is thought and readily admitted to be 'psychosomatic'. The phrase varies according to social class — 'Illness begins
little by little in the mind' according to a young painter in 1960. 'My
subconscious invites illness and takes refuge in it' according to a
thirty-seven-year-old woman writer in the same year. This is essentially the same insight: that of a complex and somewhat mysterious
interaction between mind and body. Rousseau gave this same
explanation for a rather odd illness — buzzing in the ears, palpitations, weakness — which troubled him for a number of years when
he was living at Les Charmettes with Madame De Warens (1967:
247). In 1972 a forty-year-old official of the Algerian railways also
saw his illness — a violent bout of dysentery — as a sort of price to
be paid for his success at work. Working on the enquiry into a
derailment which had caused the death of twenty-four people, he
had 'taken the affair terribly to heart'. He had to struggle to get his
point of view accepted but in the end:

> There, in front of everyone, I won. Everyone was obliged to accept my
> version. I was very tired with the work and travelling, so much so that on
> the very evening of my success, I went down with very bad dysentery,
> which started that same evening.

In the romantic view of tuberculosis, which is without doubt one
of the most familiar expressions of the 'illness of the individual', the
idea of a 'price to be paid' is also present — the price for an
exceptional personality, for passion and genius. In addition, the
individual 'welcomes' his illness; he makes room in his life for an
ailment in which he recognises himself. This idea of 'consenting to
illness' is in some way the corollary to the price-to-be-paid concept.
In the 1960s several people spoke not only of their acceptance of

illness but even of their desire for it. A young architect said, 'I have always liked to imagine the possibility of being immobilised for a while, and of being placed, through illness, in a world apart'. Such expressions convey a view also found in psychoanalysis, that of escaping into illness when the individual finds himself in an intolerable situation. In a case like this, the escape into illness is also a cry for help.

The illness, in these circumstances, even if it corresponds to a degree of withdrawal on the part of the sick person when confronted with a conflict or situation which is too much to bear, is not the real trouble. On the contrary, it is an ally, a physical reaction, almost a vital reaction which enables the individual to avoid something worse. Moreover, as psychoanalytic theory tells us — and as we all know only too well — illness brings 'fringe benefits', it allows us to escape from the sometimes unbearable constraints of everyday life. In his journal in 1942 Dr René Allendy, a psychoanalyst, remembers the illnesses of his childhood: 'I remember the pleasure of burrowing down into the bed and knowing I would have to make no more efforts or have any responsibility for an indeterminate period' (1980: 67). In 1960 a young teacher, thinking of the meaning illness could have in childhood, expresses an even more subtle view: illness gave one access to an exceptional world, much more satisfying than the everyday one; it also enabled him to find himself.

In this perspective the individual identifies biological illness with the deepest, most valued part of his personality and sets it against the social persona which is formed and demanded by the alienating society. However, in some cases, on the contrary, biological illness seen as 'illness of the self' constitutes an intolerable truth which can only lead to despair; for example, when, by its very gravity and the intensity of its threat on our life, illness such as cancer can only be seen as a failure of our whole being. It is also particularly intolerable when the individual, confronted with the failure of his own life, feels that the illness is a physical manifestation of this. Because it makes itself felt physically, illness, more than anything else, imposes a final sense of defeat.

It is, therefore, not surprising that in such cases each of us is reluctant to recognise his illness as an 'illness of the self' produced by another disorder, that of our whole personality. As Freud said, we can scarcely speak of death except to deny it. In the same way, we can scarcely acknowledge our own irremediable collapse. The meaning of illness, if it comes from within ourselves, almost always remains obscure to us. As a rule, just as we each see only the defect of our neighbour, not our own, it is *other people* who tell us that the cause is in ourselves. Then despair is replaced by revolt, by a refusal of this interpretation experienced as intolerable aggression. Susan Sontag (1979) wrote *Illness as Metaphor* as a reply to those who saw her cancer as the defeat of her personality.

5

None of the extracts so far included in this volume has addressed the issue of gender or of how concepts of health, illness and healing may vary between the sexes. In the extract which follows, Hilary Graham and Ann Oakley explore the very different ways in which mothers and obstetricians think about pregnancy and childbirth. These differences result from a long process of the medicalisation of childbirth, whereby obstetricians claimed the care of pregnant and parturient women from midwives and wise women and transferred that care from the domestic to the public domain (Arney, 1983; Donnison, 1977; Oakley, 1976, 1984). Women's thinking about childbirth has been 'medicalised' for over a century in the sense in which Jocelyn Cornwell (1984) uses that term to mean that their lay beliefs have over the years been affected by, and in part derive from, medical teaching and behaviour. Nevertheless, as Graham and Oakley show, the women think much more in terms of pregnancy and birth as 'natural' physiological processes, while their medical attendants think in terms of pathology or potential pathology. Their apparently common goal of a successful outcome for mother and baby is defined rather differently. Many social and psychological features are seen as part of the processes by the women but are ignored, and therefore not attended to, by the obstetricians.

Arthur Kleinman's model does not altogether fit the case discussed by Graham and Oakley, addressed as it is to variations in concepts derived from differences of sex and gender, as well as from differences between professional and lay sectors. The healing, if that is the correct word for the care of pregnant and parturient women, takes place in the professional sector. The women's ideas derive partly from that sector and partly from the domestic or popular sector. Those divisions are perhaps less important, however, than another; namely, that what women feel and know about their bodies sometimes conflicts with the construction put on the processes of gestation and birth by obstetricians. The former concepts derive from individual experience and also from shared knowledge and understanding among women; the latter derive from a masculinist science and treatment processes developed historically by male obstetricians. The mismatch between the women and their obstetricians reported for both the London and the York samples is associated with what are basically different systems of knowledge. These in their turn are related to the differential social position, power and interests of the two groups.

The paper was published originally in 1981.   *Eds.*

HILARY GRAHAM
ANN OAKLEY

Competing Ideologies of Reproduction: Medical and Maternal Perspectives on Pregnancy

In talking about the different ways in which doctors and mothers view pregnancy, we are talking about a fundamental difference in their perspectives on the meaning of childbearing.[1] It is not simply a difference of opinion about approach and procedures — about whether pregnancy is normal or pathological, or whether or not labour should be routinely induced. Rather, we are suggesting that doctors and mothers have a qualitatively different way of looking at the nature, context and management of reproduction. In this chapter we use the concept of a 'frame of reference' to indicate this difference. 'Frame of reference' embraces both the notion of an ideological perspective — a system of values and attitudes through which mothers and doctors view pregnancy — and of a reference group, consisting of a network of individuals who have significant influence upon these sets of attitudes and values.

We will first of all describe the main features of the two frames of reference and then go on to discuss some of the ways in which differences between them are displayed in antenatal consultations and in women's experiences of having a baby.

1. The background to the paper consists of two research projects, one undertaken in the Social Research Unit of Bedford College, University of London, by Ann Oakley, and funded by the Social Science Research Council; the other in the Department of Sociology, University of York, by Hilary Graham and Lorna McKee, and funded by the Health Education Council. Both projects are concerned with women's experiences of pregnancy, childbearing and the early post-natal period. In addition, the London project included a period of six months' observation of staff–patient interaction in a maternity hospital. Both the projects have uncovered a substantial amount of data relating to both users' and providers' views on how the maternity services do and should operate. Although the studies cover two different geographical areas and two different hospitals — a small provincial and a large metropolitan one — the two projects point to basic similarities in attitudes and experiences.

99

Obstetricians and Mothers: Contrasts in their Frame of Reference

The differences in the two frames of reference revolved around divergent views of both the nature of childbearing and the context in which it is seen. Specifically, our data suggest that mothers and doctors disagree on whether pregnancy is a natural or a medical process and whether, as a consequence, pregnancy should be abstracted from the woman's life-experiences and treated as an isolated medical event. These two issues are in turn related to two other areas of disagreement. The first concerns the way the quality of childbearing is assessed; in other words, what are the criteria of success? The second concerns the way the quality of reproduction is ensured; that is, who controls childbearing? It is these four issues (what is the nature and context of reproduction, how is success measured and how is it controlled?) that lie at the heart of the conflict between mothers' and doctors' frames of reference. Anthropologists have discussed questions about the nature, context and control of childbearing in describing the differences in the management of childbirth between Western and non-Western cultures (Mead and Newton, 1967; Mnecke, 1976; Oakley, 1977). The issues of nature, context and control have also been identified as crucial to an understanding of the historical development of Western obstetrics (Oakley, 1976). Interestingly, these dimensions have been less systematically explored in the study of the structure and processes of modern maternity care.

Nature of Childbearing

Obstetricians.   The key element in the doctor's perspective on reproduction is the status of reproduction as a medical subject. Pregnancy and birth are analogous to other physiological processes as topics of medical knowledge and treatment. The association of obstetrics with gynaecology, as a specialism, reinforces this lack of distinction between reproduction and the rest of medicine, by setting aside a special area to do with the physiological attributes of womanhood (Fleury, 1967; Rathbone, 1973; Scully and Bart, 1972–73).

Mothers.   Bearing children is seen by mothers to be a natural biological process. It is akin to other biological processes (like menstruation) that occur in woman's life. This is not to say that it is a woman's 'natural destiny' to bear children. Rather, for those women who do, the process is rooted in their bodies and in their lives and not in a medical textbook (Graham, 1977).

Context of Childbearing

Obstetricians. The obstetrician's frame of reference attaches a particular, and a limited, significance to pregnancy and birth as medical events. The doctor views the individual's career as a pregnant and parturient woman as an isolated patient-episode. Pregnancy means entry into medical care as an antenatal patient, and the end of the pregnancy, marked by discharge from maternity care, is the termination of this career. Being a patient is the woman's key status so far as the obstetrician is concerned, although other statuses she might have, for example as an unmarried person, as an engineer or street-cleaner, may affect the doctor's attitudes and behaviour *vis-à-vis* the patient by influencing his/her perception of the kind of medical treatment and patient-communication that is most appropriate (Stoller Shaw, 1974; Macintyre, 1976; Aitken Swan, 1977).

Mothers. A woman views reproduction not as an isolated episode of medical treatment but as an event which is integrated with other aspects of her life. Having a baby affects not only her medical status, it has implications for most of her other social roles. This is seen most clearly during first pregnancy and birth, when a woman becomes a mother; that is, she acquires a new social role. But even in subsequent births, her role can change as her pregnancy affects her occupational standing, her financial position, her housing situation, her marital status and her personal relationships. As Hart (1977) has shown, the new baby impinges permanently and comprehensively on a woman's life-style.

Criteria of Success

Obstetricians. The obstetrician's frame of reference gives a particular and again restricted meaning to the notion of 'successful' reproduction. Here the reference point is perinatal and maternal mortality rates, and to a lesser degree certain restricted indices of morbidity. A 'successful' pregnancy is one which results in a physically healthy baby and mother as assessed in the period

101

immediately following the birth; that is, while mother and child are still under the obstetrician's care (Haire, 1972; Richards, 1974).

Mothers. Because of the holistic way in which women view childbearing, the notion of successful reproduction is considerably more complex than the simple measurement of mortality and morbidity. Though in almost all cases the goal of the live birth of a healthy infant is paramount, success means primarily a satisfactory personal experience. This applies not only to the pregnancy and birth but to the subsequent mother–baby relationship and to the way in which motherhood is integrated with the rest of a woman's life. Unlike the obstetrician's criteria of success, these criteria — pregnancy/birth experiences, experiences with the mother–baby relationship, and experiences with integrating motherhood into a woman's life-style — are not separable or easily observable, but can only be assessed in the weeks, months or even years following birth (Kitzinger, 1972).

Control of Childbearing

Obstetricians. The medical frame of reference defines reproduction as a specialist subject in which obstetricians are the experts, possessing (by virtue of their training) greater expertise than any other social group. This expertise is not limited to any one particular area (e.g. the mechanics of the birth process) but is held to extend to the entire symptomatology of childbearing (Scully and Bart, 1972–73; Kaiser and Kaiser, 1974).

Mothers. Mothers view themselves as knowledgeable about pregnancy and birth. This knowledge stems not primarily from medical science but rather from a woman's capacity to sense and respond to the sensations of her body. Rather than being an abstract knowledge acquired through formal training, it is thus an individualised and to some extent intuitive knowledge built up from bodily experiences (Boyle, 1975; Goldthorpe and Richman, 1976; McKinlay, 1973).

Conflicts in the Frames of Reference

How do the conflicts we have seen between medical and maternal frames of reference manifest themselves? In trying to explain this, we concentrate on data relating to interaction in the antenatal clinic as this is the main forum in which mothers and medics meet. We have selected dimensions of doctor–patient interaction which illustrate and substantiate the differences between doctors and mothers already identified. These four dimensions are: (1) conflict over the status of reproduction as health or illness; (2) the question of the doctor-as-expert *versus* the mother-as-expert; (3) the issue of who makes the decisions about reproductive care; and (4) the kind of communication doctors and mothers see as appropriate to their joint interaction.

Health or Illness?

One important norm within the culture of the medical profession is that judging a sick person to be well should be more avoided than judging a well person as sick. This 'medical decision rule' is applied to obstetrics as it is to other branches of medicine; every pregnancy and labour is treated as though it is, or could be, abnormal, and the weight of the obstetrician's medical education acts against his/her achievement of work satisfaction in the treatment of unproblematic reproduction (Scheff, 1963). The 'as if ill' role was a recurrent feature in the observed interactions between doctors and patients. It was made explicit when doctors needed to explain or justify particular medical attitudes and routines to their patients. Such explanations and justifications might be called for when a doctor discussed the type of antenatal care he/she felt most appropriate for his patient, when advising on a woman's employment and domestic commitment or when prescribing medical treatment.' For example:

Patient. I'm a hairdresser. I only do three days a week — is it all right to go on working?

Doctor. Up to twenty-eight weeks is all right on the whole, especially if you have a trouble-free pregnancy as you obviously have. After that it's better to give up.

Patient. I only work three days a week, I feel fine.

Doctor. Yes, everything *is* fine, but now you've got to this stage it's better to give up, just in case.

But the most common way in which the 'as if ill' rule is mani-

2. Maternal employment *per se* is of course not related to reproductive causality, although other variables that are associated with it, for instance low socio-economic status, do show some such relationship (Illsley, 1967).

fested in antenatal care today is through the routine prescription of various tests and procedures such as ultrasonic scanning, twenty-four-hour urine collection for the measurement of placental function, and frequent internal examination to assess the competence of the cervix. The subject of tests and procedures occupies an important place in the antenatal encounter. In nearly half the encounters observed in the London hospital, there was at least one reference to technology — to one testing procedure or another. Of the questions asked by patients, 29 per cent concerned medical technology — ultrasound, blood tests, induction, and so on — and another 5 per cent concerned prescribed drugs. For some women these sophisticated procedures and forms of treatment are the hallmark of a 'proper' pregnancy. Other women felt less happy about this medicalisation of childbearing, unaware, perhaps, of the equation between pregnancy and illness until they began their careers as antenatal patients. The first antenatal visit thus comes as a considerable shock, disturbing long-held notions about pregnancy as a natural process. One London mother put the case succinctly:

> I thought, okay, first baby, the best thing to do is to have it in hospital, because it's far more of an unknown quantity . . . but it's this concern with medicine that seems to override everything else — the natural process, I mean. I mean it is something that women have always been brought up to do; everybody knows that. Okay, it's painful, having labour and everything, but it's very rewarding. It's the one pain we've been brought up to expect and not to be scared of. Before the hospital thing, pregnancy was a normal, nice condition. I'm not sure it isn't an illness now.

Apprehension about medicalised reproduction is greatest among primiparae (first-time mothers), two-thirds of whom expressed anxiety about antenatal check-ups. The focus of this anxiety is often the vaginal examination, and, for more than half of the York and London primiparae, this was their first experience of this examination.

> I'll tell you what terrified me, the internal, cos I'd never had one before and the very thought of it, oh God! For a week I was so nervous, I thought I'd get desperate diarrhoea, I was all colly wobbles and I was like that for a whole week.

The vaginal examination is of course an important part of antenatal work. Of the encounters observed in the London hospital, 28 per cent included an internal examination, but rarely was the medical rationale for the examination made explicit. Again, the 'as if ill' rule is rarely articulated by medical staff unless a procedure or a prescription is questioned or challenged by a patient. This is illustrated in the following consultation, where a patient refuses an internal examination. She has had a previous termination and her cervix is being assessed fortnightly as part of a research project designed to see whether regular internal examinations are of any use in preventing abortion due to cervical incompetence. On this occasion she refuses the examination, and the doctor asks why:

Patient. The doctor last time, he hurt me, and I had a lot of bleeding afterwards — he promised he wouldn't do it again.

Doctor. I don't care a damn what the doctor promised last time. If you lose the baby it's up to you. Do you know why we do these examinations?

Patient. I thought it was to tell the size of the baby.

Doctor. No, it's nothing to do with that. You've had a termination and this can cause prematurity, and we look to see if the womb is opening up. If it is, we put a stitch in.

The purpose of the regular internal examinations had clearly not been explained to the patient — until she challenged medical dictate.

Who Is the Expert?

A second way in which the differences between doctors' and mothers' frames of reference is manifested is in conflicts over expertise: in conflicts between doctor-as-expert and mother-as-expert. The definition and interpretation of significant symptoms was a common area of divergence between mothers and doctors. To the doctor, symptoms of importance are those that betray the patient's clinical condition: swollen fingers or ankles, blurred vision, bleeding and so forth. But the patient may very often report symptoms which worry her but which do not worry the doctor. She is reacting to her subjective experience of pregnancy, to her feelings about the physical and emotional changes that pregnancy has brought about. For example:

Patient. I get pains in my groin, down here; why is that?

Doctor. Well, it's some time since your last pregnancy, and also your centre of gravity is changing.

Patient. I see.

Doctor. That's okay. [Pats on back.]

Since it is often possible from the patient's account for the doctor to assess the clinical significance of the symptom, the patient's statement of pain may be ignored or dismissed in a joking manner.

Patient. I've got a pain in my shoulder.

Doctor. Well, that's your shopping-bag hand, isn't it?

Differences in symptom description are of course a general characteristic of doctor–patient interaction (Stimson and Webb, 1975). This kind of medical response, which may evoke considerable anxiety in the patient, was far from rare: of the 677 statements made by patients during the series of antenatal clinic encounters observed in London, 12 per cent concerned symptoms of pain or discomfort which the doctor ignored or dismissed as clinically unimportant. Mothers also state their feelings about the pregnancy and the birth, sometimes relating these to their social circumstances — a bad marriage, poor housing, for instance — and 8 per cent of the statements made by patients were of this kind. Very rarely did the doctor respond seriously to such statements:

Patient. My doctor gave me some tablets for vomiting earlier on but I was reluctant to take them.

Doctor. Are you still reluctant?

Patient. Well I feel so depressed, I'm so fed up . . .

Doctor. [interrupting] Shall I give you some tablets for vomiting?

Mothers' and doctors' different fields of expertise also compete over the dating of the pregnancy. In the London hospital, as in others, the date of the patient's last menstrual period is asked for routinely on booking-in at the clinic, and the time at which foetal movements are first felt is also requested. The routinisation of these questions acknowledges their importance, but medical attitudes to the reliability of women's information on these points tend to be sceptical. For example:

Doctor. How many weeks are you now?

Patient. Twenty-six-and-a-half.

Doctor. [looking at case notes] Twenty weeks now.

Patient. No, twenty-six-and-a-half.

Doctor. You can't be.

Patient. Yes, I am; look at the ultrasound report.

Doctor. When was it done?

Patient. Today.

Doctor. It was done today?

Patient. Yes.

Doctor. [reads report] Oh yes, twenty-six-and-a-half weeks, that's right.

Perhaps it is significant that increasingly the routine use of ultra-sound is providing an alternative medical technique for the assessment of gestation length; a medical rationale for the inflation of medical over maternal expertise is thus provided. During consultations in the London antenatal clinic, 6 per cent of the questions asked and 5 per cent of the statements made by mothers concerned dates — mothers usually trying to negotiate the 'correct' date of expected delivery with the doctor who did not see this as a subject for negotiation or as a legitimate area of maternal expertise.

Who Controls Reproduction?

The women interviewed both in York and London reported very few areas in which they were able to exercise choice about the kind of maternity care they had. From the moment they first saw a doctor about the pregnancy, decisions were made for them. As one mother in York put it:

> Well, when I went to see my doctor, he's ever so nice, he said he advised me to have it in hospital. I'm more or less putting my foot down, he said, that you have it in hospital. So I really didn't have any choice.

This lack of control experienced by mothers extended right through their antenatal careers. One sign of mothers' desires to feel in control of their reproductive care is the number of questions they ask about the progress of their pregnancy. Of all questions asked in the London antenatal clinic, 20 per cent concerned the size or position of the baby, foetal heart sounds, maternal weight and blood pressure. A further 20 per cent were questions about the physiology of pregnancy and birth in general or about related medical procedures. These are serious requests but are often casually treated by doctors with resulting confusion and anxiety in the mother.

Actual conflict between mother and doctor over medical decisions was rare in the research series, but it did characterise some encounters, and was particularly likely to do so when decisions about delivery were being made. These confrontations between mothers and doctors thus illustrate one way in which some women express a desire to control what happens to them in childbirth.

A registrar, examining a woman towards the end of her first

pregnancy, does an internal examination and comments:

> *Doctor.* It'd be difficult to get you off now — I think you ought
> to come in for the rest and to do some more water tests and
> then we can start you off. The baby isn't growing as fast as it
> was.
>
> *Patient.* What do you mean, come in?
>
> *Doctor.* Really it's a matter of *when* you come in, Sunday, I
> should think, and then stay in.
>
> *Patient.* Stay in until it's born, you mean.
>
> *Doctor.* Yes.
>
> *Patient.* I don't fancy that very much.
>
> *Doctor.* If you'd been ready I would have started you off today.
> You see, on the ultrasound it's not growing as well as it was,
> and on the water tests the oestriols are falling — it's not bad,
> but you should come in and have some water tests, get some
> rest, and then we can start you off sometime next week prob-
> ably, when you're ready.
>
> *Patient.* If my husband wanted to come and talk to you about
> inducing me, can I make an appointment for him?
>
> *Doctor.* I don't think anything your husband said would affect
> our decision one way or the other.
>
> *Patient.* No, but he would like to talk to you.
>
> *Doctor.* Yes, well he can talk to whoever's on duty, but there's
> nothing he can say that will affect us: it's a medical question.
>
> *Patient.* Yes, but he'd still like to talk it over, find out what's
> going on.
>
> *Doctor.* What it amounts to is that we won't be browbeaten by
> *The Sunday Times.*[3]
>
> *Patient.* No, I understand that.
>
> *Doctor.* If we explained to everyone, and everyone's husband,
> we'd spend all our time explaining. *I think you've got to assume*
> *if you come here for medical attention that we make all the*
> *decisions.* In fact, I think you should come in today, but I've
> already been browbeaten into saying Sunday, which is another
> forty-eight hours.

Here the doctor refuses to 'discuss' the proposed induction with the
patient, taking it as axiomatic that the most that should be expected
of him is an explanation of the reasons why he wants to induce

---

3. The doctor is referring to two articles written by L. Gillie and O. Gillie (1974) in
The Sunday Times.

labour. Interestingly, cases in the series where patients objected to induction all met with hostility from the doctor, whereas when the patient either explicitly or implicitly requested an induction this met with a very different response: in some cases the patient's request was granted, but even where it was not, the plea for induction was accepted as legitimate patient-behaviour. In asking for an induction, the patient is subscribing to two important norms in obstetric treatment: the idea that technological childbirth is 'good' childbirth, and the notion that while the doctor's superior expertise may be challenged by *refusing* medical decisions, it is *confirmed* by polite requests for them; 'begging for mercy' is how the doctors often described such requests.

The Communication Gap

Problems in communicating with doctors were commonly reported in both York and London. Mothers' comments pick out the following related themes:[4]

not feeling able to ask questions;

not having sufficient explanation of medical treatment or the progress of the pregnancy from the doctor;

being treated as ignorant;

seeing too many different doctors;

feeling rushed, like 'battery hens', animals in a 'cattle market' or items on a 'conveyor belt' or an 'assembly line'.

Asking Questions. In the London hospital observations, questions asked by patients averaged slightly more than one per encounter, and statements made by patients (i.e. not in response to anything the doctor said) slightly less. Of the women interviewed in York, 80 per cent said that they had learnt nothing from their antenatal check-ups; 40 per cent felt they couldn't ask questions — and of those who did feel they could in theory, many didn't in practice:

The nurse says, 'Now, do you want to ask the doctor anything?' And more invariably than not you say 'no' because you just don't feel you can. The

---

4. It is interesting to note the similarity between these themes and those picked out in the Standing Maternity and Midwifery Advisory Committee document *Human Relations and Obstetrics*, (HMSO, 1961).

way they ask you, 'Right, do you want to ask the doctor anything?' you think, no. All you want to do is get up and get out.

Getting Explanations.   When mothers do ask questions they usually require much fuller information than the medical staff are prepared to give. A quick 'that's normal' or 'that's nothing to worry about' is not sufficient. Take the disquiet experienced by one London mother:

> I've been getting really bad stomach pains like I'm coming on. I said that to the doctor — I said I had bad stomach pains. He said it's usual, but I mean they're getting worse. I said I'm getting pains like I'm coming on. He said you do get this. But they're getting worse. It might *be* usual but. . .

Being Treated as Ignorant.   These complaints relate to medical definitions of mothers as ignorant about medical aspects of pregnancy. One York mother, worried about contact with rubella, said:

> I mean you don't need to have done midwifery to know the complications and I wanted an answer. I think my own GP sent my blood off on the Friday and this was Tuesday or Wednesday so I knew the results were there [at the clinic]. But, 'Oh you might hear in the next few days'; it wasn't good enough for me, every hour I was thinking about it. . . Some nurses and doctors are terribly condescending. And this girl irritated me, so I said, 'When will I know the results of this rubella test?' 'It's out of your hands now, deary, the doctor knows all about it', and I did feel very irritated by that. I'm an intelligent woman and it annoyed me.

The assumption of ignorance may be a common component in doctors' attitudes to patients (Kaiser and Kaiser, 1974; Davis and Horobin, 1977) but patients in antenatal clinics are always women and the doctors are predominantly men (Ehrenreich, 1974).[5] Typifications of women as women are certainly articulated in antenatal consultations; for example:[6]

Doctor. How many babies have you got?

Patient. This is the third pregnancy.

Doctor. Doing your duty, aren't you?

Or:

5. In September 1977, 25.4 per cent of the gynaecologists and obstetricians in England and Wales listed as hospital medical staff by the DHSS were women.
6. A similar pattern of attitudes and treatment regarding female patients has been found outside gynaecology and obstetrics. *See* Barrett and Roberts, 1978.

Doctor. This is twins. . .they're growing well, but you need more rest. . .I'd advise some good books and a quiet life for three months. You're not working.

Patient. No.

Doctor. Just normal exercise — I want you to have a walk every day, but no gardening, no heavy work; postpone moving or decorating the house. If you do rest, you'll grow yourself slightly bigger babies. After all, it's this [pats her abdomen] that's your most important job isn't it?

And women, it is implied, are inherently unreliable sources of information:

Doctor. [reading case notes] Ah, I see you've got a boy and a girl.

Patient. No, two girls.

Doctor. Really. Are you sure? I thought it said. . .[checks in notes] oh no, you're quite right, two girls.

Or:

Doctor. Are you absolutely sure of your dates?

Patient. Yes, and I can even tell you the date of conception. [Doctor laughs.] No, I'm serious, this is an artificial insemination baby. [The husband is a paraplegic, and the patient's previous child was also born as a result of artificial insemination.]

Seeing Different Doctors. The problem of unsatisfactory communication with doctors is compounded by seeing a different face at every clinic visit. One London mother describes her experience:

The thing is you get such *varied* opinions — one of them says about your weight, and the next time you go I think this is it: I'm going to be told off about my weight again, and then I go and I see somebody completely different and nobody says a thing about it . . . I come out feeling completely confused.

In the York sample, 81 per cent of mothers said they would prefer to see the same doctor every time.

Being on a Conveyor Belt. All these communication difficulties are related to the organisation of antenatal clinics which tend to resemble assembly lines, if only because a small number of doctors must see a large number of patients in a short space of time. In the London antenatal clinic the average time per doctor–patient encounter was 3.9 minutes. It is rarely possible within this framework for mothers to feel that they have been treated as individuals or that they have had a 'good' experience — and such is the emotional meaning of pregnancy to women that many have high expectations of their maternity care. A York mother:

> You sort of feel, I've waited all the time, and you're just sat there . . . and I don't know, they treat you like you were just an animal, and yet it's a big thing to you. The first time in nineteen years that something happens, it's a new experience to you, although it may be everyday to them. Some of them just don't realise this.

Of all statements made by patients in the London antenatal clinic, 8 per cent were statements of worry or anxiety reflecting dissatisfaction with the kind of communication offered by doctors. Another symptom of patient dissatisfaction is the unanswered (or unasked) question that is posed to the researcher. Indeed, in the London project this was a frequent theme of the interviews. Sometimes the unanswered question is a very basic one and a source of great worry to the mother:

Researcher. Did you ask any questions?

Patient. No I didn't. You see, when it comes to that I'm very shy in asking questions.

Researcher. Did you want to ask any questions?

Patient. Yes. Is it dangerous like? Can anything happen to you? That's the most I think I wanted to ask. I'm very frightened. I just pray. They asked me — 'Any questions?' I just said 'no'. I'm frightened if anything will happen. You know a lot of people in Ireland they used to die having children . . . There's one question I'm very worried about. And I didn't like to ask it. Since I got pregnant I can't have intercourse at all. I just can't. I don't know why. It hurts. I just can't have it. . .Is it natural, I wonder? I've got a little baby book there and it says in that book that you should have no problem. It says you should have intercourse with your husband up until seven or eight months.

Patient's difficulties in communicating with doctors are rooted in medical definitions of the ideal mode of interaction with patients in which patient–passivity is central; the patient asks no questions and co-operates with the doctor in all the procedures defined medically as necessary. For example:

Doctor. [entering cubicle] Hello.
Patient. Hello.
Doctor. [reading notes] Mrs Watkins?
Patient. Yes.
Doctor. Well, how are you?
Patient. Fine, thank you.
Doctor. Can I feel your tummy? [He undoes the buttons on her dressing gown and does so.] Any complaints?
Patient. No.
Doctor. [filling in notes] Have you felt the baby move yet?
Patient. Yes.
Doctor. How long have you felt it?
Patient. Two weeks.
Doctor. [feels patient's ankles] All the tests we did last time were good.
Patient. Good.
Doctor. Okay. [Leaves cubicle.]

This mode of interaction is facilitated by the layout of many antenatal clinics, including those described by women in the York and London research projects. A cubicle system for examining patients, and the requirement that patients lie on couches ready for the doctor, militate against doctor–patient interaction as equals. In the London hospital, patients who were found by doctors sitting rather than lying on the couch were regarded as deviant; significantly, patients who began their medical encounters in this way asked more questions and were given more time by the doctor.

The most typical way in which doctors themselves exceed the kind of minimal interaction demanded by the passive-patient model is by offering certain restricted kinds of explanation to the patient. The subject of the doctor's explanation may be the physiology of pregnancy, clinic procedure or the technology of ultrasound. Particular kinds of language are used in these explanations.[7] Technical language in explanations is reserved for cases where a doctor wants to encourage a patient to agree to a particular procedure (and perceives her as unwilling to do so). Thus, in the example quoted earlier of a conflict over induction, the doctor referred to 'oestriol' tests as 'water' tests until the patient expressed hostility to the idea of intervention in her pregnancy, at which point he informed her that 'the oestriols are falling'. For other types of explanation, a form

7. Emerson (1970) has described the medical language used in vaginal examinations.

of 'lay' language is used. Examples are 'tail', 'feeling inside', 'start you off' (for induction) and terms such as 'tickling' and 'stirring up' for sweeping the membranes as a covert method of inducing labour. This lay language seems to be used fairly indiscriminately, although the doctor's perception of the social class or medical status of the patient may affect his/her choice of words. Thus one houseman regularly used the phrase 'vaginal examination' for patients with middle-class occupations, reserving the phrase 'examine you down below' for those whom he saw as working class.

In addition to this dependence on a form of lay language, the doctor also trivialises and is deliberately non-specific in his description of medical procedures. A thorough and probably uncomfortable internal examination may be trivialised to become 'a little examination' or 'a gentle examination'; induction may be given the label 'a push downhill' or 'marching orders'. For example, one patient asked, 'What do they usually do when they start you off; my last baby I had normally?' The doctor replied, 'It's nothing terrible. They do an internal and break the waters and then drip some magic stuff into your arm'. Such 'explanations' are based on an underlying typification of patients as anxious. Indeed, there seemed to be a widespread supposition among the doctors observed that the reason patients asked questions was anxiety and that, therefore, the main aim of medical explanations was to allay anxiety (rather than to give information). As the following exchange shows, joking is often used as a device for supposedly reducing patient-anxiety, although, as we have seen, it does not necessarily do so:

First doctor. You're looking serious.

Patient. Well, I am rather worried about it all. It feels like a small baby — I feel much smaller with this one than I did with my first, and she weighed under six pounds. Ultrasound last week said the baby was very small as well.

First doctor. Weighed it, did they?

Second doctor. [entering examination cubicle] They go round to flower shows and weigh cakes, you know.

First doctor. Yes, it's a piece of cake really.

We have briefly outlined here some of the main features of medical and maternal perspectives on pregnancy and birth which emerged during two research projects. We have attempted to 'explain' certain conflicts between the two perspectives by rooting these conflicts in the particular frames of reference employed by the providers and users of maternity care. The frames of reference have

114

been described primarily in terms of the differing social positions and perspectives of these two groups as they interact as *doctors* and *patients*. In outlining these conflicts in present-day maternity care, we have left unanswered the crucial question of what should be done. There appear to be two basic kinds of solution available: one which works within the existing organisation of maternity care; the other which involves working towards alternative patterns of care. The first type of solution would involve, for example, redesigning antenatal clinics so that the sense of rush and anonymity is minimised, educating doctors to be less dogmatic about the 'needs' of maternity patients, and encouraging mothers to be more articulate and more reasonable about the kind of maternity care they want. But more fundamental changes may be felt to be necessary to ameliorate the conflicts between doctors and mothers. It may be that changes *of* the system itself rather than changes *in* the system are required. Such changes might entail the development of neighbourhood maternity centres, a move back towards home delivery, a transfer of medical responsibility from doctors to midwives, and less task-orientated and more patient-orientated maternity care.

6

In terms of the elaboration of societies, there could be no greater contrast than that between the medical system encountered by women having a baby in Britain, just discussed by Hilary Graham and Ann Oakley, and the relatively undifferentiated society of the Gnau. The Gnau are the subject of this next series of extracts from the work of Gilbert Lewis, a medical practitioner and social anthropologist who lived and worked in New Guinea and the South Pacific islands. Not only is there nothing which could be called a 'professional' sector, the distinction between 'folk' and 'popular' is also less clear than in some societies. In so far as healing practices are embodied in customary behaviour in which many villagers are involved, it might be called 'folk' healing. But there are no designated healers. Any members of the group may go to the aid of the afflicted one. The comparison of this work with other societies helps to illuminate our understanding of how health, illness and healing are conceived and how they relate to other facets of the society.

The categorisations which the Gnau use for illness, which are so different from any found in a biomedical nosology, are described in the first series of extracts, taken from his paper 'A View of Sickness in New Guinea' (Lewis, 1976). There is, however, a danger that we attribute our own explanations in different cultural situations, even when we are aware of major differences. A particularly striking passage from *Day of Shining Red* (Lewis, 1980), which we reproduce here, illustrates this.

Despite the very marked contrasts, there are still some familiar themes. Of note is the idea of health as resistance, which has also been explored in detail by Claudine Herzlich (1973: 55–64). Gilbert Lewis's account of illnesses which just come and go 'nothingly' and through which life and work continues, foreshadows the view found by Caroline Currer among Pathans of illness as part and risk of living. Gnau views of illness caused by spirits or by magic will be echoed in a number of the views of causation held by the early-twentieth-century English bootworkers and their families described by Jeremy Seabrook (1973, also, pp. 201–3, 205–8, below).

Drawing on contrasts and comparisons, Gilbert Lewis raises theoretical points of general importance. These are mainly in the final group of extracts, taken from *Knowledge of Illness in a Sepik Society* (Lewis, 1975). He raises issues of what constitutes a medical system, about concepts of health, and of the 'normal' and 'natural' which we often take for granted. Such discussion helps us to make sense of the many and varied forms of healing and of thinking about illness and health which are included in this book.

Eds.

GILBERT LEWIS

Concepts of Health and Illness in a Sepik Society

Illness to the Gnau: their Main Distinctions

The point of departure for a study of medicine in another society will be the sick person, since it is what happened to him that must be explained. What do members of that society see as illness? While I was among the Gnau, I did not find or treat a wide variety of ailments. I treated people when I was able to and if they so wished; I was also brought pigs and dogs to treat on occasion. In a most general sense, nearly all the conditions I saw, which we would hold to be disorders of the body, are admitted under the heading of things 'undesired': the word they use is *wola*. This is the only word which will net or include all these conditions. But *wola* is an adjective which would correspond to our word 'bad'; I could gloss it as 'ill', but it can also mean bad, evil, wretched, harmful and forbidden, powerfully dangerous, and it is also the only word they have for aged or old (although usually in this reference it is used with a completed-action marker *bi* — i.e. *biwola*). I wish to note therefore that they lack a covering word which would differentiate illness in general from other undesirables, as 'sickness' and 'illness' do in English. It is quite common to read in ethnographies that a particular people do not distinguish illness from other afflictions or misfortune; later I will consider in what sense this is so.

But first it must be said that 'bad' or 'undesired' is not very different from the English word 'ill'. We apply the contrasting concepts of health and illness in everyday life, and often we apply them with naive certainty. The manner in which they seem black and white, clear and straightforward as general concepts, but yet at times prove obscure, subtle and uncertain when we ask how they apply to particular cases, resembles the application of other judgements of value like ones of moral good and bad. Long before medicine became scientific, health and illness existed as concepts

119

related to basic values such as life and capacity for performance. Doctors work with a knowledge of the range of normal functions and the evidence of normal structure, but the knowledge of different organs or systems varies greatly.

Medical science does not consist in elaborating these normal standards to arrive at a general concept of illness any more than it feels it should discover a single remedy for all its cases. The doctor's function, rather, consists in ascertaining what precise kind of state or event is presenting itself, on what it depends, how it proceeds and what will affect it. In the great variety of states and events called 'disease' almost the only common factor is that disease implies something 'harmful, unwanted and of an inferior character' (Jaspers, 1963: 780). Thus with *wola* as their comprehensive term for ills, they differ little from ourselves. It may be worth noting that the pidgin English '*sik*' has been very readily assimilated by them and even by speakers who have only five or ten pidgin words in all: but they certainly do *not* misuse *sik* for non-bodily misfortune.

When they applied *wola* to their ailments, I noted that someone could say either that his part was ill (a limb, tissue or organ), or that he himself was ill. In trivial things, like a cut or sore, the man is well, but part of his skin is ill. In more severe disorders, a crucial distinction is made by the sick individual. It involves his perception of himself, his body image, for he may say either that it is he who is ill, or that it is the part which is ill while he himself is well. This might seem to read things into a mere form of words; but it was indeed the supplication, repeated over weeks, of a man each time he was brought forward to confront his afflicting spirit, Malyi, that it was not he but his joints only that were ill; and the figure Malyi would, quivering, bow, bending at the legs, then rise tall and stamp its foot in sign of acquiescence. The simple phrasing of these supplications was of this general form: 'I am a fit man [literally, a good man]; it is my knees and my shoulders that hurt, they are ill — I am well. You must not kill me; it is only my knees, not me, I am well'. It was also repeated and called out by the other men who surrounded and supported him as he faced the spirit.

The distinction of illness of the self and not only of a part of the body has far-reaching consequences for their behaviour when ill. They distinguish part of the wide field of things we call illness with an intransitive verb which means 'to be sick' — *neyigeg* — he is sick. He suffers in his person as a whole. It applies to illnesses which are, for the most part, ones we would call internal, ones accompanied by pain, fever, nausea, debility or disturbances of breathing, of the bowels, and so on. It does not cover external ailments like skin diseases; nor does it cover conditions which are long-standing states of disorder (e.g. limb deformities or stunted growth or mental defect; nor insidious illness — it was not applied to a woman with a slowly progressive nerve disease of paralysis and wasting muscles, or to a man with gradual worsening heart failure. Of these insidious diseases and the long-standing disorders, they said that those who had them were 'ruined', 'wretched', not that they were 'sick' (*neyigeg*); they used the word *biwola*, the same word as that for 'old', 'aged', (i.e. *wola* with its completed action marker). Ills of the body may therefore be seen as ills of a part, or ills of the person; and the ills of the person may either be a present critical state or a completed finite condition.

Behaviour in Serious Illness

When someone is sick in the critical sense of *neyigeg*, his behaviour is conspicuously changed. It is not only altered by the physical effects of the disease but also by conventions for behaviour. He shuns company and conversation; he lies apart, miserable in the dirt or inside a dark hut, the door shut; he rejects certain kinds of normal food, tobacco and areca nut; he eats alone; he begrimes himself with dust and ashes. Further degrees of this behaviour are seen in severe illness; more extreme restrictions of food are applied, men discard the phallocrypt and lie stark naked (although in all normal life, as when bathing, they would always hide their naked penises).

The first thing to note about this pattern of behaviour is that it involves a decision, and one which the patient himself takes. The illnesses in which this behaviour is assumed vary greatly in objective severity but if someone regards himself as critically sick in his person, he adopts the behaviour. It is shown by both men and women. And he keeps it up until he thinks he is safely well. An ash-grimed man lies in the dirt and others say he is ill. I might be urged to go and treat him, but on some occasions the patient would tell me in a low and confidential voice: 'I will be well tomorrow. I feel all right and have felt so for a few days but I stayed ill like this for a little more to be sure'.

Disease may be considered from the point of view of the observer or the patient reflecting on himself. As Charcot, the great nineteenth-century neurologist, observed, 'There is a particular moment between health and sickness when everything depends on the patient, the borderline between a discomfort which is accepted and the decision "I am ill"' (quoted in Jaspers 1963; 425). This borderline is sharply defined by Gnau behaviour, and the decision is left, except for children, to the patient. In marked contrast to ourselves, they do not expect others or specialists to discern for them whether or not they are ill or when they are better. That is not the doctor's job.

What I have described represents a stereotype of how a Gnau patient should behave. Clearly, the behaviour is patterned on common features of bad illness, and some people do not need to act or mime its signs. The things which most mark it as conventional, rather than a spontaneous expression of subjective feeling, are the conspicuous and rapid griming with dirt and ashes, the marked alteration in speaking voice, the disinclination to hold conversation, the placing apart from others, even were it only to lie outside in the sun where others were gathered anyway, and the consistent association of the essential signs when shown. In addition to these, the other signs mark an illness as more or less severe: the grading of severity is shown in greater reluctance to take part in conversation; the quavering thin voice; withdrawal into a hut with shut doors; avoidance of a wider range of foods; men abandoning all attire, including the phallocrypt; and, eventually (and this on the part of the patient's relatives), the fencing off of a part of ground round the patient with bamboo poles magicked with leaves and spells, so that someone bearing ill to the patient will be struck or a spirit barred off should one seek to pass the magical barrier. The barrier also serves to alert and keep away people who might be carrying foods bringing dangers through the association of spirits with food (**Lewis, 1976: 52–60**).

The Gnau understanding is therefore very different to our own. In another book, Day of Shining Red *(1980: 136–8), we read of a totally different example which Lewis gives of how easy it is, even when one is aware of such differences, to attribute ones own explanations to events. In a particularly striking passage, Lewis describes his amazement at discovering that there were different views concerning whether birds and some animals die. A conversation about birds with a companion, a man called Sabuta, first alerted him to this:*

Well they would die if they had no food, or if someone shot them. Village pigs and dogs, yes, they grow old and die. Dogs grow grey on the muzzle, when they get old. But wild animals, birds, don't. Nor snakes, they change their skins, they go on living. . . . Butterflies die but that is because their wings get wrecked . . . I have seen dead lizards though, and they change their skins . . . Trees, palms, they're different, they grow, they dry up, wither, they die.

Over the next few days [Lewis] asked many people individually what they thought. The answers of some were similar to Sabuta's. Others said animals and birds did die, except for the wild pigs and the cassowaries which went on living, although if men should all die, they would die with them too. . . . Still others said birds and animals died; of course they did, they had found them dead in the forest. . . . Some answered the question straight out without hesitation and these unhesitating answers went both ways; others thought first before they answered and did not seem so sure of what they said. The view that trees, palms and plants have a life span, that they grow and toughen, dry out, wither, and in the end die, was held by all; it was a clear view which a number of those unsure about birds and animals mentioned in contrast to their uncertainty about the moving creatures.

I treasure the feeling of discovery I had then for three reasons. Firstly, I had presumed that something was as obvious to them as to me, and I was wrong. Yet I had lived with them more than two years without finding out so great a difference in the answers we would give to that question. Secondly, had you asked me before whether I thought a particular people might have no fixed or sure answer to the question, I would have supposed it most unlikely. 'Do birds and animals die?' does not seem a question that would be left unsettled in the general knowledge provided in some culture. Two years passed until chance revealed it to me. Thirdly, the contrast between plants and animals which some people stressed led me to make clearer a distinction I was half aware of. For human beings one aspect of being alive is consciousness, being able to move, purpose guiding action.[1] Another aspect of life lies in its contrast to death, a life as a passage of time, a span with a beginning and an end. Animals and birds can certainly move, act and choose to

---

1. Questions of medical practice and ethics have been raised over defining death with respect to the people who show no signs of cerebral activity but are kept alive by artificial respirators and tube feeding. Consider also the vulgar metaphor of 'vegetable' used to describe them or their state.

act; they have intentions and awareness. The Gnau are clear on this. Whether animals have a conscious understanding (*wuna'at*) like that of men and know things in the way that men know things is a question the Gnau answer more variously and after reflection, sometimes with subtle distinctions depending on different observations of the behaviour of wild and domestic animals; and they differentiate among the orders of the animal kingdom. But the capacity to move and to will to act attests to life. Men and beasts are alike in this respect but plants and trees are not. Man also has life in the other sense of a span with a beginning and an end, growth and decline. For this sense, the Gnau turn with more certainty to the plant world to find a parallel to human life rather than to the animal world.

Plants which grow and die in a season, and trees or palms fixed to the place where they were planted once by some known ancestor, stand witness to the sequence of growth, decline and mortality more clearly than wild animals or birds. Gnau men and women see some wild creature, it moves, is gone, and who can tell the next time whether it is the same one or another like it? Some say these creatures all must die, some say not, others are not sure (**Lewis 1980: 136–8**).

With this warning in mind, we turn now to extracts from Lewis' main account in Knowledge of Illness in a Sepik Society *(1975), and firstly to a general discussion of the concepts of disease, illness and health.*

Problems of Comparison: Illness and Disease

At the outset I wrote that only the word *wola* would cover all their ailments. The word means 'bad' and can be used in many other and much wider contexts than only ailment: a man who has recently taken part in ritual is *wolen* in the sense of being dangerous to others; a woman menstruating is *wola*, both dangerous to men and vulnerable herself. Her withdrawal from normal life, her purifying wash after her menstrual period is ended, offer parallels to the behaviour of someone sick in the *neyigeg* sense; but she is not spoken of as *weyigeg*, only as *wola*. The same would apply to a woman in and after childbirth. The area of ills of the person or self, not merely the part, is the one circumscribed by *neyigeg* and it denotes present active critical illness. The medical correlates of *neyigeg* vary greatly: it may only be a headache. It excludes long-standing slowly changing disorders or completed ones;[2] instead, they describe people with these as *biwola* — wretched, ruined or old. These are not seen as critical destroying illnesses.

In attempting to compare the boundaries they give to illness with our own, we may be led to ask if our view has clear limits. Do we define the field of medicine clearly? It may be futile or frustrating to look for equivalents for medicine in other societies if medicine is a vague concept and peculiar to our way of thinking.

In English, 'medicine' can be given the traditional meaning of the art of healing. There have been sick people ever since man inhabited the earth. Or medicine can be given the meaning it has come to have now; that is, the study of the diagnosis, treatment and prevention of disease. The traditional sense, the art of healing, implies that medicine is concerned with people or patients — with conditions of man — while the modern sense, study and control of disease implies rather the study of a thing, disease. The change of emphasis from conditions of people to a study of disease entities is attested to in the history of European medicine. It is associated especially with Thomas Sydenham, who repudiated the general supposition 'that diseases are no more than the confused and irregular operations of disordered and debilitated nature, and consequently that it is fruitless to labour to endeavour to give a just description of them'. Instead, he maintained that 'Nature, in the production of disease, is uniform and consistent. . . . The self-same phenomenon that you observe in the Sickness of Socrates, you would observe in the Sickness of a simpleton' (Sydenham, 1676). Sydenham's view has come to dominate nosology. Before him, disease had been considered as a deviation from the normal in which a healthy man through the influence of any number of factors — physical or mental — was changed and suffered.

. . . .

Today it is unusual to find a general concept of disease made explicit in medical writing: such writing abounds instead with the concepts of particular diseases. From a biological standpoint, certain kinds of change in any living species may be called disease. In

---

2. Perhaps rather similarly, we do not usually speak of mental defect or certain congenital anomalies as illnesses.

global perspective such changes may be seen to result from varied causes such as genetic change; maladaption to environment; environmental change; the predatory, parasitic and competitive habits of different organisms — bacteria for instance. The concept of disease is focused on the individual of a species.

. . . .

I have used the word 'disease' to set it in a biological frame, and I will use the word 'illness' to distinguish — and perhaps artificially to emphasise — that people recognise either in themselves or others, certain changes of body or mind as undesired, as ills, and that what particular people so recognise may vary. I wish to contrast, on the one hand, 'disease' defined by criteria of a biological nature, and applying generally to the human species, with, on the other hand, 'illness' which will be determined by the views of particular individuals or cultures — it is of a social and psychological nature. By using disease in the biological sense, we set bounds about the field relevant to our inquiry. By reference to 'illness' we examine how individuals perceive and interpret changes in their condition. The reason for making this distinction is to clarify what we are about if, for example, we wish to examine the nebulous view that disease may affect culture and culture may affect disease. A social anthropologist may quite well find that some diseases are not regarded as 'illness' by those he studies; he may find illness of the body apparently undifferentiated from other misfortunes such as a house catching fire or drought. He may urge then that medicine is a category like 'magic' or 'religion' tainted by our particular conceptual bias; hard to use in comparative study.

The sphere thought proper to medicine depends on the conceptions of health and illness which prevail in the society; these suggest for example what people expect doctors to treat. In Samuel Butler's *Erewhon* you find the problem in a nutshell:

> In that country, if a man. . .catches any disorder, or fails bodily in any way before he is seventy years old, he is tried before a jury of his country men and, if convicted, is held up to public scorn and sentenced more or less severely as the case may be. . . . But if a man forges a cheque or sets his house on fire or robs with violence from the person or does any other such things as are criminal in our country, he is either taken to a hospital or most carefully tended at the public expense, or if he is in good circumstances, he lets it be known to all his friends that he is suffering from a severe fit of immorality. . .and they come and visit him with great

solicitude, and inquire with interest how it all came about, what symptoms first showed themselves and so forth. [Butler, 1872]

Erewhon was, of course, nowhere, but the problem it suggests is this: should the medical ethnographer in *Erewhon* concentrate on the management of embezzlers or dyspeptics? In my view he should study the dyspeptics.

. . . .

Health

In most of what I have written so far, my explicit concern has been with illness, with the recognition of disease. The other side of the coin is health. The biological view of disease, which I briefly presented, in effect implied that for practical purposes health may be defined as the absence of identifiable disease or infirmity — a negative view. But among us health has much more commonly received recognition as an ideal, for example, by the World Health Organisation whose constitution begins: 'Health is a state of complete physical, mental and social well-being and not merely the absence of disease or infirmity'. Ideals involve notions that go beyond what is to what ought to be. Since their claim is to formulate what ought to be rather than what is, they cannot be verified in the sense of being shown to correspond to fact. The doctor proceeds from knowledge of the range of normal function and the evidences of normal structure; but the knowledge of different organs and systems varies greatly. The criteria of normality in medicine are both statistical and ideal; they are ideal in the sense that the proper functioning of different organs is conceived with the help of teleology — the scientist tries to determine what the relationships of different organs are, what purposes they serve; it entails the notion of proper function adequate to a purpose. Many of the most important functions of the organism are those which regulate and integrate the working of separate systems; some ideal of integration and balance, and the separate contributions of different parts to this whole comes to be involved in judgements of adequacy. In practice the doctor has no reliable positive indications of when ideal balance is achieved; instead he considers healthy the man who is free from any evidence of disease or infirmity. Health in the positive sense is an ideal 'approached but not attained' (Polgar, 1968). Polgar distinguishes this asymptotic view of health from two other kinds, which he terms the elastic concept and the open-ended view. The elastic view holds that health is an accumulated resistance to potential dangers. The view adopted is a preventive one which forsees illness as likely to happen in some form. In the open-ended view, health has no definite limits; put briefly, health is anything better than death. The implicit view of health which the Gnau would appear to hold comes closest to the elastic view in which illness is part of living or a risk of living. There is a normal course to life in which vigour and strength to resist illness waxes and then wanes; such a view makes the deaths of infants and the old more ordinary than those of people in their prime. Many of their rules of behaviour, especially their taboos, are phrased as rules of prudence by which health may be preserved. As I went round the village during the October epidemic of influenza, I came to one man sitting in his hamlet, where there were many lying scattered about miserable in the dirt, and he said: 'I have not got it. I am a hardwood post. I am well'. The idea of resistance was expressed clearly and with pride. Similarly, the notion of variable resistance can be deduced from the tentative, testing way people try out the foods that were specially forbidden them when ill, and the progressive way in which foods that were once taboo become permissable after someone has shown that he can do something, or has passed the stage of vulnerability. In old age the most enduring food taboos are raised, but people argue uncertainly that this is either because the food will not harm them, or because they are already past their prime, the food will not matter if it debilitates them since enfeeblement and weakening are natural to old age; the old are not expected to maintain or, in the same way, to husband their health. The old men have fulfilled their duties and should stand aside to watch the young men kill their game. To quote the words of a Gnau man as he invoked his ancestral dead at a hunting ritual for a grandchild:

> Now we two have long been full grown men; no longer will we kill pigs — no, these young men are growing up to hunt, we now eat forbidden foods, we have begotten children who are now grown up and adult. . . . Our children have borne children. The things of hunting are for us no longer; we eat the forbidden foods which scare game away. Shall we still kill? These young men, they must kill; they, young men, rise up and kill their game because they are still men with the good smell, the smell of youth.

The notion of health as resistance still allows it the quality of an ideal; it is desired and admired. Men and women take pride in good health. But they imagine that the malicious spirits may sometimes look on a vigorous person and say, 'There is a young man, flaunting himself, I will make him shout with pain', and strike him down in preference to a decrepit unappealing old man. I can quote a tape-recorded example of this kind of thinking, though it was expressed in joke — an old man riposting to a young man who had teased him: 'When I am dead and you come along my path I will fasten tight round you — fine young man! You come along my path — I will strike you and when the old dry *yam-mami* [i.e. an old man] comes along I'll let him be, that appetising one there, that's the one my eyes will rest on — aargh! Strike him down, that one!' (**Lewis, 1975: 146–53**)

If the diagnostic emphasis is for the Gnau on the cause, as Lewis asserts, we need to consider what is the nature of causality itself in illness, including what is natural or normal.

Natural Causes

The everyday notion of cause in our own culture is that a cause produces an effect. But in the stricter terms of logic, the word 'produces' is held to be unsatisfactory. For in alleged instances of causality, often what can be discovered in the instance in question is only that there is an invariable relation between two or more processes. A brick meets the window with a certain force; the window always breaks. This is the general notion of causality in the developed sciences — the analysis of invariant relations. In this sense, the field of taboo resembles statements of invariant relations, of uniform 'natural' laws. The danger in breaking a taboo is inherent and automatic; an analytic distinction may be made between the conceptions of the causes (spirits and sorcery) which produce or intend effects, and the causes (taboo) which involve statements of belief in natural law — invariant relations. This distinction parallels the one commonly made between personal and impersonal forces.

The Gnau say of some illnesses that they just come: *neyigeg gipi'i*, he is sick nothingly; *nag diyi*, he died by no purpose or intent. Some maladies come and go, like colds, which usually need no explanation, although particular individuals may offer one for them. Of others, for example as happened in the influenza epidemic, people say 'everyone has it'; it has a normal course, and because so many have it they do not seek to provide an explanation of why particular people have it. Ackerknecht (1946) felt that such views as these were not so much examples where illness was rationally accepted as a natural phenomenon, as examples of illness unexplained. We speak of illness as the result of natural processes that will pursue their course according to certain kinds of regular pattern which we can study by the scientific method: it is a systematic method of learning by experience. This interpretation of illness is not a matter of merely accepting that certain illnesses just occur, or expressive of a lack of concern and interest, but part of a view which is consciously held, applying equally to trivial and to tragic ailments. Although it may be analysed by only some members of our society in terms of the precise assumptions and methods by which we can find out about illness, the view prevails nonetheless as a general assumption about illness. Individual people in our society may not accept it as fully adequate to account for illness and seek religious or moral reasons for the illnesses of particular people, or even for illness in general; or individuals may feel an obscure yet deep emotional dissatisfaction with explanation purely in natural terms, but the general view remains. Our view that illness can be investigated in a purposeful, constructive, testing search for 'such general laws as can be used to link together the observed phenomena' (Singer, 1926: 89) is thus very different in sweep and consistency from the Gnau view I have just cited that illness sometimes just occurs. On a few occasions, women came to me for treatment with large discharging breast abscesses; these, it was said, sometimes happened if a child had died in early infancy; the milk swelled the breast, it was blocked and changed to pus. They did not suggest it was caused by something. It happened; they gave examples of other women to whom it had happened. The women, though some with pain and much discomfort, would continue to do their habitual jobs. I would regard this as an example of a distressing ailment accepted as a natural event. I happened to try and treat a young woman whose breast abscess was large, painful and long-lasting, and I was much surprised that no one, even when prompted by my questions about spirits, sorcery and the death of her child, ventured beyond the quite detailed natural explanation I have given for her abscess. She went about her daily life as a well person would, with none of the care and caution which someone believing herself ill by spirits or sorcery would take.

The abscess, despite its size and pain, was a mishap of ordinary life as an infected sore would be.

The abscess appeared to me sufficiently abnormal for me to expect from them some particular explanation, which I did not obtain. They regarded it as ordinary in the way that most infected sores are ordinary. The identification of a particular cause in practice depends on a variety of factors not solely linked to the immediate nature of the illness. Even common sores may in some circumstances be considered the sign of mystical harm. Perceptions of the observable cause, of the usual outcome and severity in visible ailments, like sores or burns, affect the kind of attention paid them and the degree of urgency to account for them. The words we are tempted to use in referring to such interpretations, the words 'normal' or 'natural', do not mean exactly the same, and the distinctions between them, as well as between their opposites, need a moment's care. The troubles in using the dichotomies natural/supernatural and normal/abnormal come in part because the words in English are complex and ambiguous: the concepts associated with them have changed in the course of their use, and from this comes some ambiguity. There are two aspects to 'normal': an ideal and an average one. The ambiguity may easily be recalled by remembering that dental caries are pathological but not abnormal: great strength and intelligence are abnormal but not pathological. Normality in the sense of health often implies the ideal aspect rather than the average aspect to people such as the Gnau. In discussing the concept of health and illness, I have noted that this is a common view of health and one taken by most people in our society too. The Gnau rules on correct behaviour, proper food, the dangers in objects, animals, trees, represent an ordering, or a collection of precepts which one should follow to achieve the ideal normal life.

If we take the Gnau, or indeed almost any people studied by anthropologists, we can find examples of processes like puberty or yam growth, in which the normal outcome, in the sense of average, is success, yet the activities or processes are surrounded by ritual controls and restraints. The Gnau example which springs to my mind is a short ritual done for children aged about one year so that they will learn to walk: a magical cassowary spell is blown onto nettle leaves with which the child's knees are beaten. It is difficult to maintain that magic to make a child walk has arisen from a perceived chanciness in the normal outcome, that on average only a few infants will learn to walk and that therefore magic occurs here to

131

assure a doubtful outcome, or express anxiety about it. On the other hand, it may express something about normal development in terms of an ideal outcome or the value set on its achievement. The Gnau do not have a word which corresponds to 'normal' as part of a concept of 'normality'; although, clearly, considerations of commonness or triviality, of what can be expected or understood as a direct visible sequence of dependent events, lie behind their statements that things 'just happen', in terms of *gipi'i* — nothingly — or happen without intention or some cause willing or contriving their occurrence, as with *diyi* — without cause or purpose.

The problems in using natural/supernatural have been more heavily trampled over by anthropologists. They are concisely stated by Evans-Pritchard:

> We use the word 'supernatural' when speaking of some native belief, because that is what it would mean for us, but far from increasing our understanding of it, we are likely by the use of this word to misunderstand it. We have the concept of natural law, and the word 'supernatural' conveys to us something outside the ordinary operation of cause and effect, but it may not at all times have that sense for primitive man. For instance, many peoples are convinced that deaths are caused by witchcraft. To speak of witchcraft being for these peoples a supernatural agency, hardly reflects their own view of the matter, since from their point of view nothing could be more natural. [Evans-Pritchard, 1965: 109–10] (**Lewis, 1975: 196–200**).

Lewis then explores 'our entangled conception of nature', finding it to be complex, and compares the various senses in which we use the term and the assumptions contained in them, with views of societies such as the Gnau.

Despite this distinction between the view I have called 'ours' and scientific, and the view I have called 'theirs' and might call 'primitive' or magical, there is fundamentally a similarity in that both views, ours and theirs, search for some ordering or reason in events. Events are not accepted in either view as chaotic and anarchic matters of chance. Both look to make sense of things so that people may be able to deal more effectively with them, and decide what if anything can or needs to be done (**Lewis, 1975: 201**).

Lewis turns next to analyse the explanations given by the Gnau for actual illnesses, and this leads to the issue of what constitutes a medical system.

I am using the word 'explanation' to refer to explanation of an illness in terms of causes. The causes which are involved are any of the three general kinds of cause (i.e. spirits; sorcery or destructive magic; breaking a taboo). The 'unexplained' illness is one in which they said they did not know why it occurred, or in which knowledge of any cause was denied, or in which the illness was accounted for solely by an observable directly connected sequence of ordinary events (e.g. my skin is burnt because I tipped boiling water over my leg). Thus illness in which the answer to 'what have you done to become ill?' was a description of the direct causing of the harm was called illness 'unexplained'. If spirits, magic or sorcery, or breaking a taboo were specifically indicated as the cause, then the illness was put in the category 'explained' illness. In a latter section of the chapter, I examine the detail of explanation and what is entailed in it, but for the moment 'explanation' between inverted commas refers to explanation in this limited, specific and undifferentiated sense of explanation by one or more of their three main kinds of cause (**Lewis 1975: 234–5**).

. . . .

Not all illness is 'explained'; women do not differ from men in general as regards 'explanation' of their illness — their illness is not in this sense disregarded; men over forty-five years old (and probably women over forty-five years) are more likely to have their illness 'explained'. 'Explanation' is more likely as illness becomes more severe, but in illness with an obvious cause or visible source it is less likely. Evidently, they do discriminate the general severity of illness, but there is a group of illnesses without physical signs of the disorder complained of, which they take seriously and 'explain' as much as the most medically serious of their illness. From this general background, I now move on to look in greater detail at what is involved in 'explanation'.

Cause and Illness

I have not so far distinguished the precision, source or number of assertions underlying 'explanation', or its relation to treatment. From now on I will use explanation without inverted commas: it is not intended to have a limited and special sense. The points already made about the lack of necessary connection between clinical signs

133

and the attribution to a cause may be illustrated from my observations in three ways:

1. *A given cause is not linked to a particular clinical kind of illness*; for example, the spirit Malyi was named as a cause in these illnesses: fall leading to acute renal failure and subsequent urinary infection; severe arthritis; congestive heart failure; pneumonia; infected hand from a deep splinter wound; perirectal abscess; abdominal colic and diarrhoea; abscess in the groin; a cold; hip and thigh aches.

2. The reverse of the above: *a given clinical kind of illness does not imply a specific kind of cause*; for example in twenty-five cases of pneumonia or bronchopneumonia, the following causes were explicitly suggested: named great spirits Panu'et (seven cases), Tambin, Malyi, the *mama* spirit of *wadagep* (tubers), the bad spirit of a particular water hole (all once each); undifferentiated spirits of the dead of a specific lineage or clan (eleven cases); named dead individuals (six cases); broken prohibitions (five cases); sorcery (four cases); no explicit cause recorded at all (four cases). Obviously in some of these cases of pneumonia, more than one cause was suggested. This is the third point.

3. *A given clinical illness may be attributed to a variety of causes*; for example, an old man's pneumonia (the explanations are given in the sequence in which they were brought forward): the spirit Panu'et because he had eaten mushrooms his daughter had collected from a pile of sago pith rotting beside a pool; he broke a prohibition by eating a snake killed on land belonging to his matrilateral relatives; the ancestral spirits of the local government councillor of Mandubil at whom a month before he had drawn his bow, threatening to shoot him (a covert implication of possible sorcery is involved here, not explicitly stated until after his death); the spirit of the man who had planted a palm from which he had eaten beetle grubs; the spirit of his own dead wife; ancestral spirits watching over a tract of land from which he had eaten bananas, the land having been the ground for a virulent dispute between his clan and a group of Mandubil men just over a year and a half before.

A Medical System?

Presented thus, Gnau attributions of cause in illness may appear wayward, without rhyme or reason. I have suggested that they lack a medical system in the sense of lacking a special department of coordinated knowledge and practice concerned specifically with the understanding and treatment of illness.

. . . . .

Such a focus on human sickness and the definition of a field held relevant to it, the coordination and integration of knowledge according to its value for understanding and treating sickness, is what gives some unity to 'medicine' in our society and allows us to separate it off as an institutional system. In other societies there may be no separation of a department of knowledge and practice specifically orientated towards human sickness. Illness may be treated by religious or other specialists as one of their many duties; the explanations to account for it may stem from theories or premises that have much wider relevance than to sickness alone, and whose chief significance is other than explaining illness. In such circumstances illnesses may well be managed in a rational and ordered manner. The explanations and treatment may follow logically from the ideas involved, yet to speak of a 'medical' system as a separable system would, I think, be unwarranted, for the primary or central focus of the ideas and practices is not sickness (**Lewis 1975: 243–6**).

7

By following Gilbert Lewis's account with that of Allan Young in this chapter, we as editors hope to draw attention to the contrast between the two societies described; a contrast which in itself illustrates the theory Allan Young puts forward. He offers a characterisation of medical belief systems on the basis of the type of explanatory model which they use to account for sickness episodes. At the one extreme, 'internalising systems' are based on physiological explanations; at the other, 'externalising systems' seeks aetiological explanations in which at least some causative events 'take place outside the sick person's body' (p. 140, below). His interest is then to explore what he describes as a 'core problem for the comparative study of medical systems: can types of medical belief systems be associated with types of cultures and societies and, if an association exists, how can it be explained?' (p. 142, below). In answer, he notes a connection, albeit incomplete, between simple undifferentiated societies and externalising modes of explanation, on the one hand, and structurally complex, literate state societies and internalising modes, on the other. In view of Gilbert Lewis's conclusion that the Gnau do not have a medical system at all, it is perhaps questionable to consider them within the scope of Allan Young's mode. They do, however, have arrangements for helping sufferers. Theirs is a society characterised both by lack of differentiation and by externalising modes of explanation of sickness episodes. In contrast, the Amhara people described by Allan Young have an elaborate classification of healers, outlined in this paper, where he cites their medicine as an instance of an incompletely internalising system. The division of labour described reflects a long history of contact with other societies.

In his emphasis on the division of labour, Allan Young's interests are close to those of Meg Stacey (Ch. 1, above). Many of the healers Allan Young describes fall within what Arthur Kleinman would call the 'folk' sector, but there are also 'professionals' of more than one internalising healing system present in Ethiopia.

Whatever comparisons can be made between this and other models, however, one of the strengths of Young's paper is the way in which it incorporates both theory and a specific demonstration of that theory. Thus in the contribution which follows, the reader learns more about a specific people and their beliefs, while at the same time being offered a model in terms of which this, and other such descriptions, can be understood.

The paper was published originally in 1976.   *Eds.*

ALLAN YOUNG

Internalising and Externalising Medical Belief Systems: an Ethiopian Example

Externalising and Internalising Systems

Particular beliefs about sickness and health persist because people find them useful and convincing.[1] That is to say, the beliefs enable people to decide on courses of action for (1) reversing, arresting, moderating and preventing undesirable states, and (2) exculpating the putatively sick from the stigma of deviance (i.e. responsibility for abstaining or threatening to abstain from socially expected behaviour); the beliefs are consistent with each other and with related sets of beliefs, albeit in *post hoc* and contingent ways; and the beliefs are consistent, phenomenologically, with the real events they are intended to explain. While the content and organisation of medical beliefs are, then, the product of both cultural and biophysical realities, it is culture — by determining which biophysical signs are selected and which are ignored, which objects and events are implicated in disease episodes and which are dismissed as irrelevant — which dominates in traditional medicine. For this reason (the substantive heterogeneity of medical beliefs), it is necessary to compare the medical beliefs of different societies at formal and abstract levels, first sorting them into notions about (1) pathogenic agencies: whether purposive or non-purposive; (2) places where events responsible for the onset and course of sickness episodes are believed to take place: whether inside or outside the sick person's body; and (3) linkage between these events: whether related through narrative or through image and analogy. These pairs of choices are not contraries, of course. For example the explanation of a single

1. The field research on which this article is based was conducted from January to December 1966 and was supported by a Public Health Service Research Grant and Fellowship from the US National Institute of Mental Health. Also, I want to thank Yewoubdar Beyne for reading and commenting on the ethnographic section of this paper.

disease-episode may include events taking place both outside and inside the sick person's body.

Explanations for the onset and course of sickness episodes can be usefully distinguished according to their different modes, 'aetiological' and 'physiological', of organising facts. *Aetiological explanations* have the form of narratives in which at least some medically important events take place outside the sick person's body. Such explanations (1) identify a point in time before which it is unnecessary to search for the causes of the onset of sickness episodes and (2) link agencies and events in time and through cases and effects in such a way that responsibility for the sick person's behaviour can be allocated onto causes beyond his violation. Properly exculpated behaviour becomes legitimately 'sick' behaviour; unexculpated remains socially unacceptable (e.g. insulin dependency *versus* heroin dependency in the United States). Order and pattern among aetiological facts are enhanced by the fact that alternative aetiologies which explain the same syndrome often develop in complementary and dialectical ways (Young, 1975a).

Physiological explanations of sickness work by means of images and analogies which make it possible for people to order events within the sick person's body from the onset of symptoms to the conclusion of the sickness episode (Barnes, 1974: 22, 48, 62, 92, 117, 126; Horton, 1967). Typically, physiological explanations are used to link aetiological events to the sequence of biophysical signs which mark the course of disease episodes. The physiological notions of many historical and contemporary peoples seem to have developed from observing a limited number of biophysical phenomena, in particular the following: markers which separate life from death (e.g. heat, pulsing and breathing) and imperative behaviour which is somehow mediated internally (e.g. hunger, thirst and evacuation) (Douglas, 1966; Goodfield, 1960; Turner, 1966; Turner, 1967b: 27–29; Turner, 1968). In spite of reductionist attempts to establish necessary connections between biophysical functions and explanatory beliefs (Tylor, 1873), cultures are free to choose or ignore particular phenomena. Even so, it is possible to speak of cross-culturally popular images and analogies. Probably the most widely used image is expressed in the idea that sickness is the consequence of a disturbed natural equilibrium which curers must try to restore. Equilibria are sometimes conceived in terms of static proportions (e.g. hot–cold balance in Hispano-American folk medicine — Currier, 1966) and dynamic relations between parts (e.g. in

European and Chinese traditions — Foucault, 1965: 101–32; Huard and Wong, 1968: 194–206), exclusively internal relations (e.g. Western medicine) and internal equilibria which reflect cosmic ones (e.g. in Indian and Taoist tradition — Beck, 1969; Huard and Wong, 1968: 189, 231–3). A similar image explains sickness as a reduced natural wholeness (e.g. soul loss in Spanish America — Gillin, 1948; Rubel, 1964), in South-East Asia (Chen, 1975; Tambiah, 1968), among Eskimos (Murphy, 1964: 61–3, 81), diminished life force in Africa (Jansen, 1973: 37–8). A medical belief system is not necessarily bound to a single image or analogy, of course (Hanks and Hanks, 1955).

Although it appears that most medical belief systems employ both kinds of explanations (not necessarily in combination, however), it is possible to identify systems in which the choice of medical action against life-threatening and debilitating sicknesses is dominated by a single explanatory mode. In this way, polar types of belief systems, 'externalising' and 'internalising', can be compared. *Externalising systems* concentrate on making aetiological explanations for serious sickness (Evans-Pritchard, 1956: 99–100, 104–5, 177–96, 222; Fabrega, 1970; Middleton, 1960: 70–86). Here, pathogenic agencies are usually purposive and often human or anthropomorphised. Diagnostic interests concentrate on discovering what events could have brought the sick person to the attention of the pathogenic agency (e.g. grudges repaid by witchcraft, ritual lapses punished by ancestral spirits) in order to identify the responsible category of pathogen or, even, the responsible individual agent (e.g. witch X). Often only gross symptomatic distinctions are made, since the intrasomatic link between aetiological events and sequences of biophysical signs is either ignored or not elaborated. When intrasomatic processes are used to explain sickness, emphasis is frequently given to the role of notions such as 'soul' and 'spirit' rather than to biophysical functions (from the Western point of view); when biophysical functions are used, they are often represented by simple conceptualisations such as the 'diminished whole'. The healer's therapeutic powers are typically expressed in his ability to enter into aetiology-narratives in order to compete against purposive agencies and his access to anodynes (from his own point of view) for symptomatic complaints.

In *internalising systems* physiological explanations are indispensable for organising medical strategies. Even though aetiological information is sometimes diagnostically important, diagnosis ultimately relies on the healer's ability to interpret symptoms whose form and place in the sequence of symptoms are explained physiologically. Similarly, although therapeutic success sometimes requires the neutralisation of introjected pathogens, in the end it depends on the healer's ability to restore physiological equilibrium. Typically, the physiological explanations are rationalised by a particular theory or set of theories, and emphasis is given to systematising medical beliefs in more than *post hoc* and pragmatic contexts. Western medicine, which is one instance of this type (and extends the characteristic explanation to even 'psychogenic' ailments by means of an equilibrium metaphor derived historically from a physiological context (Wollheim, 1971: 31–58), is distinguished from examples such as Ayurvedic and Unani medicine because it concentrates on micro-level processes organised according to highly elaborated machine models (Foucault, 1973; Hall, 1969).

Between the externalising and internalising extremes are systems of the type described in this article: therapeutic strategies variously emphasise aetiological or physiological explanations, and combinations of the two. However, even when physiological explanations are used, they are often weakened by the emphasis given to the motives and purposiveness (i.e. personalisation) of causal agencies and the broadly defined character of the agents' pathogenic modes (e.g. 'cutting' the heart and eating the viscera, in Amhara medical explanations).

Because medical beliefs persist as parts of larger cultural systems and the strategies of medical action which they organise and rationalise imply coordinate action in economic, kinship and even politico-jural domains, there arise two questions which constitute a core problem for the comparative study of medical systems: can types of medical belief systems be associated with types of cultures and societies, and if an association exists, how can it be explained? It is possible to answer only tentatively, and with important reservations. It does appear that structurally simple, tribal societies tend to rely on externalising systems of medical beliefs, but some caution must be shown in relying on much of the literature supporting this conclusion. Until fairly recently, descriptions of systems of medical beliefs and practices were infrequent and descriptions of medical traditions in tribal societies tended to refer to them only anecdotally and as dependent variables intended to illustrate or explain other phenomenological domains (very commonly having to do with religion, ritual, witchcraft and sorcery) in which purposive misfortune-senders and morally significant aetiological events are a natural focus. Internalising systems (at least of the polar sort I have described) are characteristic of the structurally complex, literate state societies of Asia, Europe and North Africa. Here the problem is not the descriptive literature but the kinds of distinctions which must be made between internalising 'great traditions' of medicine, characteristic of the professional medical culture and sometimes shared with the elevated strata of society, and the 'folk traditions' of the villages and the common people, mixed systems incorporating shamanistic therapies and externalising explanations. Only in contemporary Western society, where the power to cure, legitimise and explain is monopolised by professional healers, is the association with internalising systems unambiguous (Freidson, 1970a).

If these connections are accepted, the next two questions are, why do externalising systems organise medical beliefs and practices in structurally simple societies, and why do they metamorphise into internalising systems in complex societies? Two sets of circumstances help explain the distribution of externalising systems. Firstly, they are consistent with the socio-centric character of related domains of belief in tribal society. Before objects and events can become phenomenologically real, they must be ordered or structured. But ordering is the product of culture and does not emerge spontaneously from nature: people are able to organise superficially disparate phenomena because they have models for describing relations of causality, identity, complementarity, and so on (Foucault, 1970). Models working by means of analogy (in which a known complex of objects is assimilated to another less well-known complex) seem to be a primary mode of organising societies everywhere, and in simple societies it is analogy which assimilates objects and action to relations between people which is favoured (Horton, 1967: 50, 155; Tambiah, 1973). Internalising systems encapsulate sickness within the sick person's body and concentrate effort on decoding the symptomatic expressions of intrasomatic events. In externalising systems, episodes of serious sickness implicate categories or groups of people, and sickness is itself a symptom of disrupted relations, not between organs but between people or between people and anthropomorphised spirits who mirror or invert the moral order of society.

Secondly, externalising medical systems have a low degree of conceptual autonomy, in the sense of constituting a phenomenological domain which people can distinguish from coordinate jural, and cosmological, systems. That is, people can speak about particular sicknesses but not about 'sickness', about different kinds of cures but not 'curing'. Autonomous medical beliefs are unlikely to develop in societies characterised by a simple division of labour, because autonomy is probably linked to the emergence of specialists who are competent in a range of events and states approximating our sociological definition of sickness and whose putative powers unite these events and states. Further, simple division of labour means the absence of specialised politico-jural structures monopolising rights to define and decide social relations. This has important results for the development of ideas about sickness since it implies that people are 'free' to develop their aetiologies in socially and morally important ways (Thomas, 1970). That under these conditions people *do* develop explanations of sickness in this direction is a consequence of the episodic character of the serious-acute ailments which are epidemiologically prominent in these societies. Episodes of these sicknesses are efficient vehicles for communicating information since they are bounded in time and space, they separate audience from principles and incorporate shared codes; they have contest-like forms since their outcomes are unpredictable but unambiguous; and they are pervasive since they continually occur and effect all categories of people (notwithstanding the epidemiological characteristics of particular sicknesses).

Internalising systems develop when these circumstances change; that is, as the division of labour grows increasingly complex and leads to the transformation of the homogenous and self-sufficient community and the appearance of specialised politico-jural institutions and broadly competent professional healers. The assumptions here are that: (1) systematic explanations of sickness are necessary for organising medical action and defining and legitimising the extraordinary behaviour and events connected with sickness; (2) the main kinds of medical explanation are aetiological and physiological, and aetiological explanations (and externalising systems) tend to dominate in simple societies; (3) as the conditions which foster this dominance disappear, it becomes both possible and necessary for alternative explanations (i.e physiological ones) to develop. There are other changes also, but their effects on the organisation of medical beliefs are difficult to measure. These changes include the appearance of new models for analogical thinking based on mediated exchange among functionally specialised parts (taken from the money-market experience) and hierarchical dominance among functionally specialised parts (taken from the state structure). It is safest to think of these changes as fostering an ontology compatible with internalising precepts (which emphasise notions of physiology-equilibrium) and receptive to the diffusion of internalising ideas from outside (e.g. humoural notions).

The remainder of this article is intended to illustrate the argument's main points. It is a systematic account of the way an Ethiopian people, the Amhara, use their medical beliefs to explain what happens during sickness episodes. Amhara medicine is an instance of an incompletely internalising system: healing power is only partially professionalised, aetiological explanations unalloyed to physiological ones still play a prominent role for many ailments, and no single theory or set of theories rationalises disease beliefs or the practices associated with them.

The Amhara are monophysite Christians settled mainly in the central and northern provinces of highland Ethiopia. I am writing about Amhara who live around the old imperial capital of Gondar, in Begemder province north of Lake Tana. Amhara men are traditionally farmers, ecclesiastics, government functionaries, soldiers and petty traders. Artisan occupations are derogated to Muslims, Falashas (Jews) and endogamous Christian minorities. Although urbanism is well established in this part of Ethiopia, only about 6 per cent of Begemder's people live in towns with populations of over 2,000. Amhara towns are interesting demographically because of the numerical predominance of women in them, mainly beer and mead vendors. For over two millenia, the Amhara and their Tigre neighbours to the north have known a literate tradition, sustained contacts with the civilisations of the Mediterranean and Red Seas, and lived in centralised policies with specialised jural institutions.

Amhara Physiology and Aetiology

Although Amhara can identify most of the body's internal organs, they emphasise the heart and stomach for explaining sickness. The heart is primary because its pulses enspirit all other organs and it controls body movement through *jimat* cords (veins, arteries, tendons and ligaments). Over-pulsing causes excessive heat and is expressed symptomatically as fever. When the heart over-pulses for extended periods, it loses authority over subordinate organs and symptoms of

145

fatigue result. Because the heart is also the seat of the intellect, over-pulsing often leads to mental confusion. The stomach is important because it houses a colony of *wosfat* worms (ascariasis). There must be sufficient *wosfat* to turn food and drink into waste. The worms are quarrelsome and if they are too numerous for the available food and space, they attack one another and bite the stomach and the organs which lie near it. People experience this as nausea and internal pain.

Divine providence ensures that the body's organs work together in a state of harmonious well-being (*tena*). There are five categories of pathogenic agencies which cause sickness by disrupting this equilibrium. (1) Excesses of certain common-place activities: if a person eats too little food or not enough of the foods which *wosfat* crave, the angry worms attack the stomach, causing pain and bloating, and chew their way to the heart, causing great pain. By exciting the heart, they also cause fever and fatigue. Intense emotions such as sorrow, fear and anger overstimulate the heart, making it difficult to think clearly. If unrelieved, the heart deteriorates into delirium and even death. (2) Corrosive substances ingested or breathed into the body: the most important of these, known as *likift*, are innocuous substances which have been contaminated by contact with creeping animals and demons (*ganel*). When *likift* food or drink is ingested, it interferes with digestion and produces acute diarrhoea and loss of appetite by destroying alimentary worms. It may wash up from the stomach to irritate the heart, causing over-pulsing, pain, fatigue and difficult breathing. Similar to *likift* are miasmas (*gerifta*), often associated with the sun. (3) Poisons (*merz*) put into an enemy's food or drink: poisons are made from a variety of substances, including the animals which are blamed for causing *likift*. Their symptomatic expressions are nausea, vomiting, lassitude, severe disorientation and sometimes indiscriminately aggressive behaviour. (4) Wer-hyenas: these are humans who introject their spirit aspects, known as *buda*, into victim's bodies, where they eat viscera and lay eggs from which great numbers of alimentary worms hatch. The initial symptoms are nausea, vomiting and torpor. Subsequent symptoms may include possesion and bizarre behaviour associated with the hyena-like character of the *buda*. (5) Various sickness-stuff: there are ailments, often acute sickness such as influenza, whose sickness-stuff makes the heart over-pulse and destroys alimentary worms. The sickness-stuff is often objectified by the term *bashiyta* (which can be used to refer to most sicknesses).

Sickness-stuff can be contracted directly, by contagion (*telalafiy*), and (in ways not understood) through the acts of demons and *zar* spirits.

Because Amhara physiological notions are simple, they do not link aetiologies to syndromes in a highly differentiated way (although in the abstract each aetiology is linked to a typical syndrome). The pathological effects of the five kinds of casual agencies described above can be reduced to a few simple and equivalent physiological formulas. The overstimulation of the heart is central to the explanations, and they differ mainly in how this is brought about. For some it is agitated alimentary worms which are responsible; for others the worms are destroyed by an agency which itself attacks the stomach and stimulates the heart to over-pulse. Symptomatically, these differences are not very significant. Further, many of the symptoms are subjective, known mainly through the sick person's descriptions (e.g. internal discomfort) and behavioural interpretations (e.g. torpor). Amhara do use diagnostic techniques which objectify the sick person, but these tend to occur late in any diagnosis after the ailment has been substantially encoded through subjective methods. Acute ailments which have distinctive syndromes (e.g. cholera, typhus) are not linked to particular physiological explanations.

There are sicknesses which are not connected to physiological explanations. In this category are skin diseases (often caused by contact with corrosive *likift* water, miasmas, contagion and filth) and leprosy (generally traced to hereditary causes); maladies of the joints and limbs, general body pain (*wuwgat*); ailments caused by demon assault such as apoplexy, epilepsy, certain forms of madness (*ibidet*), feeble-mindedness (*muny*) and some instances of incapacitation anxiety (*aynitila*); most instances of sorcery (*sray*).

Table 1 summarises the information in this section.

Therapeutic Strategies

Healers can be distinguished according to their different therapeutic strategies. By 'strategy' I mean the choice of techniques used to counter causal agents or favourably affect anatomical arrangements and physiological processes. Amhara healers work five strategies. (1) Cures return body parts to their appropriate positions: this is used mainly in the case of broken bones, sprains, and muscle

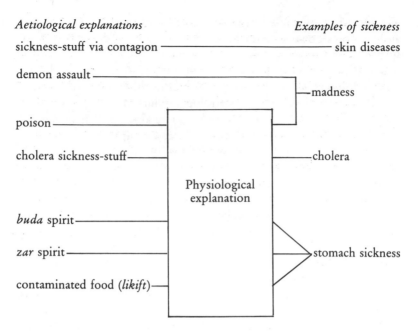

Aetiological explanations

Examples of sickness

sickness-stuff via contagion —————————————— skin diseases

demon assault

madness

poison

cholera sickness-stuff

cholera

Physiological explanation

buda spirit

zar spirit

stomach sickness

contaminated food (*likift*)

Table 1. Medical belief systems

paralysis. For example, excessive walking can dislocate the *jimat* cords which move the lower leg. This produces painful lameness (*walemta*), as the blood flows into the cords' now empty channels and prevents the cords from realigning them. Healers remove the intrusive blood by cupping, soften muscle and cords with an herbal bath, and then massage the cords back into place. (2) Diseased body parts (tonsils, uvula, teeth) are excised. (3) Cures return organs to a normal range of activity or motility. For example, in instances of high fever (*tukusat*) infusions are consumed to reduce the rapidity of heart beating and to lower the organ's output of heat; in instances of constipation (*yihod dirkot*), butter is eaten to soften the stomach. (4) Theraphy removes the causal agency from contact with the sick person. Causal agencies which have come into contact with body surfaces or visible parts such as the mouth are removed with lustrations, poultices, ointments, gargles, powders and preparations rubbed into incisions. If the causal agency is inside the sick person, it is expelled through body orifices. Emetics and purges are usually used, inhalants and fumitories are also employed, and diaphoretic and diuretic effects are sometimes sought. Medicaments are generally specific for the kind of causal agency they are intended to expel. A few pathogenic substances, such as the one associated with an influenza-like disease known as *anfula* are removed by cupping over the area of the body where the sickness-stuff is known to lodge. Poisons are a special problem. While all poisons produce similar effects, each toxic formula is believed susceptible to a specific antidote, and a generic diagnosis of 'poisoning' is insufficient for choosing an appropriate therapy. A different problem is encountered in sickness caused by a wer-hyena, since this agent is aware of the healer's strategy and consciously evades the mechanical actions of purges and emetics. The wer-hyena spirit must be coerced into leaving by a combination of argument, cajoling, and fumitories which it finds intolerable. Once it agrees to depart, strong purges are used to flush it from the body. Finally, there is the cure of the baptiser-healer (*atmakiy*), an ecclesiastic who annoints the sick with sanctified healing waters. These waters are used to force demons (who are burned by the water) to depart from the sick person. (5) *Zar* spirits lift their ailments in return for the sick person's supplications. Then, strategy (3)[2] therapies are used to flush out the sickness-stuff.

There are many therapies which are linked to their effects in a conventional way and are associated with no explicit therapeutic strategy. Often, these are anodynes effective against particular symptoms but ineffective against the sickness-stuffs which produce the symptoms (e.g. *yintil makilsol*: cionitis), and cures for complaints which are not in this instance connected to a causal agency (e.g. *saal*: cough). Sometimes, curer and client understand a sickness episode in terms of different therapeutic strategies. A herbalist for a skin disease, for example, may believe that his therapy is separating the causal agency from the sick person's body, while his client regards the relationship between the therapy and its effects as being conventional.

How Amhara Classify Healers

Amhara use a set of twenty names to categorise traditional practitioners (see Table 2). The most general term (*habesha hakiym*: 'Abyssinian' healer) distinguishes traditional curers from healers working in Western techniques. There are four categories of

2. This appears to be a misprint for (4). *Eds.*

traditional healers (grouped according to shared professional titles: Messing, 1968). (a) Chirurgeons (bone setters, uvula and tonsil cutters, tooth extractors) work strategies (1) and (2) [described in the previous section] (manipulate, excise). (b) Herbalists rely on strategies (3) and (4) (regulate organs, separate or expel the causal agency). (c) Spirit healers (whose powers come from privileged access to demons, spirits of the church, *zar* spirits, and familiarity with magic, *asmat*) practise strategies (4) and (5) (expel, supplicate causal agencies). (d) This is a miscellaneous category consisting of cuppers, midwives and tattooists. Their professional titles do not include them in any of the above categories.

Secular healers — (a), (b) and (d) — are indistinguishable from other Amhara except for their curing. Each is known to his public by his ability to treat specific, named ailments. Few herbalists, for example, offer therapies for more than three or four sicknesses. While people believe that a secular healer's success in a disease episode is proof only of healing power relevant to that ailment, they perceive a spirit healer's healing power in generic terms, competent against most ailments susceptible to strategies (3) and (4) (expel, supplicate).

Chirurgeons are distinguished according to their different organ domains — bone and *jimat* cords, teeth and jaws, tonsils and uvula. Spirit healers are distinguished from one another according to their different spirit helpers and in the case of *debtera* healers, whether they are 'strong' (*ganel sabiy* — demon-puller) or 'weak' (*trinish debtera* — minor *debtera*). Herbalists, on the other hand, are classified in a more complicated way, according to the character of the particular therapies which each owns. I concentrate on herbalists in the next paragraphs.

Amhara Pharmacology

The potency of a herbalist therapy is the product of the intrinsic power of the ingredients which make up its 'primary medicine' (*medhaniyt*) and the extent to which the herbalist has retained and concentrated these natural powers during gathering, processing and administering.

In order to prevent a medicament's intrinsic powers from dissipating during gathering, recipes often specify the particular equipment to be used, the quality of the gatherer and the circumstances necessary for gathering. For example, a recipe may indicate whether botanicals should be removed with a weighted noose or cut; if cut, whether the knife must be an 'Arab' (*arabenya*) design, previously unused, Falasha made, double-edged, or its handle made of some special wood or horn. As for the gatherer, in some recipes he is a virgin boy, or a post-menopausal woman, or naked, or facing the east. Recipes may indicate the day of the week the ingredients should be collected, and numerological details such as the number of places from which a herb must be gathered and the number of samples to be taken from each place. Finally, the gatherer may be required to repeat some common prayer a specified number of times before he cuts or digs a botanical.

Numerological instructions for processing may have the herbalist roll the preparation into *x* number of portions, or to steep the *materia medica* for *x* number of days, or to decoct to a volume of one in *x*. Equipment to be used — sometimes specified unused, sometimes worn — usually cannot rest on the ground but must be set on stones, whose number and provenience the recipe indicates (Griaule, 1930; Selassie, 1971).

Recipes often indicate the time of day when medicaments should be consumed and numerological details about how they should be taken (e.g. to be eaten seven times daily for seven days). In the case of serious illness, regimens are prescribed for the period following the expulsion of the causal agency. For example, recuperants are sometimes rested in isolated places, safe from the shadows of other humans, particularly people fresh from coitus. Recipes also direct recuperants to drink particular restoratives (*atmit*), often the broth of a cooked fowl, and to avoid the foodstuffs which were included among the *materia medica*.

A recipe's instructions are fixed. There is no theory which would enable a herbalist to introduce new elements or to explain the particular efficacy of the techniques and equipment which his recipe requires.

How Amhara Classify Herbalists

Because most of these technical details are the herbalist's professional secret, his public must evaluate his therapy according to other criteria. Aside from relying on a therapy's record of success, people evaluate a herbalist therapy according to the strength of its primary medicine, the therapist's ability to control the potentially dangerous effects of this medicine, and whether the herbalist processes and administers his medicaments.

Medicines for many internal ailments are divided into the primary medicine and its counter-medicine (*memelesha*). Strong (*hayleny*) primary medicines, particularly purges and emetics, are expected to produce violent effects, and are also associated with pungent smells and unpleasant tastes. A herbalist is expected to take into account his client's physical condition before deciding how strenuous or prolonged a therapy he can reasonable endure. A herbalist uses a counter-medicine to stop the action of a primary medicine once the causal agency has been completely ejected or after his client's condition allows no more purging and vomiting. The uncontrolled action of a strong primary medicine can itself adversely affect the sick person's heart, and it is sometimes compared with the effects of poison (just as the term '*memelesha*', 'counter-medicine', is used to refer to an 'antidote'). A herbalist's recipe is effective against a single, named ailment. A counter-medicine is less specific, but no counter-medicine is universally effective. If a healer has a strong primary medicine but no counter-medicine, his therapy can be only potentially effective since he is limited to giving relatively small quantities of the medicine. To his potential clients, such therapies are weak (*tinish*: minor) cures, assumed to have limited effectiveness, particularly against recalcitrant sickness.

A herbalist's professional title is composed of his sickness speciality and his practitioner grade. For example, the title *yianfula medhaniyt awakiy* translates as the '*anfula*-sickness medicine expert'. There are six important practitioner categories (see Table 2). (1) The least prestigious category is the 'herbal medicine giver' (*yi-medhaniyt sechi*). This herbalist gathers his *materia medica* and presents them to his client together with information for processing and administering. His instructions are always simple, with no magical elements, and often vague about relative proportions and dosages. He shreds or crumbles his botanicals before giving them so that his client will be unable to recognise them if he comes across the plants in the wild. (2) The 'herbal medicine preparer' (*yi-medhaniyt atechi*) gives his client fully processed medicaments, generally in the form of an infusion, together with information necessary for administering them. Because his medicaments have been professionally measured and processed, his therapies are expected to be more 'effective than the 'medicine-giver's'. (3) The

Table 2. Amhara practitioner titles

Shaman (*balazar*)	} Adept	}
Demon-puller (*debtera ganel sabty*)	(*awakiy*)	Seer
Minor cleric healer (*tinish debtera*)		(*tonkway*)
Baptiser-curer (*atmakiy*)		
Medicine-gatherer (*medhaniyt korach*)		
Expert herbalist (*yi medhaniyt awakiy*)		
Medicine-painter (*yi medhaniyt kabiy*)		
Herbal amulet maker (*yi kitab kitabiy*)		
Herbal medicine preparer (*yi medhaniyt atechi*)		Secular healer
Herbal medicine giver (*yi medhaniyt sechi*)		(*wogeysha*)
Bone-setter (*tagany*)	}	
Tonsil/uvula-cutter (*ankar/intil korach*)	} Chirurgeon	
Tooth-exciser (*yiters awlakiy*)	(*wogeysha*)	
Cupper (*agamiy*)		
Midwife (*awalaj*)		
Tattooer (*nikash*)		

'expert herbalist' (*yi-medhaniyt awakiy*) performs all pharmaco-logical activities himself and supervises his medicine's application. These herbalists are associated with strong medicines, serious ailments and the performance of professional diagnoses, and people assume that their recipes are pharmacologically more elaborate and complete than the recipes of other healers. Diagnosis, in the sense of evaluating symptoms prior to administering therapy, takes place in the sick person's home, among kinfolk and neighbours, and before an herbalist is consulted. In the case of therapies which aim to expel a causal agency, the medicine-expert performs his diagnosis after the primary medicine has been administered. By examining the sick person's faeces and vomit, he can judge the relevance and effective-ness of his medicine. In the evacuae, he looks for evidence of the expelled causal agency according to criteria of colour (white, green, black, and red) and consistency (liquid, viscuous, solid). The ex-pected combinations and significance of colour and consistency are generally known only to the therapist, and they have no obvious symbolic relevance beyond the therapeutic context. (4) Classed together with other herbalists is the maker of herbal amulets (*yi-kitab kitabiy*). Herbal amulets are usually the final step of a very complete therapy, and they contain ingredients used in the ther-apy's primary medicine. Once someone has suffered a serious sickness, he is particularly vulnerable to future attacks of the causal

153

agency, and the herbal amulet protects the client against a relapse. Some herbalists also give prophylactic amulets to clients who have never had the ailment in question. In addition, herbal amulets are used as the sole therapy for at least one complaint, post-parturitive haemorrhaging (*demiketir*). (5) The 'medicine-painter' (*yi medhaniyt kabiy*) applies lotions and unguents to people suffering from skin diseases. The medicine-painter's therapy includes processing and administering, but there is no counter-medicine. Medicine-painters and amulet-givers who own therapies of proven efficacy are also referred to as 'medicine-experts', (6) There are medicaments which are used in widely owned recipes for non-serious ailments (such as *enkowkow* seeds used against dwarf tapeworm) or appear as common ingredients in a wide range of recipes. Frequently, it is easier for a herbalist to get these medicaments from a professional 'medicine-gatherer' (*medhaniyt korach*) than to gather and store them himself. Sometimes a herbalist uses a medicine-gatherer because his recipes identifies a medicament only by its generic name (e.g. *sebat kelemowch*: the 'seven colours') or because he is unfamiliar with the provenience or appearance of a botanical required by his recipe.

Household Remedies

In addition to the therapies of professional herbalists, there are a variety of household remedies which are common knowledge. Cauterisation is the most common and is used mainly against certain chronic ailments, such as rheumatoid complaints (*kurtimat*), localised pain (*wuwgat*) and bubos (*ferentit*). Other household therapies are unique for particular ailments. For example, swollen lymph nodes are reduced by wrapping with a heated cloth which has been used to clean and carry the flat metal pan in which the staple *injera* bread is made. Serious ailments which are linked to self-conscious causal agencies are often treated by a combination of professional therapy (medicaments to expel the sickness-stuff) and home therapy (to draw away the causal agency). Measles (*ankalis*) and small-pox (*watetey*), for example, are attributed to eponymous spirits and are propitiated with offerings of foodstuffs. Ailments linked to demons (and sometimes to less personalised pathogens also) are drawn off by attracting the causal agency onto a sacrifice (*denkero*), often chosen with the help of a *debtera* (cleric healer) diviner. (The sacrifice, most often a chicken, is then thrown along the road side where it becomes a pathogenic danger to unwary passers-by.) There are at least two household remedies which force the causal agency to release its grip. In instances of 'bad dog disease' (*yimatfow wuwsha bashiyta*), immediately after contact with the sick dog (which includes but is not limited to animals we would label 'rabid') the person is submerged in running water in order to eject the hydrophobic spirit which has entered him. The second remedy ejects by verbal means jaundice sickness-stuff (*yililyt waf bashiyta*). The sick person is tricked into eating bat flesh (this ailment is attributed to contact with bat urine) and when told what he has eaten he is expected to spontaneously shout out the agency's name (*yililiyt waf*) and, with it, the agency itself.

Amhara Medicine as a System of Ideas

In what ways can Amhara medical beliefs be called a 'system'? Linkage can be demonstrated for certain clusters of beliefs, such as among the physiological and aetiological ideas which are used to explain syndromes characterised by internal pain, nausea and general malaise. But if we consider Amhara medical beliefs as a whole, there is no particular theory which contrasts and connects one broad range of facts with another. Further, because practitioners and their public share common sets of aetiological, physiological and nosological notions, it is not possible to sort Amhara medical beliefs into a heterogeneous 'folk' category and a well systematised 'great tradition' (as, for example, in the internalising systems of India and traditional China). There is no theory of Amhara medicine if 'theory' implies symbolic elaboration and internal coherence which go beyond reflecting arrangements taken by analogy from other phenomenological domains. Amhara medical beliefs are characterised by a discernible orientation or patterning, but patterned in ways not far removed from what seems to have been their original non-medical source. If I am correct, the core of Amhara aetiological beliefs restates Amhara ideas about the most effective ways to manipulate people in order to reach socially desirable goals in everyday life. Put briefly, these ideas emphasise reliance on physical assertiveness against obstacles whose resources are equal to or less than one's own, and ties of clientship and dependency with persons whose resources are superior. Thus Amhara aetiology-narratives are

155

organised around analogous conceptualisation of differential power: the herbalist, whose emetics and purges are described by Amhara as first weakening and then violently removing the personified sickness-stuff, concentrates on agonistic expressions of force. The spirit healer's cure adds the theme of therapeutic success through personal connections with powerful, anthropomorphised agencies. In a similar way, Amhara descriptions of the intrasomatic landscape mirror the social landscape of Christian Ethiopia: a divinely made hierarchy of position, occupation and race; a natural equilibrium sustained by life-giving power radiating from a superior and directive organ to subordinate and dependent ones, in which live the mass of indispensable and anonymous toilers, tractable if sated but aggressive and dangerous when aroused (Douglas, 1973; Horton, 1967: 50, 155 (1); Levine, 1972: 218–86).

To describe a system of medical beliefs as being without a theory does not imply that it is in some way less rational than systems with developed theoretical foundations, however. The point I want to make in this connection is that a lack of consistency among Amhara medical beliefs, or between these beliefs and objective reality — inconsistency which is less likely to occur in 'theoretical', wholly internalising systems — is apparent only in the abstract. But ordinary Amhara are uninterested in questions which would require them to frame their medical beliefs as an abstract whole. Their medical concerns are contingent and pragmatic. For example, therapies which are supposed to cure, often do not. An Amhara is most likely to see these circumstances as a vehicle for communicating new and valuable diagnostic information rather than as an experiment which discredits his assumptions about the nature of sickness and curing. What this event 'means' is that the sick person and his relatives can now choose an aetiologically more correct category of healer and a more efficacious sort of therapy.

Although Amhara can recognise ambiguities in the ways in which medical beliefs and practices articulate in the abstract, (e.g. why emetic a is effective against causal agency x but not against agency z), they are willing to assume that these can be explained away by the owners of esoteric medical knowledge, the spirit healers. There are good reasons why a man would not wish to push the matter any further. Typically, a layman (including here secular healers) conceives the necessary knowledge as too recondite for him to grasp, and dangerous to possess because of its demonic associations. A man who is tainted by such associations must expect to be feared and stigmatised and eventually forced to the periphery of common society. Indeed, even an out-of-the-ordinary interest in the epidemiology of sickness, once it becomes public knowledge, encourages people to suspect that the overly curious layman is pursuing information for anti-social reasons.

It is difficult for a layman to gain comprehensive medical knowledge because there is no practical way for it to be transmitted to him. Medical knowledge is looked on as a proprietary right. The sale of information between specialists (*debtera* spirit healers) is institutionalised, and there are regular and acceptable ways for a potential purchaser to make his interest known, for price-setting to take place, for the information to be efficiently transferred and for the donor's claims about his information to be validated to the purchaser's satisfaction. On the other hand, there are no institutionalised ways in which information can be transferred from specialists to laymen. It is unlikely that a layman could arrange things in a way that does not offend and demean the specialist-seller, nor could he make certain that his dealings did not become public knowledge and that he was not exposed as an occultist (*asmatenya*). The obstacles to obtaining information from secular healers are not much less discouraging. A man can share his knowledge with others, but unless the information is transferred between close kinsmen it must be bought with services, foodstuffs, money or other valuables. Aside from being a way to discharge social obligations, the main reasons an Amhara layman has for spending money or other resources are to gain pleasure, prestige or the means of accumulating greater resources. The purchase of medical knowledge is uneconomical on all counts since the secular healer (unlike the spirit healer) has no effective way to communicate his medical claims to a client population large enough to justify the expense of his purchase.

The Question of Empirical Proofs

Two points should be made about the empirical character of Amhara medicine. Firstly, it is efficacious, at least from a phenomenological point of view. Its greatest successes are therapies against self-limiting ailments and the transient symptoms of parasitic infections and prophylaxes against sickness episodes which are unlikely to occur anyway. Secondly, even when Amhara apprehend that therapies and prophylaxes fail, even when they choose neither to ignore the implication of the failure nor to defer its meaning to the understanding of experts, their medical system always gives plausible explanations for what has happened. Part of the plausibility results from tracing serious ailments to purposive and anthropomorphic agents which choose their victims according to social and particularistic criteria rather than biophysical and universalistic ones and which affect their victims in ways idiosyncratic and easily confused with the acts of other causal agencies. Under these circumstances, arguing from the individual episode and after the fact, is not only acceptable, it is the only way that sickness episodes can be explained. Not only are plausible explanations made when they are needed, but Amhara medical practices also give empirical proofs to support these explanations. In the case of many serious, self-limiting diseases proofs often follow as the inevitable product of the following set of premises. (1) All episodes end in a way that can be explained by weighing the balance of forces (therapeutic and pathogenic) exercised during the course of the episode. (2) The power of entire classes of pathogenic agents or entire classes of healers is not assumed to be homogeneous; that is, some spirits are more powerful, or at least more vicious or determined, than are others, just as some healers may have more formidable recipes or more helpful familiars than do others. (3) The relative power of a specific healer cannot be learned before the fact, but only contingently, as it engages the powers of a particular pathogenic agent.

Summary and Conclusions

One way to study medical beliefs cross-culturally is from an instrumental point of view. This means learning how people structure their explanations for the onset and course of sickness episodes, and how these explanations rationalise their therapeutic strategies. Systems of medical beliefs can be usefully distinguished according to (1) the emphasis given to aetiological and physiological explanations, and (2) the extent to which agencies, events and processes reflect social forms and socially recognisable behaviour. In this way, polar types of belief systems, externalising and internalising, can be described. Both systems of medical beliefs persist because they give empirical proofs of their efficacy. Cross-cultural approaches which are based on distinguishing 'supernatural' beliefs from 'naturalistic' ones are misconceived when they fallaciously imply a distinction between non-empirical and empirical systems. 'Supernatural' beliefs are better conceptualised in the context of externalising explanations. Similarly, although Western, 'scientific' medicine is an instance of an internalising system and has developed out of an historically earlier internalising system, internalising systems are not, *per se*, more scientific or rational than externalising systems. What the connection does imply is that internalising assumptions, because they make sickness a recognisable and unitary phenomenological domain, are probably a necessary but not sufficient condition for the development of scientific medicine (Foucault, 1973; Thomas, 1971).

The systematic character of a society's medical beliefs is plausibly related to certain features of its division of labour. Put simply and tentatively, externalising systems tend to be found in small-scale homogeneous societies where 'medical', 'legal', and 'moral' concerns (as the Western point of view defines them) constitute a phenomenological whole, while internalising systems are associated with the development of specialised political and jural institutions, and of professional groups into whose domains of interest medical ideas fall.

Amhara medical beliefs lie somewhere between these polar types. In many instances, aetiological explanations are necessary and pathogenic agents must be identified before the sickman or his proxies can decide on a therapeutic strategy. Even so, sickness episodes which must be traced to particular agents rarely implicate issues involving the allocation of moral responsibility within the local community (as they often do in true externalising systems). While sorcerers, poisoners and witches (*buda*) are dangers, sorcery and poisoning generally involve only the principals in some matter of personal rather than communal interest, and episodes of witchcraft-caused sickness are limited to communicating facts about categorical relationships, between Amhara and Falasha (Young, 1975a). On the other hand, only a portion of the total range of ailments can be explained physiologically, and only a segment of these *must* be explained physiologically in order for people to organise an effective therapeutic strategy. And while Amhara beliefs are systematic, they become coherent mainly in *post hoc*, pragmatic ways (and are conceptually dependent on explanatory models taken from non-medical domains) rather than through a distinctive theory or set of theories. The mixed nature of these medical beliefs is linked to social circumstances separating the Amhara from both the tribal

societies identified with externalising systems and the fully professionalised medical traditions associated with internalising systems.
Amhara society is characterised by developed politico-jural institutions, occupational specialisations, a universalising religion (introduced in the fourth century), and long (albeit intermittent) contact
with the civilisation of the Mediterranean and Red Seas. At the
same time, while ordinary people attribute generic medical powers
against most sicknesses to certain cleric healers (*debtera*), in reality
these men share no distinctive medical traditions; their medical
knowledge is mainly a compendium of secular (herbalist) recipes,
and their putative generic powers are an illusion intentionally
encouraged and exploited by many of the healers themselves
(Young, 1975b). (Historically, Galenic treatises have circulated in
Christian Ethiopia, but they are known to very few cleric healers
and have had no pervasive effect on cleric healers' understanding of
health and sickness [Strelcyn, 1975].)

8

In contrast with Allan Young, who looked at whole systems, Joan Ablon concentrates on a single, defined event and its consequences: a disastrous fire on the West Coast of America in 1964 which resulted in seventeen deaths and seventy moderate to severe burn injuries sustained by the Samoan people involved. Her focus moves from the healers to the healed and on the way in which the latter react and support their injured.

Joan Ablon's description and analysis are striking. The healers had not expected the immediate responses of the Samoans to pain and bereavement, described by doctors and others as 'stoical'. Nor had they expected what the Samoan community offered to those afflicted in the days and years following the fire. The actions nevertheless had healing consequences. The paper thus draws attention both to the role played by lay persons in the overall healing process and to the widely different conceptions and expectations that may be held by healers and healed when they are from different social and cultural groups.

Three main factors emerge as critical in the lay concepts and behaviours described. These are social position, group support and religion. Samoans occupy a lowly position in American society, having little power or wealth; theirs is a cohesive group in which members are used to sharing responsibility; finally they share a religious faith which supported them collectively and which was also a vehicle through which group support for the suffering could be expressed. Ideology and its influence on concepts has already been described by Paul Unschuld (Ch. 3, above). In the paper which follows Joan Ablon's, Caroline Currer describes reactions of acceptance of suffering that are remarkably similar and in which these three factors are also seen to be important. The discussion of the influence of social position will be echoed again by Jeremy Seabrook (Ch. 10, below).

It is perhaps the closeness of Joan Ablon's focus that lends her paper its directness. Issues of difference emerge clearly. Relating as they do to an area as apparently unequivocal as the experience of pain, these differences challenge very directly any lingering assumptions concerning universal or 'natural' reactions to illness episodes.

The paper was published originally in 1973.   *Eds.*

JOAN ABLON

Reactions of Samoan Burn Patients and Families to Severe Burns

Studies of severely burned patients emphasise the serious and complicated emotional reactions that accompany such injury (Adler, 1943; Cobb and Lindemann, 1943; Hamburg et al., 1953a; Hamburg et al., 1953b; Long and Cope, 1961; Lewis et al., 1963; Weisz, 1967).[1]

> The overwhelming significance of emotional response to burn injury on the part of the patient, the patient's family and the staff is known to every physician dealing with this form of trauma. Inextricably woven throughout the concept of burn-induced human suffering is the incalculable aspect of emotional pain and destruction. [Ollstein, Symonds and Crikelair, 1968]

Psychiatrists may be called into such cases because emotional problems are sufficiently severe as to hinder or inhibit treatment of burn injuries. For this reason, clinicians suggest that consideration of burn-associated emotional disturbances must be involved in the overall treatment plan.

The data presented here are based on materials gathered from interviews with eighteen families that the fire touched by death or injury, and with Red Cross disaster officials, physicians, nurses and attorneys who were associated with the fire victims over the following days and years. The eighteen families contacted numbered just less than one-third of those units included in the Red Cross files which comprised the master list of those affected (death to minor injury), and about three-fourths of the families who remained in the

1. The research for this paper was supported in part by the National Institute of Mental Health, USPHS Grant MH-08375 to the Community Mental Health Training Program, Langley Porter Neuropsychiatric Institute. I wish to acknowledge the generous assistance of the Disaster Service of the American Red Cross, Golden Gate chapter.

163

area at the time of the interviews. Seven persons in these eighteen family units died from burn injuries, and twenty-one others were hospitalised. Although entire families were interviewed when possible, one person in each family generally acted as chief informant, and the total number of respondents included as reporting on various topics in this paper will be eighteen. Exceptions are specified. The follow-up research was carried out five years after the fire, during 1969 and 1970. Therefore the categories of materials chosen for examination were limited to those which I realistically could expect to elicit in significant detail and with some degree of accuracy. Although Samoans rarely talk about the fire spontaneously, their memories of it and of subsequent events are quite keen and detailed. Medical personnel were eager to talk about their experiences and likewise retained clear memories of the event.

The fire occurred in a church social hall on Saturday, 23 May 1964. The 250 persons attending represented almost every Samoan church and extended family group ('relatives' by blood, marriage or adoption) of the Samoan community (Ablon, 1971a). The Samoan population of the city was estimated to be about 4,000 persons at that time. The audience, almost all Samoans, was trapped within the hall when a blaze was ignited in a container of gasoline brought by a performer for use in his fire dance. In an attempt to douse the blaze, water was thrown on the flaming gasoline, and the fire then leaped up to the curtains and rafters. The hall constituted a virtual oven for those trapped within. Although there were several available exits, almost everyone made for the front door which was partially blocked, and writhing bodies piled up at this entrance. Those who emerged from the burning building were helped by relatives or other Samoans into cars and taken to the closest hospitals — the emergency ward of the County Hospital and a nearby private hospital. When police cars and ambulances arrived, the more severely burned were piled into these. Fire fighting equipment was dispersed to the scene and the fire was rapidly extinguished. It had burned but twenty-three minutes. Six persons died that night, and eleven others died in the following few weeks.

Medical Personnel Report Samoan Response

The surgeon in charge of the emergency room at one of the two primary receiving hospitals recounted the experiences of that evening vividly. He was called from home to the hospital. As he entered the building, he was puzzled by the quiet and order in the hospital halls. Only when he entered the second-floor ward that had been quickly set aside for the treatment of the burn victims could he believe the disaster had occurred. He found there forty badly burned persons lying on stretchers and dozens of relatives standing to the side of the room. What struck him most was the absolute silence on the part of the patients and their relatives. As the diagnoses and treatment progressed, the only sounds from patients were comments of gratitude for any small attention.

On his arrival he was the only senior physician to work with the staff of interns and residents, but other hospital staff joined him within the hour. He appointed a resident to call other hospitals to inquire how many patients each could take while he examined the patients in turn to assess the severity of their burns and if they could be moved. He set up four teams to perform the eight tracheostomies that he felt were necessary. He then transferred thirty-two of the forty patients to five other hospitals, apportioning to each an equal spread of severity of burns, although he sent a high proportion of severely burned patients to a large teaching hospital that he knew was well equipped to handle burn injuries. He emphasised that the procedures of treatment and transferral were highly expedited by the cooperation of the patients and their families. The absence of complaints or questions from relatives about the treatment or transfers was paramount in the ease and rapidity of the dispersal of patients for ready and immediate care in other hospitals. He felt that the deportment of patients and relatives greatly reduced the number of casualties that occurred.

This surgeon stated that he had never before had an occasion to see so many acutely burned patients at one time. Most of the burns were external, with relatively few persons suffering from internal injuries. He remarked on the 'stoicism' of the victims and their families. Especially when informing persons of the death of relatives he was struck by the unemotional acceptance. He stated that he had no occasion to give medication to relatives for shock or grief — 'not even an aspirin'.

One physician remarked that it was a 'shocking and eerie feeling to see the silence and total acceptance of these severely burned patients'. Another physician stated that on the night of the fire he was so put off by the lack of complaint in patients who he knew must be experiencing excruciating pain that he feared it hindered his work.

A disaster official likewise used the term 'stoical' in referring to patients and relatives. He called the Samoans the 'most stoical group' he had seen in a long career of disaster work. He stated that in sudden crisis situations of this nature, Americans typically become belligerent and hostile, looking for someone or something — perhaps a doctor or a 'slow' ambulance — to blame for their loss. The need for a scapegoat is a common response. Yet here there was little weeping and no 'blame', just quiet waiting by anxious relatives.

One physician reported on his experiences the following morning when he first came to one of the hospitals where there were many Samoan patients. He found a large group of relatives there. He spoke with a prominent Samoan minister who approached him and he told him it would be better for all concerned if the assembled group left the hospital. The minister asked the group to do so and they left quietly. The physician said in his experience this was 'amazing'. The group was quiet and manageable, 'like no other ethnic group I could think of'. There were no gripes, no loud weeping, no wailing or complaints. In contrast he stated, 'Americans would have been aggressive, questioning and looking for objects of blame'.

There were great difficulties involved in identification of burn victims. Identification of blackened and charred bodies of the living and the dead was in some cases almost impossible. The unfamiliarity of Samoan names to hospital personnel created further problems for families searching for their loved ones. One woman who had been married the week before, had attended the dance with her new husband. After they both escaped from the building, he re-entered the structure to aid in rescuing others and was critically burned. In the ensuing confusion, his wife, her brother-in-law and her cousins spent almost all night going from hospital to hospital trying to locate him. After repeated trips to a number of hospitals, they finally found him. She was told he was one of several badly burned men in a small ward. She carefully looked at all of them and assured the attendants that none could be her husband. One feebly raised his arms several times. Although she was unable to identify his features she finally acknowledged this man was her husband. Two other informants related similar stories.

The most gravely burned patients frequently remained at the hospitals where they were ultimately transported that night, although some were transferred later to other hospitals where they were entitled to care through special health insurance or military service benefits. Some chose to transfer to hospitals where they could join a spouse or relative. In some instances the hospital affiliation of their private doctors or the location of burn specialists consulted by the family determined the choice of hospital.

While some few persons were treated only briefly in hospital emergency rooms the night of the fire and released that night or the next day, most faced weeks or months of hospitalisation. At the end of six weeks thirty-two persons remained in hospitals.

Physicians who treated Samoans for long-term care following the fire likewise remarked on the manner in which patients and their families withstood injury and pain. Patients were described as being stalwart and uncomplaining, no matter the seriousness of their burns. In this regard, Samoans were considered model patients. Nonetheless, one plastic surgeon remarked that he encountered problems in patient management because most of his patients did not follow directions regarding change of bandages or other necessary procedures once they left the hospital. Some would not return for follow-up visits. Some left town before the removal of stitches or before treatment was completed. This doctor felt that while he had adequately explained the procedures necessary for the patients to follow and that they understood him, they did not see the importance of carrying through the orders, and would not do so. This aspect of treatment proved difficult and frustrating for him.

The Samoan View

My interviews did not focus on pain or the pain experience as such. While there is no doubt that the Samoan patients experienced deep pain, as reported above, their outward response to this was reported by medical personnel to be 'stoical' with little or none of the external show of emotion that is typical of American patients. In the course of my interviews with Samoans, the subject of pain was spontaneously mentioned by only three respondents in their accounts of the fire and of their hospitalisation and recuperation. Two of these three respondents brought up the subject of pain in the context of explaining their refusal of skin grafts which cosmetically would have improved some of their lasting scars. These two related that other Samoans who underwent grafts told them the grafting operations were the most painful aspect of all they had suffered and

167

for this reason these two chose to forego the grafting operations. (Most who refused further corrective surgery when it was suggested to them explained their refusal in terms of lack of money or the necessary free time to undergo the procedures.) On the other hand, the two persons in my sample who were most severely burned and who underwent skin graft operations for three years following the fire did not bring up the subject of their pain. They both proudly displayed the successful results and lauded their surgeons.

There were relatively few complaints about medical care. Most persons felt they had received excellent care from the initial emergency period through the total term of treatment. Almost all of those who lost family members stated that they felt these persons had received the best care possible, but that they were just too badly burned to survive.

Distress as Expressed by Samoan Informants

Medical and agency personnel repeatedly commented on the extraordinary manner in which Samoan fire victims and their families absorbed the disaster and its effect on their lives. The caregiving services provided by the traditional Samoan large extended family met many of the urgent needs of finances, child care and general household management. The problems of household logistics may well have displaced some of the acute concerns of injury or death. Most of the respondents were parents with dependent children in the home at the time of the fire. Much of the distress expressed was caused by the total disruption of the household. Yet the extended family immediately rallied for its members. The uninjured and those who were able to be up and around again worried about juggling time for work, and for the care of children and those still recuperating rather than focusing primarily on the state of their own or others' injuries, or even of a death in the family.

Much distress was mentioned in cases where family members were listed as critical for days or even weeks following the fire. One woman who was not herself injured, recalled her anguish in living with the fact that her husband and daughter were both critically burned. For two weeks she did not know whether either one would live. She did not feel her daughter was receiving proper night care, and because she, like most Samoan women, is a nurse's aide, reported she was allowed to sit with the girl during the night to turn her every few hours and give her liquids. She and her husband talked to me about this period, shaking their heads as they relived it. After her husband began to improve, she would come each evening to his hospital room to bring him Samoan food she had cooked after returning from work. Exhausted, she would often doze in the chair by his bed as he ate. Then she would rouse herself to go to the hospital across town where her daughter still lay critically ill, and she would spend the night at her side. At 6.30 in the morning she would report for work. This woman was assisted by her mother in caring for her other seven children. Samoan friends who also were nurse's aides would occasionally sit with her daughter through the night to relieve her of that much of her burden. She spoke of this period with some wonder:

> I just never felt like that. I was feeling so funny. Here both my husband and daughter could die and I couldn't do anything about it. I never felt like that before.
> (*Have you ever felt like that again?*)
> Later, I would feel the same way when I thought about their burns, because I still wasn't sure everything would be all right.

Another woman, in recounting her three days of praying for the life of her husband before he died, said, 'I thought I would lose my mind'. Her daughter interjected at that point in the interview that she felt her mother would have had a 'nervous breakdown' at that time had it not been for strong religious faith.

Two women who lost family members specifically spoke of 'nervous' symptoms that followed the deaths they experienced. One widow reported that after her own recuperation she was 'nervous' and ate all the time and, as a result, got 'fat'. She also said that for the first time in her life she angered easily. These patterns have recurred in times of lesser stress. The second, a woman in her fifties, was hospitalised with a psychotic depression some eighteen months after her son's death in the fire:

> I felt terrible all over. I just kept thinking about it [the son's death]. It made me crazy. I went to the hospital for one month. They gave me treatments for my head [ECT]. I felt much better afterward.

This informant was the only person of all the families in my sample who actually received psychiatric treatment.

Among the eighteen families interviewed, there were four women who were widowed by the fire and three couples who lost a child. The widows all expressed to me their initial shock and grief, but quickly followed this with a recitation of the enormous amount of practical and emotional support they were given by their own and/or their spouse's relatives. The extended family, with its system of support and expectations of rapid resumption of routine household responsibilities, served as a strong force for stabilisation of the bereaved (Ablon, 1971b).

Three of the four widows have since remarried and all appear to have made a functionally successful rehabilitation. The most acute grief reactions were found on the part of two of the three mothers who lost children. These two women, both in their middle years with few other children in the home, have continued to visit the graves of their children and act out their grief in modes considered deviant by other Samoans. Probes concerning the specific elements of the grief syndrome as described by Lindemann elicited little response, as might be expected five years after the event. Many Samoans have told me that Samoans 'do not have such things'. However, it must be strongly emphasised here that such symptoms as Samoan survivors *might* have exhibited at the time are nearly impossible to assess five years following the critical event.

Continuing fears and dreams were reported by about half of the respondents. Three reported that they have repeatedly experienced dreams involving burning buildings. Two of the three reported these dreams had continued up till the time of the interviews. Seven persons reported a variety of fears related to fire, crowds or sudden accidents. Six of these stated that they are wary of attending public gatherings, and four specifically stated that if they attend a Samoan affair where there is a fire dance, they will leave the building. My own observations at a recent public event confirmed the fact that several families who were involved in the fire in the hall left abruptly when a fire dance began but returned after its completion. Several of these six persons who expressed anxieties about attending public gatherings stated that they investigate all exits before sitting down for a programme. Two women among these six persons stated that they make it a point to check all appliances at night before retiring, and are continually alert to possible accidents in the home. A few persons stated that they frequently think about the fire in quiet moments, although three couples emphatically stated that they never think about it. Two of these three couples were among those who suffered the greatest total injuries from the fire. Samoans rarely speak of the event among themselves, preferring to leave it in the past.

Response to Lasting Scarification

The personal anguish involved in physical disfigurement and scarification appears to be much less serious than might be expected, given the high visibility of the scars that most victims bear. Samoans typically are of husky build and take great pride in their size and strength. Nonetheless, statements by interview respondents suggest that scarification and the loss of strength or physical abilities engendered relatively little continuing distress. In answer to my questions about what they considered to be lasting effects of the fire, only eight persons out of fifteen who were burned remarked on slight continuing pain or a variety of physical discomforts caused by their injuries. Only six persons, four women and two men, all among those most severely burned, brought up the issue of scarification and appearance. Their concerns were expressed in a variety of ways.

One handsome young man who was in his early twenties at the time of the fire stated his cosmetic concerns the most candidly:

I look at my hands, and for a long time I was ashamed. My hands are all scarred. [Pointing to a picture of himself holding a baby.] I look at those hands and I think, my hands used to look like that, and now they look like this. I used to be ashamed, but now people know me, and my friends know that's just me and a part of me like this. I still do feel self-conscious about being with crowds and going places where there are strange people because I think that they'll look at my hands, and think — if you'll excuse me — that's a freak with hands like that.

Yet, in contrast, were the statements of one young woman who was among the most severely burned on the face, hands and arms. She was in her late teens at the time of the fire and very beautiful. She underwent three years of skin grafts. Expert facial surgery has allowed her to reappear as a still attractive young woman, but her hands and arms remain badly scarred. She recounted how her nurse forced her to look into a mirror and see her face for the first time after the fire. She screamed at the sight but came to realise that she must live with the reality. She stated that even the nurses who attended her dreaded to look at her:

At first I couldn't move my hands. I couldn't do anything. My physical therapy had to do with simple things. I had a television and sometimes as I watched TV I had a rubber ball that I would try to squeeze. They had a special knife and fork and when I would eat, the therapist would come and help me. This woman was wonderful. I remember the first time I tried to cut an egg. When I look back on this now, an egg is the softest thing to cut with a fork, but I couldn't do it. I tried and I practiced and I practiced until I was able to do all those things. My handwriting was like a child's. It was terrible. I just kept working on it. I learned how to type from scratch, but it took a long time. Now the doctors where I work say it is miraculous. They look at my hands and ask 'Who did the surgery?' I had a fabulous surgeon that has done all this work during the years. When I tell him this, he says he can do only ten per cent. The patient has to do 90 per cent. He says it is my energy. Now I type and take shorthand.

She mentioned that a friend asked her why she is not self-conscious about the scars on her arms:

I feel that I wasn't born with these scars. It wasn't my fault they are there, but they *are* there and I can't let it just change my whole life. I have to make the best of it. This is going to be what I live with and I'm learning to live with it. Sometimes new [non-Samoan] friends that I meet ask me about the scars, but Samoans never talk about the fire.

One young woman who was widowed remarked on her shame at her appearance:

I thought I would never marry again. I was all scarred. I thought how could I get married? I was ashamed. All my back and arms were scarred and I thought no one would want to marry me. [This woman in fact remarried fourteen months after the fire.]

An older woman whose arms and hands are badly scarred brought up the issue of scarification as a matter of concern to her children rather than herself:

I guess I worry the most for my children — that their mother should have to be this scarred. I've wondered if my children should have to go through life feeling ashamed. To me it wasn't so bad because I was older, but for girls such as X and Y, I think it is sad that they should have to go through life with those scars. Once, my son came home and he said, 'I almost slapped a girl today because she asked, 'Why are your mother's hands so ugly like that?'
(*Would this be different in Samoa?*)
Samoa is a small place and everybody knows what happened, so that if a

child said anything, the mother would explain and tell him not to say anything. Here it is a large place and you're always meeting new people. There's no one to tell kids what it is. For young people like X [girl described above] it is bad, but for me it wasn't so bad.

These comments dealing with the cosmetic or projected social stimulus value of their scars were in a small minority. For example, in the case of the latter woman, her own immediate concern when I first approached her for the interview was the continuing pain in one arm, not the scarification:

I told my doctor not too long ago that it feels like I have a cord in my arm and it pulls when I move it — inside at the elbow where you move your arm. It doesn't want to give. The doctor said it would cost a lot of money to remove it, and I don't have the money now.

One man whose hands and arms were badly burned and whose ears were noticeably cropped commented in a typically Samoan pragmatic way about his injuries:

I've got these scars [rubbing his arm] and my ears are this way. I could have had surgery to correct the ears, but I didn't have the money to pay for it.
(*Do the scars bother you?*)
Yes, it bothers me not having the top of my ears. You know, like if you're in the shower, water gets in your ears. It feels funny. I can't take the weather now. I used to like the cold. I would just maybe wear a little jacket when it got cold, but now I can't stand the cold. I have to wear a sweater and bundle up. I used to do steel work, but I'm not strong enough for that anymore. My hands can't close that well, so now I work in receiving, and load and unload packages.

A plastic surgeon who treated many Samoan burn victims following the fire remarked on the absence of distress. He stated that almost invariably other patients with such injuries undergo marked depression and anxiety. He is asked by patients such questions as 'What will I look like? Will I be a monster?' The patient is enveloped in self-pity. In contrast, not one of his fifteen Samoan patients asked such a question during the entire course of treatment. No depression was observed, and no medication for psychological problems was dispensed. He was overwhelmed by what he called 'the flat affect' of his Samoan patients.

Several factors appear to have contributed to the lack of anguish over cosmetic considerations. Samoans move largely in a Samoan social world. The fire was a significant event in the Samoan community. Almost every family was touched by it. Thus, the details of the fire and the personal injuries inflicted by it are well known, and to a great extent are now ignored by others. Also, the pragmatic attitudes of Samoans towards harsh and 'unpleasant' realities of life contrast with the romantic nature of cosmetic preparations regarding physical beauty as defined by American society; thus the Samoan attitudes de-emphasise the importance of physical scarification. The three informants who commented on their shame about scarification were young at the time of the disaster, and tended to associate more with non-Samoan peers than did older victims whose lives centered about their family and the Samoan community.

Contrast with Reported Responses of American Burn Patients

The medical literature is replete with accounts of emotional problems associated with severe burn injury. Hamburg and co-workers, who studied in depth 400 burn patients, detailed the nature of some of these emotional problems. They described customary behaviour of such patients:

> When a severely burned patient is admitted to the hospital, he not only is in a state of severe physical pain but also is undergoing serious emotional disturbances. Many of these patients are difficult to manage because of their inability to adjust themselves to their physical status and to their surroundings. Their emotional instability is reflected in their behaviour; some are noisy, loud and demanding and others are markedly depressed and sullen, and generally refuse to cooperate with staff. [Hamburg *et al.*, 1953a]

In the assessment of reaction to specific fire stress and associated grief, materials for comparison were sought for the Cocoanut Grove fire, which occurred in a Boston night-club in 1942 and resulted in the death of 492 persons and the injury of some 142 others. Members of the staff at the Massachusetts General Hospital published a series of papers in 1943 that chronicled the hospital's receiving of fire victims and the condition and care of the thirty-nine patients who survived the first night following the fire. These papers offer detailed materials appropriate for a comparison of some facts as reported to me by physicians, nurses, agency personnel and

Samoans who were present during the period of emergency treatment of victims of the fire described here.

Beecher (Beecher, 1943) stated that initial contact with the thirty-nine Cocoanut Grove patients revealed that few except the comatose lay quietly at rest. The outstanding characteristic of the living group was hyperactivity to the extent of mania in some cases. This hyperactivity was attributed to three major causes: (1) pain resulting from burns, mucous irritations by irritant gas, and physical injuries resulting from the panic of the scene; (2) fear and hysteria, as a result of the traumatic experience and panic of those with and without physical injuries (alcohol consumed previous to the fire also contributed to this condition); and (3) anoxia, which may give rise to excitement, loss of self-control, or even manic behaviour. Beecher discussed the considerations involved in diagnosing the cause of the hyperactivity in each case in order to decide the appropriate therapy. Hyperactivity resulting from one or another of each of the above three causes would indicate a different therapy.

The physicians involved in treating Samoan burn patients described a *lack* of hyperactivity of the fire victims as they awaited treatment. It might appear, then, that some of the alternative precipitants of hyperactivity that Beecher proposed, such as pain, fear and hysteria, might less likely have been present in the cases of Samoans because of their high tolerance for pain and what we consider to be highly traumatic or stressful situations. Doctors speak of their 'stoicism' and 'flat affect'. The psychological set of the Samoan may have precluded the complicating psychologically induced physical reactions Beecher described for Cocoanut Grove victims.

Cannon's review of the social service activities at the time of the Cocoanut Grove fire noted that the personal and social aspects of the patients' problems were acute and distressing:

> For them the experience of sudden shift from well-being and gaiety to painful and serious injury, and for many the death of some loved ones, created deeply disturbing complications that needed special psychiatric attention. Deep grief experience came to many patients at a time when they were enduring physical suffering, and, immobilised and isolated, they could not act for themselves. [Cannon, 1943: 809]

Because the fire at the Samoan dance described here occurred in a relaxed and joyous context quite similar to that of the Cocoanut Grove fire — a Saturday night dance and social event in the company of spouses and loved ones — a similar stage was set for ensuing deep emotional distress. Lindemann (1944) and Cobb and Lindemann detailed their neuro-psychiatric observations of the Cocoanut Grove patients. Of the thirty-nine patients admitted, seven died within the first sixty-two hours. Of the thirty-two in the patient population, most were included in the reported screening and follow-up activities that covered psychotic problems, psycho-neurotic problems, and problems that later developed because of bereavement.

> This report deals rather with the problems involved in the emotional adjustment of the patient to the disaster, with all its implications — disfigurement, lasting disability, loss of work, bereavement and disturbed social situations. We wanted to learn how to recognise those patients who are liable to emotional disorders, to prevent such disorders if possible, and to help those who had become victims of untoward emotional reactions. [Cobb and Lindemann 1943]

These investigators found at least fourteen patients presented neuro-psychiatric problems, but observed that this was well within the experience of psychiatrists in general hospitals, where they estimate that between 45 and 55 per cent of the patient population presents psychological factors in its problems. In all patients with clear-cut neuroses and psychoses, such problems were suggested by their histories. The investigators noted that severe emotional disturbances where no indicators appeared in histories seemed attributable not so much to the impersonal trauma of the fire as to problems in personal and social relationships involving conflict and guilt.

Cobb and Lindemann catalogued a common syndrome of somatic and psychological symptoms experienced by bereaved patients. They concluded that the work of grief, with its disabling disturbances, can be delayed but not avoided.

Adler (1943) reported psychiatric observations of forty-six Cocoanut Grove victims who were treated at Boston City Hospital. While twenty of these patients manifested no psychiatric complications at any time afterwards, twenty-five presented symptoms of general nervousness and anxiety neuroses lasting at least three months. At the end of nine months, thirteen still suffered from general nervousness and anxiety neuroses. Adler found that bereaved patients who had lost relatives or close friends exhibited no higher percentage of these psychiatric complications than patients who did not.

While no systematic psychiatric evaluations were made of the Samoan patients, statements of medical personnel intimately involved with care of these patients present a marked contrast with the findings of Beecher, Cobb and Lindemann, and Adler. Although it could not be denied that the patients experienced pain and distress, these physicians did not detect emotional problems during the treatment period that they would label as psychiatric complications.

Cultural and Religious Factors

By all accounts, Samoans as individuals and as family groups appeared to have absorbed the disaster amazingly well. Samoans present a marked contrast to most Americans in their undemonstrative acceptance of pain, death and calamaties. Many informants say offhandedly that despite painful events of whatever magnitude, the mechanics of life must, after all, go on.

Samoans were queried as to their own explanations for their unusual strength in handling the stresses of the fire. Repeatedly they referred to the Samoan proclivity for hard work and their deep religious beliefs. Samoans expect to have to work hard in life. They know they must get over difficulties that are normal expectations of life. Informants emphasised these points:

Samoans are used to taking things and having to work hard. When bad things come you just have to get through them. When Samoans have problems, they just don't complain and run to a doctor with every little thing like Americans do. People who lost somebody held up pretty well. Maybe for a month or so they just wanted to stay to themselves and think a lot about it, but after that they just have to move on.

Americans are crazy. They get so worried. In the paper or on television they get so upset about some little thing that would be nothing for us. We take such things for granted.

When you come here everything is bills and money and you have to work hard. So, I guess we feel that you have to get over things and stand on your own feet.

Secondly, informants frequently stated that people bore up under their losses because Samoans are very religious, go to church and have faith. Samoan Christian churches, which mushroomed with the influx of Samoans migrating to the mainland cities in the past fifteen years, serve as the social as well as the religious centres of the Samoan population in all of the West Coast cities. Samoans are zealous church-goers, and household prayer and Bible reading are routine for most families. One informant stated the religious case for the extraordinary management of the stresses at the time of the fire:

> The Samoan people are very religious. At home we're raised with church and people have faith. You can build on this, and even in this country, it is true. The Samoans are God-fearing people and people who go to church. So they had strength and faith for this, too.

Another who was among those most acutely burned and who, despite three years of skin graft operations, bears severe lasting scars, stated:

> It was just the man up there. We prayed to thank him that we survived because we know that here all these people were wounded and dying and we lived. We were just thankful to be alive.

A woman who was severely burned and lost a daughter in the fire was asked how she got through this period:

> Well, I was strong, and God helped me. I just prayed to God all the time, and I said that if you help me I'll just do everything and I'll get well. I examined myself and prayed that God should help me.
> (*How did the rest of the people get through it?*)
> It's because God helped them.

Samoan clergymen ministered faithfully to patients. The choirs of most of the ten Samoan church groups that existed at that time made regular Sunday afternoon rounds to all of the hospitals to sing hymns and pray over Samoan patients. This was greeted with amazement and respect by hospital staff and non-Samoan patients.

Some fire victims spoke of being consoled by the fatalism of 'God's will' being worked out in the disaster. This was the message of the ministers and priests who came to them. Indeed, one prominent Samoan minister who counselled with many survivors, emphasised to me the significance of their religion to the bereaved:

> They had to forget. I would talk to them and then they would even forget that they had a family member who died — or after a while they would thank God that this happened to them.

Indeed, at the time of the death of a Samoan, religion is the chief consolation for the survivors. In the very act of withstanding the sacrifice of their loved ones, Samoans frequently feel they are able to show their dedication to God and Jesus. The continual reaffirmation of their faith allows some survivors to speak of the time of death as their happiest hour of sacrifice accompanied by understanding and blessing (Ablon, 1970).

One plastic surgeon who attended the largest number of fire victims commented on the power of this religious fatalism for his patients. He felt they unquestioningly accepted whatever happened and phrased this acceptance in such statements as 'What is fate is fate', and 'Whatever God wills'. He gave the example of informing a husband of the death of his wife. He, in turn, passed on this word to a group of relatives waiting outside. They immediately fell to their knees in prayer, and then left without demonstrating what the surgeon considered to be observable external signs of grief.

A third factor contributing to the Samoan response to the fire is the bulwark of available family and community support. This element may be more apparent to the non-Samoan observer than to the Samoan who takes for granted the extraordinary emotional, social and financial support offered by the Samoan extended family and the larger Samoan community (Ablon, 1971b). Medical and agency personnel never fail to remark with wonder on the spontaneity and extent of this support. Members of the large Samoan extended families moved in to aid fire victims with household management, funeral arrangements and long-term nursing care. A detailed discussion of the social aspect of these indigenous caregiving activities is in preparation.

This paper has described Samoan comportment and response to injuries and acute stresses resulting from a catastrophic fire. The accounts of Samoan fire victims and non-Samoan medical and agency personnel describe stoical and accepting attitudes that proved highly functional for facilitating emergency treatment and toleration of long-term hospital care and incapacitation. Samoans regarded the injuries and deaths resulting from the fire as aspects of life that they must bear, sanctioned by a Christianity that dictates an acceptance of God's will as non-reversible fate. Furthermore, forthcoming family and community support offered the individual an extraordinary, multi-faceted security. When compared to cases of American patients reported in the literature, Samoans offer a variant response to the stresses generated by severe burn injuries. These data suggest that the total Samoan support system may in effect preclude many of the emotional problems that are observed routinely in association with severely injured and bereaved burn patients.

9

The preceding paper by Joan Ablon graphically described behaviour in the face of disaster quite unlike that which American biomedics had anticipated. In the paper which follows, Caroline Currer discusses another example of a minority ethnic group whose concepts of health and illness are at variance with biomedicine and whose illness behaviour is therefore unexpected in biomedical terms. Caroline Currer writes about Pathan women, from the North-West Frontier of Pakistan, now resident in an English industrial town. The original misconceptions on the part of British professional people about this population included the notion that *purdah* and lack of English language would lead to isolation and depression. The assumption that sample surveys and individual interviews were an appropriate methodology to use also turned to to be misconceived.

Notions of individual separateness of the person from others and especially from kin did not apply: appropriate research methodology and their concepts of health and illness had to be seen in this light. The women's lives were guided by understandings of how to think of and handle illness and suffering which were intimately associated with their status as wives in patriarchal Islamic households in which they observed relatively strict *purdah*. Caroline Currer in this paper shows how the women's illness behaviour and their health concepts can only be understood in their own terms and having regard to the structural positions they occupy: as women in Pathan migrant society and as immigrants within English society. She draws out implications for the interface with biomedical care.

Eds.

CAROLINE CURRER

Concepts of Mental Well- and Ill-Being: The Case of Pathan Mothers in Britain

Introduction

This paper arises out of a research project which set out to explore the reasons for an apparent discrepancy between expected *illness behaviour* and suggested *incidence of depression* amongst a section of the migrant population in Britain.[1] Amongst other hypotheses put forward for this discrepancy (such as lack of access to health care) it was suggested at the outset that *differences between lay and professional concepts* of depression (and of mental illness generally) might account for it. Thus the project was designed in such a manner that conceptual issues were at least left open and, where possible within the context of the study, explored in their own right, so that they could be analysed as one of a number of possible contributing factors. The study also set out to investigate whether a *conflict between the childrearing ideals of mothers and of health care professionals* might be a factor in increasing feelings of depression on the part of mothers. Many matters of infant care are concerned with health and are seen to come into the proper sphere of expertise of health professionals. So this aspect of work was concerned with norms of maternal behaviour in a context that is defined as within the purview of the medical system in Britain but is also very firmly within the private domain.

The mothers' and health workers' ideals of child care could be expected to conflict because each had been born and reared in

1. An earlier version of this paper was presented at the workshop on Lay Culture and Illness Behaviour organised by Dr Bert Tax and his colleagues at Nijmegen, Netherlands, July 1984 (Tax [ed.], 1985).

   The research project on which this paper is based was entitled 'The Mental Health of Pathan Women in Bradford' and was funded by the DHSS, whose support is gratefully acknowledged. Two unpublished reports have been prepared: Currer (1983a) — a full report; and Currer (1983b) — a shortened version of the major findings for use by practitioners in the Health and Social Services. A thesis and various publications are in preparation.

different countries with different social and cultural contexts.[2] All the mothers had migrated recently (within the previous ten years) from the North-West Frontier of Pakistan. They form a distinct cultural group known as Pathans and a subgroup of the population of Asian women living in Britain, the section of the population for which the incidence of depression is suggested to be high — see, for example, Knight (1978), Wilson (1978) and the discussion by Jane Schofield (1981) — whilst reported admissions to mental hospitals (a measure of one type of illness behaviour that may be defined as appropriate in such circumstances) are lower than average (see Cochrane, 1977, discussed by Littlewood and Lipsedge, 1982). Incidence of depression is, it is argued, highest amongst those women who are most secluded. Seclusion is seen as leading to isolation and this to depression. Pathan women are strong Muslims and the most strictly secluded of all Asian women insofar as they are the strongest adherents to the practice of *purdah*.[3] Thus, although they cannot be said to be 'typical' of Asian women (indeed, such are the variations of culture within this designation that such a claim could not be made for any subgroup), Pathan women do form an extreme, and one that could be expected to illustrate the issues to be explored most clearly.

Arthur Kleinman's model (Ch. 2, above) is helpful in attempting to understand the research questions within a theoretical framework. In examining the issues described, the study was exploring the interface between the arenas within a health care system.[4] In

---

2. A variety of anthropological works could be cited to illustrate the variation in ideals of childrearing across cultures. For an example relevant to the present study, see Parekh (1974: 45, 57). Although relating to Indians, there are strong overall similarities with the Pathans described here. My personal experience of rearing a child in Pakistan convinced me of the differences and potential conflicts for mothers in such a situation.

3. *Purdah* is the social system by which women are secluded from men and from public life. Although its practice is not restricted to Muslims, many Muslims see *purdah* as religiously sanctioned within Islam. For discussion, *see* Sharma (1980), Papanek (1973); and, regarding *purdah* observance in Britain, Saifullah Khan(1976).

4. I have discussed these within the terms of Kleinman's model as separate arenas within a health care system. The geographical boundaries of each of these arenas were, for my respondents, very different from each other. Thus the boundary of the professional NHS sector technically extends across Great Britain, although in practical terms for respondents it extended to the specialist children's hospital, some 30 miles away, and antenatal care was within the city, and most everyday consultations within a few streets. The popular sector of the system extended, however, to Pakistan, from whence the advice of close relatives might be sought and thereby exert an influence on illness behaviour in very practical ways. Some aspects of the folk sector likewise extended to consulting religious healers in Pakistan, either in person or through other family members by means of letters.

Britain a biomedical system is available to all the population through the National Health Service (NHS), which thereby represents the main part of the *professional* sector of the health care system for the majority of people. Ethnic minority groups, as part of the general population, have access to this system,[5] as well as to other healing systems which operate. These others include some specifically Asian healers who, in view of their lack of legal recognition in Britain, probably fall within the *folk* sector of the health care system, although in Asian countries they form part of the professional sector.[6] Within the *popular sector* of the health care system, we find the lay referral systems of the group under study (based on their families and social networks) as well as their own conceptual framework within the terms of which health and illness are understood. This sector corresponds to Stacey's private/domestic domain (Stacey, 1982).

The initial research questions had been concerned both with illness behaviour and with the ways in which illness is defined, insofar as the use of psychiatric hospital admission rates itself embodies a professional sector perspective, albeit in very crude form. Those admitted to psychiatric hospital are those acknowledged to be mentally ill in the terms of the biomedical system. To explore the apparent discrepancies, it was therefore necessary to look at the concepts of health and illness of the women concerned. Although this was not the sole focus of the work, the study of lay concepts of mental well- and ill-being therefore became an important part of it, and it is these aspects of the study which are particularly the subject of this paper.

Research Methodology: a Cultural Product

It was the aim of the study to interview women in the community, selected in a way that had no relation to health status. Sampling

---

5. I am not by this implying that such access is in practice equal with that of the indigenous population. *See* Pearson (1983) and Brent C.H.C. (1981), for a way into the debate concerning ethnic minorities, racism and the health service.
6. *See* M. Aslam (1979) for an account of the organisation and work of hakims in Britain. Daniel Freidman (1982) suggests that the main factor unifying folk healers is their lack of legal recognition and status. In fact, my respondents had not, they said, consulted these organised healers, although they had consulted religious authorities and local folk 'experts' such as masseuse or untrained but experienced midwives.

proved difficult since there is no record of Asian families that is broken down into their areas of origin or cultural background, to be used as a sampling frame. Names are not sufficiently distinctive. Moreover, I wished to avoid identification with official agencies, such as would have been necessary had health records been used. The work therefore proceeded on the basis of personal introduction, hoping for a snowball effect, and guarding against the danger of becoming involved with only one network of women by seeking separate introductions into each area of the city in which there were known to be Pathan families living.

During the fieldwork period of a year (1980–81) 105 visits were were made and 91 interviews conducted. Contact was made with fifty women, of whom four did not wish to be included in the study. The remaining forty-six were divided into *focus respondents* and *additional respondents*. There were seventeen of the former and twenty-nine of the latter. The focus respondents were those women who fulfilled the research criteria (Pukhto speakers with at least one child under five years). The research schedule was completed with these women, who were the 'focus' of the study. The additional respondents were women who were present with the focus respondents during interviewing. This was not a distinction made prior to interviewing, but one forced by the progress of the research. It reflects a major modification of methodology which was, as I see it, necessitated by the culture of the population under study. In the search for lay concepts, I wished to avoid overstructuring the interview process. Thus it became necessary to let this process, and hence the methodology itself, be dictated by the social norms of the women involved. Interviews were conducted in Pukhto by a Pathan Research Assistant (Fatima Khan) and myself. These interviews became conversations and were seen by the women as social occasions, albeit with a direction and purpose. The research methodology had conceived of the women as individual entities for inclusion in the sample — I had hoped for at least thirty to be interviewed in depth. Although aware of the existence of social networks and their importance as support mechanisms (probably of particular relevance in the mental health of women), the initial approach was still individualistic, seeing these as optional extras. In fact, women were rarely to be found alone and certainly not when entertaining outsiders. As interviewing progressed, occasions arose when women were alone, and these were used to cover certain aspects of the schedule which were particularly individually orientated and which might be especially biased by the presence of others. But generally it was necessary to adapt the approach to interviewing in a group setting. Not all members of each group fulfilled the research criteria; moreover, the groups were *ad hoc* and membership varied from one visit to another.

This shift in research methodology draws attention to an important issue in the attempt to investigate lay concepts cross-culturally. A number of the methodologies we employ are, I suggest, largely culturally determined. Magdalena Sokolowska (1973) has drawn attention to the individualistic orientation of curative medical systems, and Arthur Kleinman (1978b) suggests the need for a new terminology and methodology in the investigation of lay understandings. In this study, I gained an awareness of the dynamic nature of the social representations concerning health and illness and of their grounding in the group as a consequence of the change of research orientation. Because the interview schedule was long, the average number of contact visits per household was five and the average span of interviewing was four months in the case of focus respondents. I was therefore able to see changes in the norms of health behaviour, and to attribute these to intervening experiences of members of the network. Unfortunately, the study was not set up to be a longitudinal one and therefore systematic analysis of such changes could not be made. Nevertheless, interviewing over a period of time and in group settings, as we did, made me aware in a very immediate sense of their existence. Culture and the social representations of health and illness are *dynamic*, they are *influenced by health experiences* — in this case, not only by the health experiences of the individual but those of the group also. This is of course not a new idea (for example, see Herzlich, 1973). It is, rather, one of the advantages of using the concept of representations which by definition involves a dynamic element in contrast to the oft-used notion of attitudes. When presenting the work to practitioners it seems important to emphasise that the notion of a 'Pathan attitude to . . . contraception (or whatever)' is misleading.

The Data: Some Limitations and the Description of Health Behaviour in the Women's own Cultural Terms

Thus the data was collected by means of a series of conversations in Pukhto which usually involved a number of women. These conversations were unstructured except insofar as the interviewers were guided by a detailed list of topics to be covered. Although rarely covered in order, these topics were grouped into areas: (1) pregnancy and childbirth; (2) rearing young children; (3) the women's own background and world; (4) health and illness; and (5) experience of stress. The use of a tape recorder was suggested, but this was not acceptable as it was seen to violate the observance of *purdah*, and in many cases the taking of notes was also unacceptable since it emphasised the formality of our contact, which, although initially explained and agreed, was subsequently underplayed by respondents. Interviews were therefore recorded immediately afterwards directly onto the tape recorder by means of both of us recalling in order the sequence of conversation. This we did in English noting, where it seemed important, the Pukhto phrases or words used. Because a translation process was involved at this stage and recording was by means of recall, no linguistic or other detailed analysis of the data can be attempted in the exploration of concepts. However, the psychological test scales used: the General Health Questionnaire (GHQ) thirty-item scale (Goldberg *et al.*, 1970) and the Langner twenty-two-item scale (Langner, 1962), were translated into Pukhto, administered verbally but uniformly and replies noted in the interview situation, with notes on Pukhto usage. Again, detailed analysis of semantics is not possible even with these responses, but we can come closer in this case. These scales were used when we knew the woman well and when we found her alone. Only thirteen women agreed to respond to them, possibly because of the change in style of interviewing necessitated.

In analysis, the third area — (3), the women's own background and world — emerged as data concerning social situation, while areas (1), pregnancy and childbirth, (2), rearing young children, and (4), health and illness, became focus topics. Data concerning stress, (5), was drawn not only from direct questions in this area (in fact, apart from the psychological test scales, this often revealed little) but from each of the other topic areas. Much of the data from the study concerning women's experiences and practices in situations such as giving birth, rearing young children and visiting the doctor has been presented in an accessible form for health and social workers in order to present an 'inside view' of the lives of a group of women who are often not understood by health workers (Currer, 1983b). In the context of the Pathan women's own lives, health behaviours which appear from the professional's perspectives as irresponsible, irrational and sometimes uncooperative can be understood. This paper does not address this aspect of the work except to explain that the study was not primarily or only concerned with issues of conceptualisation.

Issues of Conceptualisation

These issues did emerge with some force from the work, however, and relate to several of the major themes in the literature. Pathan women viewed both health and illness, happiness and unhappiness as part of the natural order, as a part and risk of living (cf. Lewis, 1975; Ch. 6, above; Seabrook, 1973, and Ch. 10, below). Any feeling that to be healthy was an overall aim or ideal in life was lacking (although health was valued when it occurred) as was any attempt to apportion blame for illness (cf. Ablon, 1973; Ch. 8, above). Explanations of causality were given and included ideas of the 'evil eye' (cf. Lewis, 1975; Seabrook, 1973; Chs. 6 and 8, above, and 10, below), as well as environmental and hereditary explanations, but these were not emphasised. The definition of an illness was linked to the ability to work (cf. d'Houtaud and Field, 1984; Ch. 12, below). The women's value, in their own eyes and those of their community, lay in their ability to care for their husbands and children and manage the home. Many minor illnesses occurred which were not allowed to interrupt this, so women claimed, 'I have not been ill'. Social position and religion emerged as the factors which most powerfully influenced concepts, particularly responsibility for becoming ill. These are themes that emerge strongly in Joan Ablon's work (1973). Apart from issues of health maintenance (mainly in respect of the children) relating to taking precautions against temperature changes and ensuring a correctly balanced diet (defined according to the classification of foods as hot or cold), the women felt little responsibility for the occurrence of illness (cf. Pill and Stott, 1982; Ch. 13, below; Herzlich, 1973). Their responsibility (and this was marked) was *to behave correctly in face of illness*, as, indeed, in all other social situations. Social life was in all matters emphasised over individual well- or ill-being. However, it was in this context important to obtain verification of an illness episode — and here the professional biomedical system provided a reference point — since this could make possible the relinquishing of role obligations and mobilise a caring community (cf. Cecil Helman's,

1978, discussion of the difference between colds and fevers — Ch. 11, below).

These lay concepts are the focus of this paper and will be discussed in more detail with illustrations from the interviews. Firstly, however, it is important to describe how it became apparent from the study that some of the concepts and definitions used to indicate a condition as defined within biomedicine were inappropriate to describe the women's experiences.

The discussion of the translation and use of the two screening tests which follows has more than a negative importance however. The use of items which were inappropriate pointed me clearly to the types of explanation used by the women themselves. As had been the case with the overall methodology of the study, so again in struggling to translate terms and items into Pukhto phrases and idioms in a meaningful way, I was forced not only to realise the partial inappropriateness of one framework but in addition to an awareness of another to put in its place. This discussion is not a methodological digression therefore; it leads directly into a deeper understanding of lay concepts as well as pointing to some of the central issues in any attempt to translate not only words but meanings and concepts.

The Use of Psychological Screening Tests: Issues Raised by Translation and Discussion of Items

Two psychological screening tests were used as part of the study: the GHQ thirty-item scale (Goldberg, 1970) and the Langner twenty-two-item scale (Langner, 1962).[7]

The purpose of using the scales in the context of this study was in order to obtain some rating of the mental state of respondents *in the terms of biomedicine* to set alongside the respondents' own self-descriptions which would be *in their own (i.e. popular sector) terms*. This was seen as necessary because the initial research questions contained the suggestion that secluded women in the community were suffering from depression which was unrecognised by themselves and/or their doctors and/or under-reported. There was a further suggestion that the incidence of depression amongst groups

7. I am indebted to Dr John Bavington of Lynfield Mount Hospital, Bradford, for his supervision of the psychiatric aspects of this project, particularly the use of the scales. We are both grateful to NFER, Nelson, for their permission to translate the GHQ into Pukhto.

of secluded women was higher than amongst other groups of women in the community. The small size of sample and its unrepresentative character (in statistical terms and in respect of the total population of Pathan women) meant that the study could not hope to make any definitive statement on this comparative issue. It would, however, be possible, it was hoped, to compare the women's self-ratings and descriptions with their own 'scores' using the rating scales, and to use these scores as a biomedical profile of the mental state of the group of women interviewed, just as their self-descriptions would give us a profile of the group in popular sector terms.

The two scales chosen were ones which had been previously used with Asian respondents and were reported to be reliable in this context (Cochrane, Hashmi and Stopes-Roe, 1977). Their aim is to detect psychiatric disorder among respondents in community settings. The manual of the GHQ states 'to the extent that the questionnaire score gives an assessment of an individual's position on an axis from normality to undoubted illness, it can be thought of as giving a *probability estimate* of that individual being a psychiatric case' (Goldberg, 1978: 6, original emphasis). The concept of psychiatric disorder on which they are based is firmly within the biomedical tradition (see Goldberg, 1978: 5). In this study they were to be used rather differently to the optimum recommended; for example they were to be administered verbally rather than self-administered by respondents[8] and they were not to form part of a medical consultation. These factors, together with the small number of women who agreed to respond (thirteen), reduced the emphasis that could be placed on the scores themselves.

In the event, the one woman who saw herself as ill, was seen by others to be so and who had also completed the tests, did in fact score highly on them. Another woman who saw herself as ill did not complete them. A number of the items *were* seen by the women as symptomatic of unhappiness, and it is possible therefore that this led to an agreement between the different types of assessments in this instance. The issues which emerged most clearly from the use of the scales, however, were areas of difficulty and dissonance.

Language is of course a cultural product, embodying many of a peoples' cultural assumptions about life (Parekh, 1974: 77, 80). It is

---

8. Although Pukhto was the mother-tongue of respondents, it is not a language in which many people are literate. Respondents who were literate were literate in Urdu, not Pukhto. The tests therefore had to be used verbally.

not surprising therefore that translation is not a straightforward process (d'Houtaud and Field, 1984: 57n). Thus translation of the items of the scale in itself highlighted assumptions upon which a number of them are based. In Pukhto there are fewer words to describe variations in emotional state than there are in English. No equivalent term exists for 'nerves' and 'nervousness'. I repeatedly found that Pukhto contains fewer abstract concepts and that questions had to be contextualised. For example, when asked 'have you recently been taking things hard?' (GHQ, Q18) respondents would ask for elaboration, saying 'what things?' The women also took literally questions that were asked generally. For example, 'have you recently been managing as well as most people would in your shoes?' (GHQ, Q6) elicited the response that no one else was in their place as they were their husband's only wife. Thus even when the words were equivalent, the sense was not always so.

In addition to issues raised by the translation, there were items which had a special meaning due to the women's social position. As women with young babies, all had restless disturbed nights (GHQ, Q3) but this was not indicative of any mental disturbance on the part of the mothers. Further, GHQ question 5 'have you recently been getting out of the house as much as usual?' clearly has a special meaning for women who are in *purdah*. It is again a question that has a different meaning for mothers with young children and it is of interest here that P. N. Nott and S. Cutts (1982) suggest that these two questions (3 and 5) be omitted in using the GHQ with post-partum women. My contention is that social factors other than the presence of young babies influenced the Pathan respondents in addition to those relating to motherhood. These items show a direct influence of social factors on response; others showed a more indirect influence in so far as the women were unable to understand the items as stated and had a different view of the ideal. For example, GHQ Q4 contains assumptions concerning the value of work: 'have you been managing to keep yourself busy and occupied?' None had any difficulties in this respect as they had an average of four young children to care for, but even if this had been different they did not view 'keeping busy' as desirable. Work was ever present and to be done, but if ever there was little to do they would not suffer any guilt at being unoccupied. However, the strongest discrepancies related to GHQ questions 25 and 26 concerning hope. These items were repeatedly questioned and discussed by respondents. Life, like health and happiness, was in the hands of God. Hope and despair were therefore seen as irrelevant. They could not therefore be taken as indications of well- or ill-being. In view of the centrality of notions of hopelessness to the definition of depression, this difference seems of importance. Compare the description of depression, quoted by George Brown and Tirril Harris (1978: 22): 'Aaron Beck has described its central core in terms of the self seeming worthless, the outer world meaningless, and the future hopeless, and many psychiatrists would probably agree with this', with a typical comment by one Pathan respondent, 'It is not for us to feel hope. The future is in God's hands. How can we know what it will hold?'

As already stated, some of the concepts implicit in the scales used did relate to women's understandings of mental well- and ill-being. For example, concentration (GHQ Q1) was seen as important, and women told me that excessive thinking could turn their brain bad. One woman had thought all the time about her relatives in Pakistan and her mother's death and these thoughts had driven her 'mad'. Concepts of 'facing up to' difficulties (GHQ Q20) translated literally and were important — they seemed to tie in with notions of the important factor being one's behaviour, how one faced up to things. Feelings of being under pressure were also common (cf. GHQ Q14, Q21) and ideas of heaviness denoted sadness.

Such were the striking differences in respect of some of the other items, however, that it is important that one does not assume that any such list of items is automatically indicative of the same state of mind (however defined) in respondents from a different cultural background. The fact that I was forced to administer the scales verbally gave these women an opportunity to question items and to give their perspective. This might well have appeared merely as a negative score had they been completing the scales alone. I turn now to the women's views, drawn from discussions with all the women interviewed and not only from the test scales, although this draws also on what I learned through discussion of these items.

The Definition of Illness

For the women interviewed, there seemed to be two dimensions of illness. The first related to how they felt in themselves. The second was defined by whether or not they were able to work. Thus I was told both 'we do not have time to be ill. I have not been ill at all' and 'whether we are well or ill, happy or unhappy, we do our work'. In the former statement, the fact that work had not stopped meant that they claimed not to have been ill. In the second, illness was something that might be contained and overridden in the interests of work. The important thing was not whether or not the women felt unwell, but that they should fulfil their obligations within the family. This is not, of course, an orientation limited to Pathans but one that has been described elsewhere as characteristic of mothers generally (see Graham, 1982).

Inevitability

Illness (in both senses) and health, unhappiness and happiness were all accepted as a part of life. There was an absence of any feeling that health was 'normal' or even ideal and illness was pathological, insofar as both were seen as one's fate. However, such acceptance did not lead to apathy in the face of illness. Most sought treatment for disorders and wished to be free of them. The important factor was never how they felt as individuals but how they behaved in the face of illness or unhappiness. The focus was on the social aspects of illness, not individual implications.

Sadness and happiness were two sides of the same coin of living and were integral to the definition of their work. For the women's work was, apart from the physical caring for her children and husband, concerned with '*ghum/shadi* (lit., sadness/happiness), a common Urdu phrase which sums up the purpose of the visits the women paid each other. They were for congratulation and condolence. There was always a birth, wedding or death within the families of members of the community on which those concerned were to be congratulated or commiserated. Both happiness and sadness were a part of life, and to be accepted as such.

Concerning mental state, all the women referred to periods of unhappiness which were seen as a part of normal life. These had some direct cause and were temporary. Some also referred to temporary periods of unhappiness or restlessness which seemed without direct reason but just came from time to time. These two were temporary and considered a part of normal life. Some spoke of more severe periods of depression (the word in Pukhto for depression is the same as that for unhappiness). Thus one said she had been unhappy for three years when she first came and another for four or five months 'at first'. The period was a specific one and the cure in both cases had been 'getting used to it'. Another woman felt that she was just coming out of a bad patch and had been 'better since Ramzan'. In all but two cases, such periods of unhappiness did not interfere with their work. These other two women, however, defined themselves as 'ill', although interestingly others did not. Their family and acquaintances did not agree that they were 'ill' but saw their personalities as at fault; they did not cope well with the inevitable and normal difficulties of life. Both Fatima, representing a lay Pathan perspective, and I, representing a more 'professional' one in respect of training as a psychiatric social worker, agreed that these women were depressed beyond the normal and in need of outside help.

Correct Behaviour in the Face of Unhappiness

Concepts of silence and endurance emerged repeatedly when women were discussing what was for them the major issue — not how they felt but what they did about it. 'I place it [my unhappiness] quietly on my heart', 'we are sitting here, standing here', 'we pass the time'. These were common phrases. The silence and stillness was not, however, an angry or rebellious one, but one which took in all manner of adverse circumstances. It was made possible by the women's lack of any responsibility for changing these circumstances. Sitting and accepting them were all she was required to do. It might be hard — some women spoke of having 'thin hearts' meaning that they were not good at facing difficulties well. Some said that talking of their unhappiness helped — but there were variations in whom they could discuss it with. Generally matters such as personal unhappiness would not be widely spoken of (in contrast to adverse circumstances that might be bemoaned publicly), and women who complained freely about personal or domestic matters were looked down on.

In view of the lack of outlet for distress, it is hardly surprising that there was a belief in the sense of protecting oneself or being protected from stressful situations or knowledge. Thus a woman with triplets was not told that she had given birth to three sons for several days after the event, at her husband's insistence. She was grateful for this. Mothers who became distressed at visiting their babies in hospital were encouraged to let their husbands take over as daily visitors rather than being told to 'control themselves'. News of the worsening condition of one mother's baby was kept from her by her husband and she was proud of his consideration of her.

The whole community told the story for a long while of the way in which a family who were throwing a big party had been prevented by God from playing a tape from Pakistan before the party. Had they heard the news it brought of the death of a close relative, they would have had to cancel the event.

Purdah too was seen as a form of protection. The women distinguished between work and worries, practical tasks and responsibilities. Even when her early childhood had been marked by the deaths of her uncle, father and brother in close succession, one woman spoke of that as a time without sadness because it was a time without responsibility. She was one of the few who felt the weight of responsibilities now since her husband had been ill and she had had to assume many responsibilities on behalf of the family in the absence of suitable substitute male kin in the locality. This problem is one that is associated with migration. Her difficulty in doing this was not helped by the way in which her assumption of many 'male roles' (such as shopping) was frowned upon by others. *Purdah* is a system, like many closely defined ones, in which the deviant — however good their reasons for deviating — is not viewed with sympathy.

Most women saw themselves as having few responsibilities, few decisions to make and, on a scale of any significance, few worries. I was told that they could not affect anything and thus it mattered not at all whether they hoped or not: 'I have no hope at all, it is all right', and again, 'death is always first, therefore there's always hope' were two apparently unreassuring statements which to the women concerned summed up the whole situation in respect of hope for the future.

The attitudes of acceptance of misfortune that I found amongst Pathans are reminiscent of Joan Ablon's description of Samoan people's reactions to a fire disaster in which many were burned (Ablon, 1973, and Ch. 8, above). It would be interesting to know whether Pathan women's acceptance would extend to this kind of physical discomfort as it did to mental strain and considerable unhappiness. Similar factors to those discussed by Joan Ablon can be identified in accounting for this acceptance. In both societies there were social networks which were supportive in a practical sense. Pathans and Samoans both had social positions at the bottom of a social structure which they were therefore powerless to change. In the case of Pathan women, this powerlessness was not only within the wider society but within their own community, which is strictly sex-segregated and in which they are seen to have few responsibilities. Furthermore, religious beliefs encouraged acceptance of their fate and of the will of God and offered considerable support to members through prayer, reading and pilgrimage.

Answering the Initial Research Questions

The study set out to understand illness and childrearing behaviour amongst an immigrant group in terms of their own concepts, and to present this as a coherent world view to health workers of the dominant culture. It also set out to understand why the women's health behaviour was not consistent with what might have been expected in view of a supposedly high rate of mental illness. The hypothesis that different concepts of well- and ill-being between the service providers (representing a biomedical perspective in the professional sector) and those supposedly needing treatment (representing a Pathan perspective in the popular sector) was put forward as one possible explanation. Our findings did support this hypothesis to some extent. The situation was complex, however, and other factors were also important. These were:

Lack of access to health care.

As a consequence of *purdah*, and the lack of separate facilities for women in the NHS, over half of the women were only treated by their doctors through their husbands. This led to an under-reporting of illness and distress, and to misdiagnosis. In the case of mental illness which is often judged by the patient's appearance, many signs were missed. It was also not possible for women to report unhappiness when they thought their husbands would not approve.

The initial assumption that had been made by many writers that seclusion leads to isolation and this to depression was not borne out by the findings.

In this study, the most clearly depressed women (as assessed by themselves and the research team) were not isolated. They were members of close networks in which interaction was frequent but within which they were rejected personally. Where seclusion was socially and religiously sanctioned, women were lonely but not necessarily depressed, as their very conformity united them within a very real community. They accepted their powerlessness to change their situation and did not rebel against it.[9]

The exploration of conceptualisation did lead to an understanding of an aspect of illness behaviour amongst Asians that is often reported.

This is the somatisation of mental illness (discussed by Philip Rack, 1982: 101–5). Although we found a ready acceptance of the link between emotional and bodily states, it was the latter that was emphasised. Treatment was sought not for the causes of mental illness where these were seen to lie in unhappiness but for its effects in the nature of headaches, lack of sleep, and so on. I felt that this emphasis tied in with the overall importance of the social rather than the individual. For the women concerned, it was important that they should continue to work, to care for their children and to maintain social relations. Lack of sleep or the existence of headaches were more of a problem to them in these aims than unhappiness. They did not seek to apportion blame for either illness or unhappiness or to alter either social circumstances or episodes of illness that to them seemed inevitable. They did seek to maintain correct social behaviour in the face of all adversity. Illness and health, sadness and joy were all, therefore, of less importance than their effects.

9. It is important to note that my findings in this respect cannot be generalised from the Pathan women interviewed to other groups of Asian women. While I had thought that the extreme example offered by Pathan women might show up the issues more clearly, this may in fact not be so. Women with more contact with the host society and who aspire to be part of it in a way that these respondents did not, may well be depressed as a result of isolation due to seclusion or to a lack of acceptance by members of the host society. Moreover, they may lack the close social networks that I found among the women interviewed. I am also told that the time when children are at school and are teenagers is one of more conflicts for mothers than when children are small. Lastly, there are signs that many Pathan women in Pakistan accept *purdah* less completely than my respondents appeared to.

10

From concepts to be found in modern Britain amongst a minority ethnic group, the next chapter takes the reader back between fifty and a hundred years to ideas of life and death within the indigenous British population, amongst a family who moved from a village in Northamptonshire into the town of Northampton to work in the boot industry there. In his foreword to *The Unprivileged* (1973), the book from which these extracts are taken, its author, Jeremy Seabrook, introduces the account as follows:

> For a long time my family passed on to each succeeding generation a knowledge of its history, its customs, ideas and values, and for as long as anyone can remember the transition from one generation to another had been accomplished without hiatus, as the received ideas were accepted and assimilated without question. But towards the middle of the twentieth century the process of transmission began to break down.
>
> This book deals with the falling into obsolescence and decay of a way of life once believed by those who shared it to be the only admissible form that human life could take.
>
> The material is drawn mainly from oral tradition, but I have supplemented it with my own observations over a period of about twenty years. I cannot vouch for the accuracy of all the events, and do not accept responsibility for the judgements on past members of the family.

The themes and issues which emerge from this account with great clarity are themes which are found in many of the other papers. The mode of explanation described is surely an 'externalising' one, in Allan Young's terms. Echoes of Gilbert Lewis's account of the Gnau can be heard throughout. There is also evidence concerning the relationship between social position and concepts, a point made by Meg Stacey, Joan Ablon and Caroline Currer, together with attitudes of resignation and acceptance of both suffering and joy as inevitable, again reflecting Caroline Currer's findings. It is interesting to wonder, with Gilbert Lewis, whether the ideas of sickness held by these people could be described as constituting a medical system in Arthur Kleinman's terms at all, so intertwined are they with other views of life and death. But a system for dealing with illness and misfortune they most certainly are.

It is salutory to remember how recent is the current dominance of biomedicine, as well as questioning its pervasiveness outside the professional sector. Paul Unschuld, on the one hand, and Claudine Herzlich and Janine Pierret, on the other, introduced historical perspectives in Chapters 3 and 4. Jeremy Seabrook introduces a rather different sort of historical perspective, recording in detail the concepts of one 'popular sector' (Kleinman, pp. 32–4, above). In some ways they are reminiscent of views found in an undifferentiated society such as that of the Gnau. They were views held by one group of the poor and powerless in a highly differentiated society in which biomedicine was already remarkably advanced both in power and prestige.

Eds.

JEREMY SEABROOK

The Unprivileged: a Hundred Years of Family Life and Tradition in a Working-Class Street — Extracts from Chapter 2, 'Ideas'

Human life was so important that the whole natural world was subservient to it, and betrayed constant portents and warnings and clues about the future for anyone who knew how to interpret them. It was remembered that blossom had appeared on the plum tree in the autumn of the year before my grandmother died, a sure sign of approaching death. For them nature had a profound meaning for human life, not, as for the Romantic poets, in the imagined harmony between its moods and their own, but in the innumerable omens and indications to be found there foreshadowing the future. It was possible to anticipate a death, to predict the course of a marriage or the progress of a newly born child from conditions prevailing in the natural world at the time of an illness, a wedding or a birth. The world had for them a wholeness and coherence which it has since lost. It was not Arcadian or sentimental. The real fear in which their superstitions held them — and at least fifty common phenomena were considered certain forerunners of death — was a grim and joyless feature of their lives. But everything had meaning. The flight of a bird, the flowering of the trees, the colour of the moon represented something more than mere scenery to be stared at uncomprehendingly for its picturesqueness through a car window on Sunday afternoons. There was a profound connection, not always pleasant or beneficent, between human life and the most insignificant wild flower or the smallest insect. Corn-poppies induced sleep and blindness, drooping blossoms introduced into the house presaged death. I remember as a child my mother's sudden, bewildering anger one day when I picked up some trampled daffodils abandoned on the muddy cobbles from a market flower-stall: 'Pick up a flower, pick up sickness', and she thrust them vigorously from me into the gutter. My grandmother, seeing a solitary crow perched on the clothes-line, would prophesy a death before the week was out. And since she always turned immediately to the deaths columns in the local paper every evening, she rarely had much difficulty in establishing a link between some omen and the death of someone she knew.

Even the fire burning in the grate — ancient elemental source of so many superstitions — was frequently consulted as an infallible means of divination. If the fire burned at the first match, your love was said to be burning brightly or your sweetheart smiling. If the fire burned itself out at the centre, leaving a hollow surrounded by half-consumed coals or wood, this meant certain death to someone in the household. The old women who no longer moved from the fireside restlessly fingered the poker, ready to destroy unfavourable omens in the hearth. As the cinders fell through the horizontal bars into the fire-basket, they were closely examined: if they were short and square they represented cradles, or births; if elongated they stood for coffins. Sparks flying up the chimney were souls going to heaven; sparks flying out into the room showed that someone was 'having his spite out on you'. When a shred of soot-covered plaster fluttered in the draught at the back of the fireplace a stranger would soon arrive at the house, and when the flame burned blue frosty weather could be expected. These were not simply quaint or curious superstitions, deferred to absent-mindedly, out of habit, in the way that some people touch wood or throw salt over their shoulder: these were of crucial significance in their whole view of the world. Almost every manifestation of nature presaged or symbolised something else. And because those who believed in them believed with such conviction they were a great source of strength. They united the family in an unshakeable faith far more effectively than formal religion. In later generations, as the universal superstitions became weakened and finally suppressed, private and incommunicable neuroses burgeoned in their stead. Their irrational beliefs were like a hereditary poison, which, if it no longer manifests itself in blains and pustules on the surface of the skin, nonetheless continues its toxic effects insidiously and invisibly. Previously there had been no one like Aunt D., who was persecuted by everyone in the street, spied on as she ate, watched as she sat on the lav, whose house was entered at night by people intent upon rearranging her furniture and playing her piano. Cousin G., with her imaginary pregnancies and empty tumescent belly, became a figure of fun to all those who could not understand the nature of her suffering, and who, when they were not making mock-solicitous inquiries about her condition, were telling her to pull herself together or to snap out of it.

Ellen Youl, like everyone else of her generation, knew that the moon shining on the face of a sleeping child was likely to cause madness. When her children had warts, they could be charmed away by being rubbed with some meat that afterwards had to be buried. As the meat rotted in the earth, so the warts would disappear. (Although if she had been as poor as she was reputed to be, some of her descendants uncharitably suggested, she ought to have found a better use for any spare pieces of meat with a dozen children to rear.)

A bird tapping at the window, a picture falling from its hook for no obvious reason, a dog howling on its chain throughout a long summer afternoon, a bat at dusk thudding against a dusty windowpane, all these things warned of approaching death. Meat handled by a menstruous woman would go bad. During the last war the family was scandalised by the fact that my mother looked after a butcher's shop unaided by any male, and for this reason custom diminished appreciably. For many years no member of the family would go to the Co-op because of 'all them gals handlin' the meat when they're like that . . .'. If you ate from a plate resting upon another you were drowning a sailor at sea, and if the wind changed while you were pulling faces, you would be left with the disfiguring rictus for life. There was a vast and complicated network of relationships between apparently unconnected events and phenomena: if a farmer burned holly, his cows would go dry; if you deliberately killed a spider, you would never 'live and thrive'. Sheet lightning ripened the corn, cow dung used as a poultice cured boils and abcesses, a potato under the mattress was proof against rheumatism — such beliefs were the last vestiges of a way of life in complete harmony with natural surroundings.

. . . .

None of them ever doubted life after death. This was not really surprising. The consumptive young wives, the sons who didn't come back from the war, the children who died of a mysterious and unspecified 'fever', would have made nonsense of their lives if they had not believed that death represented a continuation of the many truncated and incomplete relationships of their earthly existence.

203

Preoccupation with contriving meals, keeping a job, obtaining credit, precluded the luxury of deep and rewarding relationships, and the family was full of people who reproached themselves half a lifetime for not having appreciated a mother or sister while she lived. There had been no time. And the image they had of life after death was a direct and idealised extension of their daily life.

. . . .

In spite of their harshness, nearly all of the men lived in a childish dependence upon their women, and they were unable to cope with real illness. It was always the women who hid the first symptoms of cancer or consumption, who concealed the emaciated arms and the blood-stained handkerchiefs, throwing themselves into their work with increased energy, as though the effect of routine everyday things would be to render their imminent collapse or death impossible. But the men had only to be afflicted with a sore throat for them to exact a constant, unflagging solicitude from their wives, and unless the women shared their own anxiety and preoccupation, they were taxed with indifference and accused of 'wanting them out of the way'.

. . . .

They have always been suspicious of hospitals, workhouses, institutions and asylums, which loomed like a physical threat over the streets, buildings they never came to terms with. Hospitals are still places to die in. It is still believed that they 'use you', they cut you up, they experiment on you, they give you drugs never before administered to human beings. For twenty years Ellen kept an unworn elaborately embroidered nightgown locked away in a drawer 'just in case'. This meant in case of sudden illness and an unexpected removal to hospital. The only gesture she could make against the alien world that had the mysterious power to take possession of you and carry you off as soon as you became ill was to die with dignity. When at the age of eighty-seven she fell in the back garden and broke her thigh while knocking down plums from the tree with a line prop, her overriding worry was not the pain she felt but the fact that somebody had produced an old darned calico nightie for her, and no one paid any attention to what were considered the ramblings of an old woman in pain about the special nightgown that had lain so long in the bottom drawer of the wardrobe, waiting ceremonially to adorn her death. Behind her agitation lay again a sense of inferiority of her own ways and her own life, the feeling of shame at even the things she wore.

. . . .

Resignation characterised their attitude towards life, and they were only sustained by an incontestable belief in some fundamental though unrevealed cosmic justice. 'It was sent.' And they believed that the life of each individual is made up of an equal amount of hardship, joy, suffering, pleasure. The ostensible disparity between the lives of people merely indicated the submerged nature of those equalising factors they knew to exist. Justice will always be established sooner or later, wrong always atoned for, good inevitably rewarded. ''Tain't long', Ellen would say, folding her hands confidently over her darned pinafore, ''tain't gunner be long 'fore I see all them as 'ave shit on me an' rubbed it in punished for their wickedness.' She was convinced that she would be a triumphant witness of the downfall of the woman who had persecuted her from the strap-shop, the pawnbroker who had taken advantage of her poverty and despair. Many of them believed that justice was not confined to heaven, but would also invariably be established on earth, and when confronted by evidence to the contrary — as when children died, or cheats, in defiance of their constantly recurring dictum, manifestly did prosper — they did not allow their beliefs to be undermined. They may have voiced an occasional and hesitant doubt, but they preferred in the long run the comfort of unshakeable convictions to frequent disturbing reassessments of their position, and all doubts became in retrospect merely symptoms of weakness. 'It'll find you out in the end' was their cry. If you told a lie, your tongue would drop out; if you took something which did not belong to you, your fingers would stick to it; and although such ideas are perpetuated today only in the lore of children — as in the threat to the unmoved child who says 'I don't care' that Don't Care was hanged, or the threat that if you masturbate your hair will drop out and you will go mad, or the idea that if you throw bread on the fire you are feeding the devil — only a few generations ago these beliefs prevailed in every age group.

The conviction that every human being knew joy and sorrow in equal measure often enabled them to derive some comfort from the misfortunes of the rich: they would stand all day waiting for the funeral cortège of local gentry or factory owners so that they could make sententious remarks about equality, as though the fact of the mortality of the rich somehow attenuated their own poverty and privation. Their idea of justice was as cruel and inflexible as the laws which at one assize alone in Northampton less than a century and a half ago could sentence twenty-eight men and women to death. Still strong is the belief that natural calamities — earthquakes, storms, floods — are a direct consequence of human wrongdoing. At the time of the Skopje earthquake in 1963 the family's country-dwellers were unanimous in their declaration that 'it must be caused by some folks' wickedness somewhere'. It has to be accounted for. With those who still work on the land an inclement season calls forth the same strictures on increasing crime and lawlessness. Human transgression is likely to be visited with punishment in unpredictable and apparently unconnected ways. Sexual crime may blight the crops or result in the death of an innocent child. The phenomenon of the adulteress abandoning her lover as soon as her child begins to show symptoms of serious illness was familiar to the family. They are not easily brought from this conception of justice. The crops do fail, and children do die. The belief in causal links between seemingly unrelated phenomena could not be discarded without destroying the completeness and coherence of their world. When they are confronted with inexplicable death or suffering they will search anxiously for some event within their own immediate experience to account for it, and in their need they will sometimes ascribe it to things in no way commensurate with the degree of suffering involved: a farm or street accident may come to be blamed upon insistent demands for higher pay in industry. It is another act of hubris, another example of people getting too big for their boots, and consequently responsible for all kinds of unhappiness and misery.

. . . .

It was only a hundred and fifty years ago that the last known attempt was made in Northamptonshire to ascertain the guilt or innocence of a woman suspected of witchcraft by throwing her into the river, and of course with us, too, such deeply rooted beliefs could not be cast off with indifference. My great-aunt had a daughter who was simple-minded. She would sit on the doorstep sadly watching the clumsy, elephantine girl, and swear that she had been 'overlooked' when she had been with child. Nothing would convince her that the girl's affliction was not the direct result of a neighbour's malevolence. When pressed to reveal the identity of the malefactor she would close her lips tightly and shake her head and say it would be more than her life was worth. One or two older members of the family still assert that they are able to work harm against those they dislike simply by the power of their will. 'Anybody as has crossed me', Aunt Poll used to say solemnly, 'I'm only gotter wish sommat on 'em, and sooner or later, you can believe it or believe it not, but sommat 'll 'appen to 'em.' Sometimes she even claimed to be afraid of her own power, and whenever misfortune befell anyone she knew, she would remember some occasion on which she had had cause to wish them ill. Momentary impatience with a child crying in the street late one night led to its contracting a fatal disease. Aghast at what she had done, she tried to make amends by showing herself full of solicitude and kindness for the bereaved mother. She surprised and embarrassed the afflicted woman by presenting her with an elaborate expensive wreath. The surprise and embarrassment were intensified by the fact that Poll was renowned for her meanness, and since she had scarcely ever spoken to the family in question apart from some trifling complaint, her gift was even more unaccountable.

One kinswoman who had a child with a club-foot believed that she was being punished for something she had done wrong. She could not imagine what her crime or sin had been, but this did not diminish her sense of guilt. Of course, when children misbehaved or were ungrateful it was a frequent histrionic gesture for their mothers to call them a punishment or 'their cross', but in this case there is no doubt that her bewilderment was real. And as a result she expended upon her son an overwhelming expiatory affection, which made him even more dependent upon her than he might otherwise have been, and when she died he survived her by less than a year. Similarly, when Ellen's husband ill-treated her — when he struck her or failed to come home at night — she would ask what she had done to deserve a man like that. Everything that happened to them had to be understood in terms of reward or punishment, and it sometimes seemed that the crippled child or Edwin Youl had no more human reality than their afflictive or compensatory role in the lives of those around them. Edwin Youl had been sent for no other reason than to try her. With such a view it is not surprising that she never made any effort to understand him. His alcoholism was only considered in so far as it related to her own life. Its destructive and corrosive tyranny over her husband did not concern her, and her repeated magnanimous pardons were intended only to contrast her own virtue with his wanton depravity. The possibility that she and her husband had simply chanced to meet and had made an unsuccessful marriage would have been quite unacceptable. Nothing was gratuitous. Nothing came to disturb the order and meaning of her life, even if violence had to be done to reality before it conformed to that preconcerted order and meaning.

Although they were all convinced that they had been 'put there' for a purpose (a purpose which they never ventured to define and which it often wasn't 'given to us' to understand in our ignorance), their lives were in fact so uncertain and insecure in every way that many of them sought refuge in the spurious reassurances of fortune-tellers and the stars. Nearly all of their superstitions connected with the natural world were warnings of imminent death, sickness or loss, and they sometimes needed to be comforted by the belief that legacies and dark strangers and rich relatives were not crowded out of their future by the suffering and hardship which they all anticipated, and which, they affirmed grimly in a rare and sombre concession to anything resembling a sense of humour, it didn't need a fortune-teller or a soothsayer to foretell.

. . . .

In the formation of their ideas and opinions and beliefs they were subjected to so many haphazard and contradictory influences that their outlook was often inconsistent, compounded, as it frequently was, of shreds of superstition, half-understood aspects of Christianity, fragments of ancient ritual and custom. For them the notion of 'freedom' had very little meaning. They were as they were by accident, adventitously, passively. If they had embraced their idea of the world as a conscious act of choice, fully understanding at the same time all those things they were rejecting, then they could perhaps be said to have done so freely. But in fact the alternatives were never placed before them.

. . . .

They may have lived in harmony with their surroundings, but the unquestioning assimilation of ideas effectively smothered the development of any independent thought.

. . . .

The development of any individual skills or abilities, the realisation of distinctive attributes or qualities were not considered to be the purpose of human life. They stood like fallow or uncultivated fields, strangled by weeds and stones, choked by whatever by chance found its way there.

11

The last two papers concerned lay concepts in Britain: firstly, those of a minority ethnic group and, secondly, those that existed earlier this century. Cecil Helman's paper concentrates on the present and on the ethnic majority. The author is both general practitioner and social anthropologist. This contraction of an original paper (Helman, 1978) reports on his research into folk beliefs persisting in an urban English context: an area of research that has, Cecil Helman claims, been largely neglected in favour of medical anthropological research either in the non-Western and non-industrialised world or, in a Western context, in ethnic minority or relatively isolated rural communities. By contrast, Cecil Helman's respondents live on the outskirts of London and receive treatment for most ailments from him and other general practitioners in a manner typical within the British National Health Service. The impact of the lay beliefs described lies not in their lack of familiarity, at least to readers of similar cultural origin, but in Cecil Helman's articulation of them as a belief system.

Like Joan Ablon, Cecil Helman is interested not only in the concepts of a group of patients but also in the relationship between these concepts and those of the healers. His focus is different, however, in that it is on the process of interaction between these belief systems. His conclusion is important, for it challenges views which would see these as necessarily in conflict due to their different starting points. Helman finds a difference between the folk model and that of biomedicine, but notes a moving together of them. There is adaption on both sides, evidenced in the use by doctors of folk terminology and in the incorporation of biomedical concepts, partially understood, in the folk model. This is a facet of the 'medicalisation' of which Jocelyn Cornwell speaks (Cornwell, 1984), but involving modifications on the part of the healers too. The general differences noted are of special interest, underlining as they do a point made earlier by Stacey (pp. 16–23, above) with reference to the work of others as well as to that of Cecil Helman, concerning the effect of the structure of professional–client relationships on health concepts and behaviour. The point about mutual adaptation between belief systems is one that is worth keeping in mind. Although most people working in this field are aware of the dynamic nature of cultural beliefs, there is still a tendency to portray them as static rather than emphasising the dynamics of the cultural process. Cecil Helman's paper gives an illustration of this interaction.

Eds.

CECIL G. HELMAN

'Feed a Cold, Starve a Fever': Folk Models of Infection in an English Suburban Community, and their Relation to Medical Treatment

. . . .

This paper — which arises from my own experience as a family physician — describes a folk model of illness in an ordinary English suburban community on the outskirts of London; it outlines certain widely held beliefs about illness related to perceived changes in body temperature in such a community — beliefs which can be summarised in the pharse 'Feed a cold, starve a fever', and which to some extent are common throughout the British Isles.[1] Although the suburb is now part of the great metropolis, it is a study of the 'ethnomedicine' of the area, which in Hughes' definition is 'those beliefs and practices relating to disease which are the products of indigenous cultural development and are not explicitly derived from the conceptual framework of modern medicine' (1968: 88). It is also a study of the effect of these beliefs on the diagnoses and treatments given by the general practitioners (GPs), the local representatives of biomedicine, to their patients. The material was collected in a four-year period since 1973, during which time I have worked as a GP or family physician for the British National Health Service (NHS) in Stanmore, Middlesex. Many of the present-day inhabitants, now in their sixties and seventies, moved into the area as young couples in the 1930s, while others are their descendants, or new arrivals mainly after the last war. It is a predominantly middle-class suburban community, with strong values of order, balance, and social respectability. . . .

---

[1] A number of notes and references exploring in greater detail points raised in the course of the paper can be found in the original paper (Helman, 1978). *Eds.*

General Practice in Great Britain

Under the British NHS the entire population has access to free medical care, at both general practice and hospital levels. Each patient belongs to the 'list' of a GP in their area, though there is some choice as to which doctor's list they can join, provided it is still within the area. Consultations between patients and family physicians are free of charge and take place at specified times at the surgery or by house-call for emergencies at other times. A small fee is paid by the patient for each item of drugs prescribed by the doctor; the fee is paid directly to the pharmacist who dispenses the drug. It is estimated (Levitt, 1976) that there are about 26,000 GPs in Britain, and that each one has an average list size of 2,347 patients. Levitt estimates that about 75 per cent of symptoms are treated by the patients themselves, without going to a doctor (1976: 95), but of those who do seek professional medical treatment for ill-health, the NHS GP is the first point of contact for about 90 per cent of these people (1976: 97). The GP is therefore the main interface betwen biomedical concepts of disease and lay beliefs about illness.

. . . .

'Illness' and 'Disease'

The analytical distinction between illness and disease is one that has been made by several authors (Cassell, 1976: 47–83; Eisenberg, 1977; Fabrega, 1973b: 91–3, 218–23, and 1975: 969–75; Lewis, 1975: 146–51; Mitchell, 1977). In general the term 'disease' has been used to describe the pathological processes and entities of the biomedical model; diseases are defined 'on the basis of deviations and malfunctions of the chemical and physiological systems of the body' (Fabrega, 1975: 971). . . .Each disease in biomedicine is 'an abstract biological 'thing' or condition that is, generally speaking, independent of social behaviour' (1975: 969). . . .To the Western-trained doctor, therefore, the aim of therapy is primarily the identification and treatment of these named diseases, using the scientific paradigm and definitions of modern biomedicine — which is the culturally-specific system of the West for explaining and treating ill-health. By contrast, 'illness' is an altogether vaguer term, embodying the patient's subjective perception, or sometimes the perception of those around him, of a condition of impaired well-being. Fox (1968), Fabrega (1973b) and Foster (1976), all of whom have studied the medical systems of the non-Western world, point out how illness in those regions has many dimensions: social, moral, psychological, as well as physical. Explanations for ill-health are part of wider systems for the explanation of misfortune, which usually embody a variety of aetiologies. . . .In dealing with what constitutes 'illness' here in the West, the literature is less helpful. Fabrega (1975: 973), Cassell (1976: 47–83) and Eisenberg (1977), have all pointed out that in the West it is possible to feel 'ill' without having an identifiable disease in biomedical terms, and to have a biomedically defined disease without feeling ill (e.g. a raised blood pressure, or early carcinoma). Biomedicine can be seen as the world-view of a professional sub-culture, the medical profession. Contrasted with this, is the patient's perspective of subjectively experienced ill-health; in Eisenberg's pharse, 'patients suffer "illness"; physicians diagnose and treat "diseases"' (1977: 11). Diagnosis is therefore the ordering of the patient's experience into the disease entities of biomedicine, but neglecting those that do not fall within this classification. . . .It is therefore a problem of two partially overlapping schemes of classification, whereby the symptoms and signs of illness/disease are grouped into pathological entities, in both folk and biomedical models.

However, a major drawback of many studies of illness in the urban West, both in Europe and North America, is that folk beliefs about illness have not been studied as systems but rather as a vague area of subjective symptoms and signs beyond the territory of biomedicine. It is not only in the non-industrialised world that folk models of illness have strong moral and social dimensions, and where patients ask the question 'Why me?' as well as 'How?' In addition, folk theories of what constitutes 'normality' also form part of such models, and these definitions of 'normality' often bear little relation to the biomedical definitions. A further point is that the rational and scientific nature of biomedicine, in practice, is often overestimated. . . .However, not only is there wide variation in medical practices in different Western communities but also within the same country. My research indicates that in Great Britain, at least, biomedicine at the GP level is more flexible than had been realised; and that due to the process of 'negotiation' at the consultation (see Stimson and Webb, 1975) the 'operational' model of the

GPs bears a closer resemblance to the folk model, in some respects, than to the official model of biomedicine that exists in hospitals, medical schools and medical textbooks.

Colds, Chills and Fevers

The phrase 'Feed a cold, starve a fever' is a common aphorism in the area. It arises from a folk model, or scheme of classification, of illness which is widely accepted by the patients, and it relates to those conditions of impaired well-being which the patients perceive as disequilibrium, and regard as 'illness', and which concern perceived changes in body temperature — either 'hotter' than normal or 'colder'. In general, these feelings of abnormal temperature change are purely subjective; they bear little or no relation to biomedical definitions of 'normal' body temperature as 98.4°F or 37°C, as measured orally on a thermometer. The conditions where the patient 'feels hot' are classified as *Fevers*; those where he 'feels cold' in his body are classified either as *Chills* or *Colds*. Both *Fevers* and *Colds/Chills* are states of being — both classified as abnormal — which in the folk model have different causes, different effects and thus require different treatments.

There are two important principles underlying this folk classification of 'illness-misfortune': (1) the relation of man with nature (i.e. with the natural environment) in Colds and Chills, and (2) the relation of man to man, which exists within human society, in Fevers.

. . . .

In Figure 1 I have listed the common groups of symptoms which relate to, or are accompanied by, perceived changes in body temperature. There are four diagnostic categories in all (see Figure 2); the basic division is between 'Hot' and 'Cold' conditions, but in addition there is a further division into 'Wet' and 'Dry' conditions. 'Wet' conditions are those where the temperature change is accompanied by other symptoms, and with a seemingly abnormal amount of 'fluid' being present — either still within the body, or else emerging from its orifices; this 'fluid' includes sputum, phlegm, nasal and sinus discharge, vomitus, urine and loose stools. The symptoms here include nasal congestion or discharge, sinus conges-

Figure 1. The folk classification of common 'hot' and 'cold' symptoms

	Hot	Cold
Wet	(1) Ear, nose and throat *Fever + nasal congestion* *or discharge* (2) Chest *Fever + productive cough* (3) Abdomen *Fever + diarrhoea and* *abdominal discomfort* (4) Urinary system *Fever + urinary frequency* *and burning* (5) Skin *Fever + rash + nasal* *discharge or cough*	(1) Ear, nose and throat *Cold + nasal congestion* *or discharge, watery eyes,* *'sinus' congestion* (2) Chest *Cold + non-productive cough* (3) Abdomen *Cold + loose stools and* *slight abdominal discomfort* (4) Urinary system *Cold + slight urinary frequency* *but no pain*
Dry	*Fever + dry skin, flushed* *face, dry throat, non-* *productive cough*	*Cold + shivering, rigours,* *malaise, vague muscular aches*

Figure 2. Diagnostic categories

	Hot	Cold
Wet	Hot Wet	Cold Wet
Dry	Hot Dry	Cold Dry

Figure 3. Temperature change

	Hot	Cold
Wet	Fever | Fluid	Cold + Fluid
Dry	Fever	Cold

tion, productive coughs, 'congested' chests, diarrhoea and urinary frequency. 'Dry' conditions are those where the abnormal temperature change is the only, or the paramount symptom, such as a subjective feeling of being cold, shivering or rigours, on one hand, and a feeling of being 'hot', perhaps with a dry throat, flushed skin, slight unproductive cough and possibly delirium, on the other. Skin rashes usually occur on the 'Hot' side of the classification. Other, subsidiary symptoms — including pain — may occur in one form of another on both sides of the temperature division.

Thus there are four basic compartments into which most common symptoms relating to temperature change can be fitted (see Figure 3): Hot/Wet (Fever plus Fluid), Hot/Dry (Fever), Cold/Wet (Cold plus Fluid), and Cold/Dry (Cold). Obviously, these compartments are not watertight; there is always some overlap between divisions. In addition, not all conditions associated with abnormal temperature changes have been included; only the commonest, as encountered in general practice.

'*Chills*' *and* '*Colds*'

These are explained as being due to the penetration of the environment — across the boundary of skin — into the human organism. They are part of the relationship of man to the natural environment; in particular, to the idea of 'danger without' and 'safety within' the boundaries of the human body. The causes of these illnesses are areas of lowered temperature in the natural environment — either as damp or rain (i.e. Cold/Wet), or cold winds and draughts (Cold/Dry). In general, Cold/Wet conditions in the environment may cause Cold/Wet conditions in the body, and Cold/Dry may cause Cold/Dry conditions of illness, though the division is by no means rigid. Dampness is considered dangerous in most situations, as is rain. Wind is dangerous if it is lower than body temperature, and is called a draught. Wind at body temperature, or above it, poses no threat, and is merely 'fresh air'. Night air, though, whether warm or cold, is considered dangerous by many of the older patients; it is different in quality from day air, and often 'the children get sick if you leave the bedroom windows open at night'.

These cold forces in the environment are impersonal and not linked to any social relationships.

The protective boundary of the human being is skin, but also clothes. All areas of skin, though, if exposed to damp or draughts, can be penetrated by the cold ('the damp goes right through you', 'I was chilled to the bone'). The actual *route of entry* of the cold, is through the skin itself. Some areas of skin are more vulnerable than others: in particular, the top of the head, the back of the neck and the feet. These parts of the body must be specially protected from draughts and damp. Colds were explained as occuring when any of these areas were inadvertently exposed to damp or draughts; for example, after 'getting one's feet wet', 'walking around with damp socks on', 'going outside with damp hair', 'going out into the rain without a hat on', 'stepping into a puddle', 'getting caught in the rain', and so on. Among men there is a particular sense of increased vulnerability to 'head Colds' after a haircut — when the back and top of the head are unprotected against environmental cold by their normal covering of hair.

I think it is significant, incidentally, that the two most vulnerable areas to cold — the head and the feet — are, in a sense, the most *public* parts of the clothed body, and the parts most passive to being acted upon by the environment. I would argue that the hands and face, while both 'public', are considered less vulnerable as they actively manipulate the environment, and in a sense 'join' the person to the environment.

. . . .

Although Colds do not, at least in the view of older patients, originate in other people, they are caused — as one middle-aged patient put it — 'by doing something abnormal'. . . .There is the strong implication of personal responsibility for the condition, which has been caused by one's own carelessness, stupidity or lack of foresight. You get a Cold when you 'don't dress properly', 'go outside after washing your hair', 'allow your head to get wet', 'walk barefoot on a cold floor', 'wash your hair when you don't feel well', and so on. Making oneself, or part of oneself, vulnerable to cold causes one to 'catch Cold'. Colds, therefore, are a by-product of one's personal battle with the environment. They are one's own responsibility, and no one else could be blamed for them. If, despite adequate precautions such as proper clothing, and so on, one still got a Cold, it was still your responsibility. Poor people tended to get more Colds as they are 'less responsible'.

Once the cold has penetrated the boundaries of the human organism, it can travel. It can move from the damp head, down to the nose (causing a 'runny nose'), the sinuses ('Sinusitis', 'a head Cold'), the chest (causing a slight cough — 'a Cold on the chest'). It can travel even further downwards to the abdomen, to cause vague abdominal discomfort and possibly slight loosening of the motions, or to 'the bladder' to cause discomfort and slight frequency, but no burning sensation or fever. From damp feet it can migrate upwards to cause the 'stomach Chill' or a 'Chill on the bladder' already mentioned, or even further upwards to the nose, chest or sinuses. All of these symptoms are accompanied by a subjective feeling of cold, shivering and possibly by some muscular discomfort. In addition, a direct draught can also cause the Colds and Chills, but this occurs less frequently; usually a direct draught on the lower back (while 'sitting in a draught') causes a 'Chill on the kidneys', which is described either as a muscular pain in the lumbar region or vague lower-back discomfort, perhaps with some urinary frequency.

In general, *Chills* occur below the waist ('stomach Chill', 'bladder Chill', 'kidney Chill') and *Colds* above it (a 'head Cold', a 'Cold in the sinuses', a 'Cold on the chest', a 'Cold that's gone to my chest'). In the battle with environmental cold, one should strengthen one's own defences by dressing warmly, avoiding draughts and damp, and building up the body's strength from within, by good food and patent 'tonics'. If you 'did not eat properly' you were more liable to develop a Cold. People took tonics to 'build themselves up' against the threat of cold; older patent tonics used included Parrish's Food, ViDaylin, Cod Liver Oil and Malt Extract, and Virol, and newer ones include Brewer's Yeast, Multivite, Haliborange, Sanatogen and, of course, Vitamin C. As one patient put it, if you went outdoors after having taken a tonic 'you felt warm inside'; the tonic was an ally in one's battle with cold. Most important of all allies and body strengtheners, though, was food.

. . . .

The area of Stanmore is known by the patients as a damp, dangerous area as far as Colds go. People in the area are reputed to suffer many respiratory infections and to be 'bronchial'; this is said to be due to 'dampness' retained by the clay soil in the area, which is the residue of marshes drained in the 1930s.

Treatment of a Cold or Chill is your own responsibility; it is your own problem, and is less likely to mobilise a caring community around you than a Fever. As in all Hot–Cold and humoural systems, treatment aims primarily to fight cold with warmth, and to move the patient from Cold (or 'colder' than normal) back to 'normal', by adding heat in the form of hot drinks, hot-water bottles, rest in a warm bed, and so on — and in giving him the means to generate his own heat, especially by ample warm food ('Feed a Cold, starve a Fever'), as well as tonics and vitamins, which are also perceived as a type of nutriment. In addition, he must if necessary be shifted from the Wet to the Dry state — not by expelling or washing out the fluids, but by drying them up. These fluids are considered part of the body, and should be conserved, with the aid of nasal drops, decongestant tablets, inhalations, and drugs to solidify the loose stools. Older remedies used as decongestants include goose fat, Vick and Friar's balsam. Pain accompanying these symptoms is to be treated by analgesics such as aspirin, anadin, paracetamol and several others. By these various methods, both folk and medical treatments aim to restore the previous equilibrium and a 'normal' temperature.

The only social dimensions of Colds and Chills are the implications of personal carelessness that they carry, and also for the social embarrassment of a red nose, rhinitis, blood-shot eyes, and so on. 'For appearance's sake' said one patient, 'you get rid of them as soon as possible!'.

'Fevers'

Illnesses in this group are all characterised by conditions which begin with, or are accompanied by, a feeling of abnormally raised body-temperature. In general, they are more severe, longer-lasting and potentially more dangerous than those in the 'Cold' group. All are said to be due to the actions of entities known as 'Germs', 'Bugs' or 'Viruses'. These terms are not used in the strict biomedical sense; to most people, who have never looked down a microscope and seen 'a Germ', and who have no other perceptual evidence for their existence, Germs remain a hypothesis, a theory of causality. Although the terms are borrowed from biomedicine, folk theories of Germs are rooted in the folk classification of Fevers and Chills rather than in modern microbiology.

When asked about the attributes of Germs, most patients give the following description. Germs are described as living, invisible, malevolent entities. They have no free existence in nature, but exist only in or among people. They are thought of as occuring in a cloud of tiny particles, or as a tiny, invisible, single 'insect'. They traverse the spaces between people by travelling in the air or in the breath. Germs causing gastrointestinal symptoms are seen as more 'insect-like' (Bugs), and are larger in size than those Germs causing other symptoms. Germs have personalities; these are expressed in, and can be recognised by, the various symptoms they cause. (For example, 'I've got that Germ, doctor — you know, the one that gives you the dry cough and the watery eyes', or 'the one that gives you diarrhoea and makes you bring up'). The Germ, however, may only reveal its true personality in stages, during the course of the disease.

In their effect, Germs are single; you are only attacked by one

221

Germ at a time, which selects just you to attack ('I've got a Germ, doctor'). 'Your Germ' can infect other people, but part of it will remain with you until it is expelled or you are cured. The same individual Germ cannot be in two places at the same time. Germs are amoral in their selection of victims, but once they attack they can only cause harm. There are no 'good' Germs or 'normal' Germs; all Germs are bad, whether they are 'Bugs', 'Germs' or 'Viruses'. Viruses and bacteria are generally lumped together, and no attempt is made to differentiate them clinically.

The *routes of entry* of the Germs into the body are via the orifices; particularly, the larger ones of mouth, nose or anus, though sometimes they can enter via the ears or the urethra. These orifices are the natural breaks in the body's defences and boundaries (cf. Douglas, 1970a: 145). The Germs can enter the mouth in a 'moist wind', perhaps causing a painful throat en route; or through the anus from a dirty lavatory seat. In general, Germs that enter the body in this latter way cause diarrhoea and vomiting, and are usually termed 'Bugs', while the remainder of the Fevers are caused by Germs or Viruses (these terms are used interchangeably) that enter via the mouth, though this division is not absolute.

Once having entered the body, and crossed its boundaries, the Germ signals its presence by a *Fever*, and later by other symptoms. It can expand to inhabit several parts of the body simultaneously, or it can move in sequence form part to part ('It's gone to my lungs', 'I can feel it in my stomach', 'It began as a sore throat, but then went down to my tummy', 'It's moved to my chest', 'It's breaking out in the skin', or as one patient with a peptic ulcer said, 'I got the 'flu, but then it flew to the ulcer and that blew up').

The cardinal attribute of Germs is their externality. They originate *outside* the individual, but not outside human society. They may wander from country to country, or through a community, but they are always transported by people. Here, the inside/outside dichotomy can be seen to refer to dangers outside the organism, but which still originate in other people — not in the natural environment. In fact, Germ infection implies another person, and the social dimension of life. Infection with a Germ implies a *social relationship* (of whatever duration) with another person. Infection is an inherent risk in all relationships. Different types of relationship imply different types of risk, different types of infection. For example, measles, mumps, chicken pox, and so on, indicate relationships between children (school or family); influenza usually occurs after sustained contact between adults (relatives, friends, neighbours or work-mates); urinary infections are sometimes linked to sexual relation-ships; and tuberculosis infection implies contact with 'unclean' people, such as slum-dwellers or recent immigrants. The risk, however slight, of Germ infection appears to be inherent in all relationships, but neither party is to blame for the infection. There is no malevolence or *maleficium* involved; that is, the Germ has its own volition and cannot be directly controlled by its host. The victim of a Germ infection is therefore blameless; there is not the slight implication of irresponsibility found in Colds and Chills. The patient is the passive victim of a Germ that is 'going around', and his illness is not in any way linked to the moral order (with the exception of certain venereal infections). Because of this blameless-ness, the person has a socially acceptable reason for withdrawal from all his social networks, work obligations, and so on.

Fevers create a caring community around the victim. Because Germs can be dangerous to contacts, one of the obligations of close relationships is to undergo these risks when called upon to do so. This is especially true of families with children, or with adults who become, as it were, 'temporary children'.

Fevers attack especially the weak, the old and the poor. With regard to the latter, there is a strong association with dirt (which is conceived of as concentrated, or condensed, Germs) and Germ infection, particularly in very poor people. To some extent this may be due to their type of social relationships, as well as to the dirt and disorder associated with poverty.

Germs can be 'immunised' against; the 'immunising' drug or chemical is seen as a force that is introduced into the patient's body, with his permission, and resides there, ready to combat the Germ should it enter the body. It is, in a sense, an internal talisman against infection.

The Fevers that are covered by the classification above are those that occur most commonly in the population in Stanmore, and which are frequently seen in general practice (see Figure 1). They include such conditions classified biomedically as influenza; bron-chitis, pneumonia; pharyngitis; tonsilitis, urinary tract infections; some forms of gastroenteritis; and the childhood fevers — all of which are accompanied by a subjective feeling of being 'hot', as well as certain other symptoms. In all of these the Germ is con-ceived of as being within the body itself. Local skin infections, which usually do not cause a Fever, are therefore, not included here.

223

As with Colds and Chills, Fevers may occur in either the Dry or the Wet state. Wet fevers (Hot/Wet) are the presence of a Fever, plus Fluid — whether as excess phlegm, sputum, nasal discharge, tears, urine, loose stools or sweat. Dry Fevers (Hot/Dry) are characterised by merely 'feeling Feverish', perhaps with a flushed skin, dry mouth, and a slight cough. A rash may occur in either state and so may pain or discomfort.

In summary, Fevers and Germ infections seem to be associated with three qualities. (1) *Externality*: penetration of the body by an external, living entity. It is easier to conceive of the Germ as a living entity, I think, because it originates in living people, unlike Chills and Colds. (2) *Heat*: that is, the Germ itself is 'hot', and brings its heat into the body. It is also easier to conceive of a 'hot' entity being alive. (3) *Liquidness*: the majority of Fevers seem to be related to the presence of excess fluid. It is as though the Germ matures into a 'hot liquid' inside the body.

The treatment of Fevers, in the folk model, aims firstly to move the patient from the Hot state back to a 'normal' temperature, and secondly to move him from the Dry to the Wet state (see below).

Methods of dealing with Germs — the living, malevolent entities who temporarily invade and disrupt the body, or parts of it — fall into three main categories:

1. *Expulsion*. In all these methods fluids are used to 'wash out' or liquefy the Germ, so that it can be 'washed out of the system'. Fluids are taken in by mouth as a form of treatment, and the appearance of a more Wet symptom indicates that the Germ is being diluted and 'washed out', usually via the orifices through which it entered the body. . . .For example, the aim in chest infections associated with Fever is the expulsion of fluid from the chest, carrying with it the infecting Germ — 'getting if off your chest', 'coughing up the muck', 'clearing the chest', 'getting it [the phlegm] out of your system', and so on. . . .A variety of fluids are used as expectorants here; including tea, honey, hot water, cough medicine and other liquids. . . .'I gargled with salt water to get the catarrh out', said one patient, 'and I always swallow a bit of it to loosen the cough'.

. . . .

2. *Starvation*. As in the phrase 'Feed a cold, starve a fever'. I think the implication of this advice to reduce the food intake of a feverish patient is that as the Bugs or Germs are living entities, to

starve their host is to starve the Germs, and they will eventually die or leave the body, and so end their possession.

3. *Killing the Germs In Situ.* Since the Second World War, and the discovery of the anti-microbial drugs, it has been generally accepted by most of the patients that antibiotics and sulphonamides are the specific agents for killing the Germ *in situ*, without the need to expel or starve it. This is particularly true of those Germs causing high Fevers and severe illness, which do not respond to home remedies. The drugs are taken into the body as an external force to kill the Germ *in situ*, in a battle lasting up to ten days.

The signs of expulsion, death or starvation of the Germ are a return to what is perceived as normal body temperature, a subjective feeling of being less ill and the appearance of excess liquid being expelled from the body (as phlegm, nasal catarrh, urine or loose stools), which then gradually dries up — as well as the disappearance of all other associated symptoms.

. . . .

It should be noted that this description of 'Germs' as hypotheses, or theories of causality, of illness in the folk model in Stanmore, has a similarity to equivalent theories of disease causation in many non-literate societies, particularly with spirit possession. In these societies 'spirits' take the place of 'Germs' as causal entities of disease, and like them are invisible, amoral, malign and capricious in their choice of victims. The victim is therefore blameless, and possession by these pathogenic spirits is a culturally accepted experience, and a way of mobilising a caring community around the ill person (see I. M. Lewis, 1971: 66–99). However, a much wider range of disorders are caused by these spirits than those included in the Fever/Colds model described above.

Impact of the Biomedical Germ Theory of Disease on the Folk Model

There is an increasing difference, as regards the Germ explanation of disease, between older and younger patients in the area — especially those born during or since the Second World War, who constitute the first 'antibiotic generation'. . . .'Fevers' and 'Chills' in the folk classification, that would previously have been treated by folk remedies alone, are now brought to NHS doctors — particularly

GPs — for diagnosis and treatment. Nevertheless, the basic conceptual system of the Fevers/Colds/Chills model has remained largely
unaltered; Germs are still hypotheses, and there is little lay knowledge of their characteristics, or of the difference between Germs
and Viruses, terms which are used interchangeably by the patients.
The main differences between younger and older patients regarding
the folk model, are as follows: the conception of Germs as active
causative agents of illness has spread to include several (though not
all) conditions on the Cold side of the classification. Younger
patients are more likely to blame Germs or Viruses for these
conditions. Because Colds and Chills are due to these active agents,
they can be killed, expelled or starved like the Germs causing Fevers
— hence the increasing demand, on the part of the patients, for
specific 'anti-Germ' drugs and the pressure put on doctors to
prescribe antibiotics for even minor viral infections. While a Cold is
now often considered to be caused by a Germ, some sense of
personal responsibility for the condition still remains: bad clothing,
inadequate nutrition, exposure to damp or cold — all make you more
vulnerable to Colds, as before. Nevertheless, on the Cold side of the
spectrum, the amount of personal responsibility for illness seems to
have declined. At the same time, 'Cold' illnesses have become more
social in origin, effect and dangers; they now arise more from within
human society, and create more of a caring community around the
victim than previously. Colds and Chills are now dangerous to
other people, especially children and the very old. Young mothers
often ask, 'My child's got a Cold — can she mix with other
children?', or remark, 'I didn't go round to her place yesterday
because her child's got a Cold'. It seems that there is an increased
sense of danger in human relationships, and they are now all tinged
with a new anxiety, the threat of infection. Whether or not this new
fear expresses or echoes other stresses in the social system, one
cannot be sure. Nevertheless, in a small way, the threat of infection
is used to avoid social contacts, or to mobilise a perhaps unwilling
community around the patient. This 'medicalisation' of Colds and
Chills extends also beyond the original confines of the folk classification; for example, a wide range of mood changes, from aggression
to depression, are now being ascribed by patients to Germ infection. In this medicalisation of internal moods, the folk Germ theory
provides a useful escape route to the patient — 'I'm feeling low and
depressed. I must have picked up a Virus', or 'He was rather
aggressive on Sunday, and I wondered if he hadn't picked up a

Germ — so that, increasingly, the hypothesis of Germ infection is now being used to explain behaviour changes. Depression due to Viruses, is now added to 'post-Viral depression', in the folk classification of younger patients. Also, both 'stomach Chills' and 'bladder Chills' are now increasingly being ascribed to Germ infection, except by the older generation; they are now often thought to be due to 'a Germ in the water [urine] rather than 'a chill on the bladder', or to a 'stomach Bug' rather than a 'stomach Chill' or 'something you ate'. In both cases, the infection requires active medical help to destroy or expel the Germ. In general, as the hypothesis of 'Germ infection' has spread to cover a wider range of illness and behaviour, illness has become more social and dangerous, and the process of seeking medical treatment for it is increasingly common.

. . . .

Diagnosis of 'Fevers', 'Colds' and 'Chills'

The initial diagnosis of 'illness' is usually made by the patient himself, and expressed in the terms of the folk model ('I've got a Cold'), and is usually dealt with by self-medication. However, there is a hierarchy of advice as to the diagnosis and the treatment required. This hierarchy includes friends and relatives, the local pharmacist, the doctor's receptionist, and finally — in the minority of cases — the doctor (see Dunnell and Cartwright, 1972: 96–8 — 57 per cent of adults questioned in their survey regarded the local pharmacist as a good person to ask advice of when not feeling well) The threshold at which the doctor is consulted varies with individuals and between social classes; the impression is that under the NHS the threshold for consultation is dropping for most conditions. Diagnosis, as given by the GP, is the organisation of the patient's symptoms and history into a named and standardised entity, the biomedical disease. The patient's symptoms and experience pass from the private to the public domain, and become a recognisable part of the biomedical model of misfortune. For this to be acceptable to both sides, a consensus must be negotiated; diagnosis, as Fabrega (1975: 972) has said, 'is an attempt to establish a consensus for purposes of action'. No diagnosis would be acceptable to patients, it appears, unless it was to a large extent consonant with their world-view, and particularly with their interpretation of illness. The impact of biomedical concepts on this world-view are less than had been thought. Despite exhortations in medical textbooks — for example, 'D[octor] should never forget that P[atient] is already equipped with all kinds of ideas about the nature of disease. Many of these are stereotypes, and attacking them is an essential part of any therapeutic strategy' (Crystal, 1976: 49) — the language and concepts used by GPs in consultations with patients suffering from Fevers/Colds/Chills was in the idiom of the folk model, not the biomedical one. The patients usually presented lists of symptoms, often accompanied by questions like, 'Is there a Bug going around?'; 'I'm feeling ill: is there a Virus around?'; 'Have you had anyone else come in with a tummy Chill?'; 'Is there chicken pox in the area?'; 'Have there been any children in recently with German measles?'; and so on. The answer from the GP was usually in the affirmative, and the patients were relieved to find that there is a 'Bug going around', and they are blameless and not socially deviant in their behaviour; they also no longer feel uneasy or unsure of their condition, particularly as their illness is now a disease within the biomedical world — and, by definition, capable of being cured, or at least palliated. The diagnosis given by the GPs, which provided a unified explanation of the patient's vague feelings of illness or unease, were also couched in the folk idiom; for example, 'you've picked up a Germ'; 'You've got a 'Flu Bug'; 'It's a Viral infection'; 'It's just a tummy bug — there's one going around'; 'It's just an ordinary Cold'; 'I'm afraid it's gone to your chest'; 'Oh yes, is that the one where you've got a runny nose, watery eyes, and you lose your voice? I've seen a dozen already this week'; and so on.

These explanations do not satisfy all patients; nevertheless, the majority find such diagnoses, although vague, a satisfactory diagnosis of their condition. Even if a more precise and 'biomedical' diagnosis is given, if often turns out to be also vague and non-specific. This is partly due to the fact that diagnosis in general practice, where the average consultation time between GP and patient is 5 to 6 minutes (Marsh and Kaim Caudle, 1976: 132; Morrell, 1971: 454) is usually based on traditional rather than modern forms of biomedical divination — such as listening, looking, feeling, touching, smelling, and so on; and by numerous questions relating to the patient's feelings, experiences and behaviour up to that point in time. A minority of patients are referred for hospital investigations, such as blood tests or X-rays (also a form of 'seeing'), or referred to specialists in out-patients departments. In general practice precise differentiation between viral and bacterial infections is often impossible to make (due especially to the time factor involved), or else unreliable. Aetiological agents of infection are often loosely termed 'germs' or 'Viruses' by the GPs when speaking to patients, rather than a precise definition of the type of bacterium (e.g. Streptococcus, Staphylococcus) or virus (Coxsackie virus, ECHO virus) responsible for the condition. . . .The effect of the vagueness of diagnosis from the perspective of the patient is, I think, to confirm and strengthen the 'illness entities' — clusters of subjective symptoms and behaviour changes — that constitute the folk model illness, rather than imposing precise biomedical 'diseases' on this lay model. This vagueness of diagnoses given extends also to the anatomical model used by both patients and GPs; in order to achieve a diagnosis based on mutual understanding, broad areas of the body are coalesced into: 'a chest infection'; 'a tummy bug'; 'a cold in the head'; 'gastric 'flu'; 'an infection in the sinuses'; or 'a urinary infection'. So, to a large extent, as far as diagnosis goes, what might be termed the 'operational' model of the GP, in practice bears a closer relationship to the folk model than to the official biomedical model of hospital medicine, and may therefore serve to reinforce that folk model. The entities into which the patients' symptoms are organised in diagnosis often bear a closer resemblance to the symptom groupings of the folk model than to biomedically defined diseases.

. . . .

Treatment commonly prescribed by general practitioners for disorders within the Fevers/Colds/Chills model can also be seen to 'make sense' within the conceptions of that model. More important, though, is that many of these prescribed treatments cannot be fully justified in scientific, biomedical terms; for example, the use of antibiotics, cough medicines, anti-pyretics or nasal decongestants for the viral infections that comprise most 'Colds', 'Chills' and 'Fevers' (Garrod and O'Grady, 1968: 225–427; Goodman and Gilman, 1965: 313–14; Harman et al., 1976; Harrison, 1976; Wilkes, 1974). It is almost as if, in some cases, the patients are treating themselves, using the doctor as a source of folk remedies — rather than a pharmacy, or a supermarket.

. . . .

Discussion and Conclusions

Although the conditions that fall within the Fevers/Colds/Chills model are in general trivial and non-life-threatening, they are extremely common in the population at large and are frequently encountered in general practice. As such they provide a useful source of data for any study of the persistence of folk beliefs about illness in a Western, urban community, a community long exposed to information about biomedicine and which is in frequent contact with the medical profession. The creation of the National Health Service in 1948, which brought free medical care to the entire population, also converted the entire population into potential patients. A wide variety of folk beliefs and folk remedies relating to illness, which, largely for economic reasons, had remained untouched by the medical profession prior to 1948, were suddenly brought into contact with the concepts and treatments of biomedicine. The Fevers/Colds/Chills model described above is just one example of such a folk system. Despite the impact of information about the true nature of microbial infections, the basic underlying classification of 'Fevers', 'Colds' and 'Chills' seems to have remained largely unchanged. It is suggested that a reason for this is that GPs in the area studied (and presumably in other parts of the country) give their patients diagnoses and treatment which clearly 'make sense' in the terms of reference of the folk model. Biomedical concepts are tailored to fit in more closely with the patients' model in the consultation; partly to avoid 'cognitive dissonance' in the interpretation of the illness, and partly because most conditions in the Fevers/Colds/Chills model are self-limiting and not life-threatening — so that in treating them symptomatically the GPs are less concerned to be biomedically 'scientific' than they would be in more dangerous conditions. The rushed consultation times of only a few minutes per patient also make it difficult to be more scientifically exact in diagnosis and treatment, and afford the doctor less opportunity to dispute or tamper with folk models of illness. ('My job', as one GP put it, 'isn't to educate — it's to cure'.) The effect of these factors is to reinforce, in the patients' minds, many aspects of their traditional folk models of illness, and the traditional remedies used for them.

It would seem, therefore, that in some respects the 'operational model' used on a day-to-day basis by the GPs is closer to that of the lay model than to the official biomedical model of disease as found in hospital medicine, the medical textbooks and the medical schools. However, this effect on the prescribing habits of GPs is by no means always benign; many of the drugs prescribed have undesirable side-effects, both in the short- and long-term. Antibiotics, antipyretics and even antihistamines may all cause dangerous side-effects. In addition, the cost of NHS prescribed drugs is spiralling in Britain. If six million gallons of cough medicine are annually prescribed by NHS doctors, in the face of biomedical doubt as to its pharmacological effectiveness (Wilkes, 1974), a case might be made for the much wider use of harmless 'placebo' drugs — at least in those conditions known to be trivial and self-limiting. The increased use of traditional remedies by patients should be encouraged, provided that they are free of harmful side-effects and that the doctor is confident that biomedical treatment cannot improve on the traditional remedies, in safety or in effectiveness. If life is being 'medicalised' as Illich has suggested — that is, brought under the aegis of the biomedical model of misfortune — then at least one can ensure that the treatments prescribed are not dangerous to the patients in any way. As the common conditions within the Fevers/Colds/Chills model are now firmly within the biomedical sphere of influence, at least in Britain, it is important that doctors should be more aware of the traditional medical systems of their patients, and of the effect of these systems on their own prescribing habits.

Contrary to its original intention, the NHS in Britain may have reinforced the 'folk healer' aspect of its GPs; a much wider range of life experience and misfortune is now being dealt with by GPs — not only a wider range of illness and disease than formerly but also psychological crises, life crises (such as bereavement, divorce, etc.), and all the normal biological landmarks, such as birth, childhood, puberty, menopause and death. In an age of preventive medicine, the GP deals increasingly with healthy people (as biomedically defined), for immunisations, ante-natal clinics, cervical smear clinics, baby clinics, and so on. The more intimate and long-term relationship between GP and patient that this brings about does not seem to have drastically changed folk models of illness. The Fevers/Colds/Chills model is one example of this, but undoubtedly there are many others that remain to be studied, with the eventual aim of improving health care, with less side-effects to the patient.

12

In Chapter 4 we reproduced in English translation work by Claudine Herzlich and Janine Pierret which was in the Durkheimian tradition, thinking about health and illness as 'social representations'. The work by Alphonse d'Houtaud which follows is also in this tradition. Inspired by Claudine Herzlich's *Health and Illness* (1973), Alphonse d'Houtaud used the methods of the sample survey to try and find out how lay people conceived of health. Claudine Herzlich had not manipulated her samples of Parisians and Normans statistically. She was more interested to establish what representations were present among the people she talked to. Alphonse d'Houtaud's addition was to relate his respondents' concepts to such variables as age and socio-economic status. A critical paper from this work is available in English (d'Houtaud and Field, 1984).

What follows is a translation (with which Mark Field helped) of an article discussing a later repetition of this work. In this second study Alphonse d'Houtaud used closed rather than open-ended questions. This paper compares the responses of the two samples. Some methodologists may wish to disagree with his preference for the closed questions.

It is important to note that, whether the questions were open or closed, the respondents were asked them when they were attending for a regular health check. Whether women or men, old or young, lower or upper class, they were all self-selected to accept biomedical routines associated with the mode of health care delivery available to them.

Two features are particularly relevant for this volume. One is the way in which approaches to health, such as the fatalistic, which other authors have shown to be dominant properties of a particular ethnic group (see Caroline Currer's account in Ch. 9, for example), are to be found among members of this population in Lorraine. It demonstrates well the plurality of beliefs about health and healing in advanced industrial societies which Paul Unschuld discussed in Ch. 3.

The second is the variation by socio-economic group which appeared in Alphonse d'Houtaud's first study and reappears here despite changed methodology. It supports the case made by the those who argue for a relationship between health beliefs and practices and the structure of a society and people's position within it. In particular, the more positive and egocentric approach of those in positions of greater power and wealth compares markedly with the more negative and sociocentric definitions among manual workers who have fewer resources and less self-determination available to them.

Alphonse d'Houtaud's work has inspired others in various parts of Europe, and his enquiries have been replicated. In work in Nijmegen, Netherlands, Bert Tax and his associates repeated some of the d'Houtaud questions with different results. These differences await full explanation. Perhaps these are associated with religious differences, perhaps with the sample being taken outside the context of a health examination or perhaps with the higher levels of unemployment which pertain since d'Houtaud's study together with differing occupational structures in the two locations. The workshop which Bert Tax organised in 1984 showed how widely the study of lay concepts of health is now pursued on the mainland of Europe (Tax, 1984).

The paper from which this translation is taken was published in French in 1981. *Eds.*

ALPHONSE D'HOUTAUD
MARK G. FIELD

New Research on the Image of Health

Introduction

In a follow-up to a study on the image of health based on the open-ended answers of 4,000 respondents among the 72,513 who underwent a health examination at the Centre de Mèdecine Prèventive of Vandoeuvre-lés-Nancy (north-eastern France) from 21 January 1971 to 15 May 1974, we were able to continue this type of research based this time on closed questions administered to 11,002 persons among those who underwent a similar type of health examination in 1978.[1]

The first phase of this investigation was the major concern of two publications in French (d'Houtaud, 1976, 1978) and of a third one in English (d'Houtaud and Field, 1984). The second phase has already been the subject of a fourth publication in French (d'Houtaud, 1981). Here we propose to give, in English, the highlights of that publication.

The population we studied (5,247 men and 5,754 women) includes 56.4 per cent under the age of 40 (2,966 aged eighteen to twenty-nine and 3,156 aged thirty to thirty-nine); among the older respondents there are more between the ages of forty to forty-nine (2,556) than among those fifty to fifty-nine (1,692) and those of sixty plus (490); a few respondents did not give their age.

When we examine the socio-economic categories of our respondents, we find that the three most numerous groups are middle managers (cadres moyens) (1,902), employees (employés) (1,417), and skilled workers and foremen (1,817). Semi-skilled and unskilled workers together (921) are almost equal in numbers to the higher managers and professionals (cadres superiors, professionnels

Based on a translation by Dorothy Parkin.
1. This study was carried out with the help of R. Gueguen, Statistician, at the Centre de Médecine Préventive at Vandoeuvre-lès-Nancy. The work was done with the help of a grant from the Caisse Nationale d'Assurance Maladie.

235

libérales) at 906.[2] Among those 1,844 not actively employed in the labour force are housewives, the retired, students, and so on. Let us note that 1,259 did not give their socio-economic category and that the other respondents are distributed among service personnel (personnel de service) (548), owners of business, tradesmen and artisans (patrons, commerçants, artisants) (109) and other occupations (137). Let us also add that between 1974 and 1978 farmers and farm workers (salaried) were not, any more, eligible for the health examination through their special insurance funds and that, from one investigation to the other, the proportion of men to women was reversed.

Research Methodology

Among the eighteen themes proposed in that second investigation as items in four closed questions (Table I), ten were copied *verbatim* from the forty-one themes that emerged through a content analysis of the 4,000 answers to the open-ended question of the first investigation. The other thirty-one themes of that investigation were regrouped into eight more synthetic and logically complementary themes. A fifth question with two items permitted us to tap the fatalistic and voluntaristic tendencies of the respondents (Table II).

The eighteen themes in the four questions ask the respondents for two types of reponses:

> one allows them to differentiate their views by responding with a YES or a NO to each item; the other one forces them to select only one item in each question through an exclusive CHOICE such that the percentages of items in each one of the four questions total 100.

Among the 'yes' or 'no' responses, the eighteen items are comparable one with the other (each respondent being able to express

---

2. We have here translated '*ouvriers qualifiés*' (lit. qualified workers) as 'skilled workers', '*ouvriers spécialisés*' (lit. specialised workers) as 'semi-skilled workers', and '*manoeuvres*' as 'unsakilled workers' since we believe these to be the nearest equivalents in common use. In the French classification used by d'Houtaud, the 'qualified worker' is one who, having completed a specific training, has received a certificate of professional (occupational) aptitude (CAP) or its equivalent as a result of competence demonstrated over a specified length of time. The 'specialised worker' is one who works in a determined specialty, but without ever succeeding in obtaining a certificate of professional (occupational) aptitude or its equivalent. The specialised worker is not entitled to the same wage level as his qualified colleague.

Table I. Numbers and % obtained for the 18 definitions of health, in decreasing order, from 11,002 respondents

Definitions of health	Numbers			%		
	Yes	No	NR	Yes	No	NR
1. Hygiene	9,555	464	583	90.5	4.2	5.3
2. Living and working conditions	9,187	979	836	83.5	8.9	7.6
3. To feel well in one's skin	9,166	909	927	83.3	8.3	8.4
4. Equilibrium	8,646	1,130	1,226	78.6	10.3	11.1
5. Top of one's form	8,336	1,269	1,397	75.8	11.5	12.7
6. Precautions	8,259	1,600	1,142	75.1	14.5	10.4
7. Good morale	8,063	1,513	1,426	73.3	13.7	13.0
8. Medicine	7,897	1,728	1,377	71.8	15.7	12.5
9. Not to be sick	7,800	1,796	1,406	70.9	16.3	12.8
10. Physical resistance	7,721	2,063	1,210	70.2	18.7	11.1
11. Joy of living	7,495	1,839	1,658	68.1	16.7	15.2
12. To be able to face all problems	6,942	2,449	1,611	63.1	22.3	14.6
13. Leisure	6,803	2,533	1,666	61.8	23.0	15.2
14. To know oneself well	6,686	2,568	1,748	60.8	23.2	15.9
15. Work	6,292	3,088	1,622	57.2	28.1	14.7
16. Personal unfolding	6,199	2,804	1,999	56.3	25.5	18.2
17. Luck	4,570	4,870	1,562	41.5	44.3	14.2
18. Not to feel one's body	4,094	4,769	2,139	37.2	43.4	19.4

Table II. Fatalistic and voluntaristic tendencies regarding health (% choice)

Question V. Which of the following two formulations, all things considered, do you favour?

1. If one is going to be sick, there is not much one can do about it	18.9
2. One can always avoid a sickness	73.8
No answer	7.3
Total	100.0

several 'yeses' of 'noes' in each question). Among the responses by 'choice', the percentages are valid, in the strict sense, only inside of each question.

These then are the essential dimensions that will now permit an examination of the results of this research and their interpretation.

Overall Principal Results

'Yes' and 'No' Responses to the Eighteen Items in Decreasing Order

Before attempting to organise the eighteen themes proposed in four closed questions, it is preferable to present them in Table I in decreasing order of 'yes' responses obtained from the 11,002 respondents. Looking at the percentages, the order of the 'no' responses and of the 'no answers' does not increase as regularly as the decrease in the 'yes' responses: those who hesitate (i.e. those who do not answer one or the other of the items) may be seen as the attenuated shadow of those who disagree as we go down the list. However, certain terms seem to have been less readily understood or to have evoked reticence.

In any case, there are not even 10 per cent who disagree or hesitate when acknowledging the role of *hygiene* in maintaining health. Furthermore, the first third of the list of themes attains over 75 per cent support, whereas the last third does not reach 62 per cent, *luck* and *not to feel one's body* following well below 50 per cent.

The Exclusive Choices of the Items in Each of the Four Closed Questions

When we examined the scores of the exclusive choices of the items in each of the four questions, we divided these questions into two sets. One is more orientated towards the query, 'Where does health come from?' (QI and QII). The other set was more orientated towards the query, 'What is health?' (QIII and QIV). Moreover, in each set, one question proposes substantive expressions (*To remain in good health comes from...* and *What corresponds best to the definition of health?*; the other question proposes more active verbs and phrases like: *To enjoy good health is...; To be well is...*).

Comparing the scores for the items in the four questions shows that their position in the presentation does not seem to have influenced the informants. Thus, in first position, we find the lowest score (*not to feel one's body*) as well as the highest (*hygiene*). Lastly, there are the 42.9 per cent *good living and working conditions* and 7 per cent *leisure*. The greatest disperson of choices is in the third question; the smallest, in the first.

The most popular themes were *hygiene* (more than half of the informants), *good living and working conditions* and *to feel well in one's skin* (physical well-being), each with more than 40 per cent. The least popular were *not to feel one's body* (3 per cent), *personal unfolding* (5.1 per cent), *leisure* (7 per cent), *to be lucky* (8.6 per cent), *work* and *to know oneself well* were equal at below 10 per cent (9.7 per cent). Around 25 to 30 per cent, we find *equilibrium* (30.7 per cent), *to be at the top of one's form* and *not to be sick* (each 25.4 per cent). Around 20 per cent we find *physical resistance* (21.6 per cent), *medicine* (19.9 per cent), *take precautions* (19.6 per cent), *to have good morale* (19.5 per cent). There remains *joy of living* (14.6 per cent), slightly ahead of *to be able to face all problems* (13.7 per cent).

Where Does Health Come From?

Next we took up the themes presented in Questions I to IV but arraying them in a descending order of choices: the percentages were then recomputed on the total for each one of the series (eight and ten items).

The first series derives its homogeneity from the question which it answers: *where does health come from?* This question synthesises the two introductory formulas *to remain in good health comes from. . .* and *to be in good health is. . . .*

More than half of the actual choices (taking into account the 8.4 per cent 'No answers') touch on hygiene and on living and working conditions (48.6 per cent): together these two themes aim directly at the social environment, on which, according to one respondent in two, human health closely depends. How can it (environment) be improved? Negatively, it is the task of medicine and precautions (19.8 per cent, nearly one-fifth of the choices). Positively, it depends on some kind of fatalism, either that of our body (10.5 per cent for *physical resistance*) or more general indeterminate factors (4.3 per cent for *luck*); or it is the result of human activity, either the more classic one of *work* (4.9 per cent) or the more modern one of *leisure* (3.5 per cent), the most neglected of the eight items in these two closed questions.

What is Health?

The second series seems to give a more direct response to what health is in itself: *what corresponds best to the definition of health?* and *to be well is. . . .* Here we find five passive expressions and five

239

active verbs.

The first two themes together receive as many choices as the next three that follow and more than the last six combined. Direct references to the body (*to feel well in one's skin*; *not to be aware of one's body* — 21.9 per cent) or indirect references (*to be at the top of one's form* — 12.7 per cent) account for more than a third of the choices (34.6 per cent). Three references to feelings of psychological well-being (*to have a good morale*; *joy of living*; *personal unfolding*) account for nearly one-fifth of the choices (19.5 per cent), to which can be added the admonition *to know oneself well* (4.8 per cent), for a total of almost a quarter of all choices (24.3 per cent). There remain the positive and pragmatic criterion *to be able to face all problems* (6.9 per cent) and the negative and *posteriori* criterion *not to be sick* (12.7 per cent).

Major Tendencies Relating to Health

Having established the overall results, we must now trace the major tendencies relating to health, for the overall sample of course, but mainly at the level of its age groups and socio-occupational categories.

Fatalistic or Voluntaristic Tendencies Relating to Health

The fifth question attempted to draw out more general attitudes with regard to health: fatalistic or voluntaristic (Table II).

Table III combines these two attitudes and the responses in the two preceding series of themes, and we have underlined the percentages surpassing 20 per cent for the fatalistic attitude and over 80 per cent for the voluntaristic attitude.

Quite naturally, *luck* (42.6 per cent) is exceptionally prominent on the fatalistic side, followed far behind with *not to be aware of one's body* (29.6 per cent), then *physical resistance* (27.3 per cent), *work* (26.1 per cent), *not to be sick* (24.0 per cent) and *a good morale* (23.8 per cent).

Not less logically, on the voluntaristic side come *precautions* (89 per cent) and *to know oneself well* (87.6 per cent). Lagging considerably behind are *good living and working conditions* (83.4 per cent) and *to feel well in one's skin* (81.2 per cent).

Between the two groups, one clearly fatalistic, the other volun-

Table III. Fatalistic and voluntaristic tendencies according to the two series on themes of health (%)

	Fatalistic attitude	Voluntaristic attitude	Total
Health comes from			
1. Hygiene	19.6	<u>80.4</u>	100.0
2. Good living and working conditions	16.6	<u>83.4</u>	100.0
3. Physical resistance	<u>27.3</u>	<u>72.7</u>	100.0
4. Medicine	19.3	<u>80.7</u>	100.0
5. Precautions	11.0	<u>89.0</u>	100.0
6. Work	<u>26.1</u>	73.9	100.0
7. Luck	<u>42.6</u>	57.4	100.0
8. Leisure	19.0	<u>81.0</u>	100.0
Health is			
1. To feel well in one's skin	18.8	<u>81.2</u>	100.0
2. Equilibrium	17.4	<u>82.6</u>	100.0
3. To be at the top of one's form	<u>20.8</u>	79.2	100.0
4. Not to be sick	<u>24.0</u>	76.0	100.0
5. Good morale	<u>23.8</u>	76.2	100.0
6. Joy of living	<u>20.2</u>	79.8	100.0
7. To be able to face all problems	<u>20.6</u>	79.4	100.0
8. To know oneself well	12.4	<u>87.6</u>	100.0
9. Personal unfolding	<u>21.2</u>	78.8	100.0
10. Not to feel one's body	<u>29.6</u>	70.4	100.0

taristic, there are intermediary themes. Orientated towards fatalism there are three themes with just over 20 per cent: *to be at the top of one's form* (20.8 per cent), *to be able to face all problems* (20.6 per cent), *joy of living* (20.2 per cent). And around 80 per cent, *medicine* (80.7 per cent) and *hygiene* (80.4 per cent) lean towards the voluntaristic side.

Correlations Between the Two Series of Themes on the Origins of Health and on What Is Health

The comparison of these two series of themes with the fatalistic and voluntaristic attitudes invites an enquiry into the correlation between these series. This is the aim of Table IV, where each term in one series is related to each in the other. More precisely, in the percentages in the rows as well as those in the columns, it is those who have chosen a theme who have also chosen one or the other of the themes in the other series; these percentages are similar to the choice in each of the four closed questions. Since in Table IV the choices within each of the two questions are only correlated with the choices in the two questions of the other series, Table V provides as a complement a matrix of the choices by a permutation of questions on the horizontal axis with questions on the vertical axis. For the sake of symmetry and to make it easier to compare the data, some of the correlations cited in the previous table have been used again for the two questions where there has been no permutation.

In addition, in each row as in each column of the two tables we have underlined the highest correlations of themes so as to emphasise them. We indicate at least those which are found simultaneously in rows.

Thus in Table IV a concentration of high correlations is found between:

— *Top of one's form* and *not to be sick*, on the one hand; *physical resistance* and *medicine*, on the other.
— *Not to be sick* and *good morale*, on the one hand; *to take precautions* and *work* and *luck*, on the other.

Similarly, we can see correlations as follows:

— *Not to feel one's body* with *physical resistance* and *luck*.
— *To feel well in one's skin* and *equilibrium* with *hygiene* and *good living and working conditions*.
— *Leisure* with *to feel well in one's skin* and *top of one's form, joy of living*.
— *Good living and working conditions* with *joy of living, being able to face all problems*.

In Table VI we examine the correlations:

— *Good living and working conditions* with *work* and *leisure*.
— *Work* with *luck*.
— *Medicine* with *precautions*.
— *Not to feel one's body* with *personal unfolding* and *top of one's form*.
— *Not to be sick* with *good morale* and *top of one's form*.
— *Equilibrium* with *to know oneself well* and *to be able to face all problems*.

Table IV. Correlations of the themes on health. Percentages of the two themes by the same respondents by rows (where does health come from?) and by the columns (what is health?) respectively

Where does health come from? (%) / What is health? (%)	Hygiene	Working living conditions	Physical resistance	Medicine	Pre-cautions	Work	Luck	Leisure	Totals
	54.3	42.9	21.1	19.9	19.6	9.7	8.6	7.0	
1. To feel well in one's skin — 41.6	62.1 / 46.1	56.1 / 53.6	20.1 / 39.3	18.1 / 36.5	17.0 / 35.6	9.9 / 41.3	6.8 / 32.6	10.0 / 57.7	100.0
2. Equilibrium — 30.7	64.0 / 34.1	53.3 / 36.7	21.2 / 29.8	20.7 / 30.2	20.4 / 30.8	8.5 / 25.5	5.1 / 17.6	6.8 / 28.4	100.0
3. Top of one's form — 25.4	54.5 / 24.2	43.1 / 24.8	26.4 / 31.0	26.1 / 31.8	20.3 / 25.7	10.2 / 25.5	10.2 / 29.6	9.3 / 32.4	100.0
4. Not to be sick — 25.4	54.2 / 24.8	30.7 / 17.9	29.2 / 35.0	30.4 / 37.9	24.5 / 31.3	11.2 / 28.9	15.6 / 45.6	4.2 / 14.9	100.0
5. Good morale — 19.5	59.5 / 20.5	35.8 / 15.6	25.2 / 22.4	20.2 / 19.1	25.0 / 24.0	15.0 / 29.1	14.1 / 31.0	5.2 / 14.1	100.0
6. Joy of living — 14.6	57.7 / 15.1	51.4 / 17.1	18.3 / 12.4	21.4 / 15.3	20.8 / 15.2	10.9 / 16.0	9.5 / 15.9	9.9 / 20.3	100.0
7. To be able to face all problems — 13.7	59.7 / 14.8	54.2 / 17.0	21.2 / 13.7	20.4 / 13.7	18.5 / 12.8	12.6 / 17.5	6.1 / 9.6	7.3 / 14.1	100.0
8. To know oneself well — 9.7	63.- / 10.9	41.3 / 9.2	16.9 / 7.7	19.8 / 9.3	37.5 / 18.3	9.8 / 9.5	4.2 / 4.7	7.4 / 9.9	100.0
9. Personal unfolding — 5.1	69.8 / 6.1	52.4 / 5.8	19.2 / 4.4	15.1 / 3.6	17.7 / 4.3	7.9 / 3.9	10.7 / 6.0	7.2 / 4.9	100.0
10. Not to feel one's body — 3.0	64.9 / 3.4	34.3 / 2.3	30.8 / 4.3	17.7 / 2.5	13.1 / 2.0	9.2 / 2.7	21.8 / 7.4	8.2 / 3.4	100.0
Totals	100.0	100.0	100.0	100.0	100.0	100.0	100.0	100.0	

Table V. Correlations of themes of health complementing those in Table IV. Data obtained through permutation of half of the themes on the horizontal axis with half of the themes on the vertical axis: % of choices for the two themes by the same respondents, in rows (9 verbs) and columns (9 nouns).

9 verbs	9 nouns (%)	Hygiene	Work	Medicine	Leisure	Personal unfolding	Good morale	Joy of living	Equilibrium	Top of one's form	Total
9 verbs (%)		54.3	9.7	19.9	7.0	5.1	19.5	14.6	30.7	25.4	
To be lucky	8.6	56.6 / 8.7	13.1 / 11.4	23.9 / 9.9	6.4 / 7.6	6.0 / 10.7	31.0 / 14.1	15.9 / 9.5	17.6 / 5.1	29.6 / 10.2	100.0
To have physical resistance	21.1	58.9 / 22.5	10.4 / 22.5	22.4 / 23.0	8.3 / 24.6	4.4 / 19.2	22.4 / 25.2	12.4 / 18.3	29.8 / 21.2	31.0 / 26.4	100.0
To take precautions	19.6	57.4 / 20.7	7.5 / 15.4	30.2 / 29.5	4.8 / 13.6	4.3 / 17.7	24.0 / 25.0	15.2 / 20.8	30.8 / 20.4	25.7 / 20.3	100.0
To have good living and working conditions	42.9	61.7 / 48.1	11.5 / 50.6	17.9 / 37.6	9.0 / 54.3	5.8 / 52.4	15.6 / 35.8	17.1 / 51.4	36.7 / 53.3	24.8 / 43.1	100.0
Not to feel one's body	3.0	64.9 / 3.4	9.2 / 2.7	17.7 / 2.5	8.2 / 3.4	10.5 / 6.4	15.2 / 2.4	12.1 / 2.5	27.6 / 2.8	34.7 / 4.1	100
Not to be sick	25.4	54.2 / 24.8	11.2 / 28.9	30.4 / 37.9	4.2 / 14.9	3.6 / 18.2	27.0 / 36.1	12.5 / 22.0	23.8 / 20.1	33.1 / 33.4	100.0
To know oneself well	9.7	63.1 / 10.9	9.8 / 9.5	19.8 / 9.3	7.4 / 9.9	6.1 / 12.0	22.0 / 11.3	13.9 / 9.4	44.2 / 14.2	13.8 / 5.3	100
To be able to face all problems	13.7	59.7 / 14.8	12.6 / 17.5	20.4 / 13.7	7.3 / 14.1	4.1 / 11.5	22.7 / 16.4	16.5 / 15.7	37.0 / 16.9	19.8 / 10.8	100
To feel well in one's skin	41.6	62.1 / 46.1	9.9 / 41.3	18.1 / 36.5	10.0 / 57.7	6.1 / 51.9	15.4 / 33.9	17.4 / 50.4	33.2 / 46.0	27.9 / 46.3	100.0
Totals		100.0	100.0	100.0	100.0	100.0	100.0	100.0	100.0	100.0	100.0

— *Joy of living* with *being able to face all problems* and *feeling well in one's skin.*

A comparison of the results in Tables IV and V and those in Table III shows that the predominantly voluntaristic themes are more often highly correlated with each other; the same is true for the predominantly fatalistic themes.

A Scalar Structure of Attitudes, Underlying Health perceptions

This comparison of the results of Tables III, IV and V suggests the hypothesis that attitudes are distributed according to a scalar structure which we have tried to express in Table 10. In row and column, this consists of the list of eighteen themes in an order which we shall explain. For each theme in the columns we have shown the correlation, the highest with a plus (+) and the lowest with a minus (–), with the other seventeen perceptions of health. In other words, for the supporters of the chosen response in each theme, we show the other theme which the largest number of them had chosen, and the item chosen by the smallest number.

We have modified empirically the order of the themes simultaneously on the two axes, to obtain the best diagonals of highest (plus) and lowest (minus) correlations. In this respect, the result seems more satisfactory at the top and bottom of the vertical listing. We designate horizontally (at the bottom of the table) the zone of themes 1–7 as A and the 13–18 zone as C. Here the concentrations of '+' and '–' are clear cut. In B we have themes 8–12, which change less regularly. Indeed, up to and including theme 10, the 'plus' is still above the 'minus'; from no. 12 onwards, it is already below; no. 11 is at the cross-over point of this distribution as it contains two equivalent weaker correlations.

The significance of this is that the themes in zone C define health is a more negative way (*not to be sick, not to feel one's body*) or by reference to *luck* and *medicine*. The zone A themes, on the contrary define health in a much more positive way.

On the right-hand side of the table, we have suggested a grouping of the themes: four groups of four or five definitions of health. The first two correspond to the more positive and egocentric pole; the second two to the more negative and sociocentric pole.

In group 1, the first five themes are *good living and working conditions; leisure; to feel well in one's skin; joy of living; equilibrium.*

Table VI. Maximal and minimal correlations of each of the 18 themes with one of the 17 others according to the choices of the respondents: towards a scalar structure of attitudes relating to health

	(1)	(2)	(3)	(4)	(5)	(6)	(7)	(8)	(9)	(10)	(11)	(12)	(13)	(14)	(15)	(16)	(17)	(18)
To have good living & working conditions (1)	╲																	
Leisure (2)		╲	+															–
To fee well in one's skin (3)	+	+	╲	+														
Joy of living (4)				╲														
Equilibrium (5)					╲													
To know oneself well (6)					+	╲	+						–			–		
To take precautions (7)						+	╲					–		–			–	
To be able to face all problems (8)								╲										
Hygience (9)									╲									

Table VI. *continued*

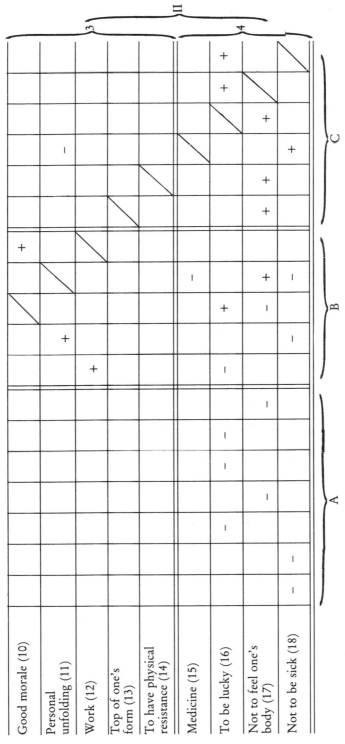

In group 2, four themes have in common self-observation with a view to prevention and prediction for the future: *to know oneself well*; *to take precautions*; *to be able to face all problems*; and *hygiene*, this latter to some extent following on logically after the preceding attitudes.

In group 4, we find the two negative verb phrases combined with *luck* and *medicine*.

As for group 3, it contains, as well as work, two more psychological references (*good morale*; *personal unfolding*) and two were physiological references (*top of one's form*; *to have physical resistance*).

Table VII shows a schematisation of the tendencies according to which health is defined, following the grouping in eighteen themes in Table VI. There are four groups of criteria, ranging from the most personal to the most impersonal.

Table VII. Positive and negative poles between which the more and the less personal criteria are distributed

I. More positive and more egocentric criteria of health	1. It is the social milieu at the service of personal success
	2. These are initiatives based on prevention and prediction, orientated towards the future of the individual
II. More negative and more sociocentric criteria of health	1. These are criteria of psycho-physiological adaptation and social competence
	2. These are more impersonal criteria whereby one relies on society or on chance

The Scale of Definitions of Health According to the Sociological Parameters of Age and Socio-occupational Category

Tables VIII and IX show choices of the eighteen themes on health and on the fatalistic attitude according to age groups (Table VIII) and the six socio-occupational categories (Table IX).

In Table VIII we see that the five themes of group 1, in Tables VI and VII are clearly predominant among the youngest age group;

Table VIII. The choices of 18 themes on health and of the fatalistic attitude according to age groups

No. Theme	18–29 years	30–9 years	40–9 years	50–9 years	60+ years
1. Good living and working conditions	51.7	52.0	41.6	38.5	31.4
2. Leisure	10.8	8.2	6.3	4.1	4.4
3. To feel well in one's skin	49.8	49.9	40.2	35.1	33.8
4. Joy of living	17.8	16.3	13.7	13.4	9.5
5. Equilibrium	33.4	34.7	31.3	28.0	27.5
9. Hygiene	60.5	60.3	60.2	57.3	57.3
11. Personal unfolding	5.8	6.0	4.9	4.5	2.9
13. Top of one's form	27.8	26.9	26.8	24.9	24.4
6. To know oneself well	8.5	9.8	11.1	12.7	13.7
7. Take precautions	20.4	19.8	22.0	22.6	28.6
8. To be able to face all problems	11.6	13.3	17.6	18.1	15.8
10. Good morale	15.3	16.2	23.3	29.1	35.7
12. Work	7.5	9.8	12.2	14.7	14.9
14. Physical resistance	20.9	19.7	25.1	27.9	26.5
15. Medicine	21.3	21.8	21.2	23.9	23.4
16. To be lucky	6.9	8.5	11.3	10.9	13.5
17. Not to feel one's body	3.2	3.3	2.9	3.1	5.0
18. Not to be sick	27.0	23.8	28.3	30.9	31.8
0. Fatalism	19.3	21.3	19.8	21.5	20.6

and that the four themes in group 4 and the fatalistic attitude are predominant in the older age groups.

The division is less homogeneous in the two intermediate groups. Three themes in group 2 and three themes in group 3 increase with age, whereas the fourth theme in group 2 (*hygiene*) and two in group 3 (*personal unfolding*; *top of one's form*) predominate among the younger age groups.

To summarise, the five most positive and egocentric definitions of health, to which *hygiene*, *personal unfolding* and *top of one's form* are quite close, draw more choices among the younger age groups. On the contrary, the four most negative and sociocentric definitions, the fatalistic attitude, together with the six other themes

Table IX. Choices of the 18 themes of health and of the fatalistic altitude according to the 6 socio-occupational categories

	Top management	Middle management	Employees	Skilled workers/ foremen	Semi- and unskilled workers	Personal service workers
1. Good working and living conditions	52.7	53.6	50.6	49.0	40.8	40.8
2. Leisure	9.3	10.0	6.8	8.6	6.9	5.7
3. To feel well in one's skin	52.9	52.6	47.2	37.6	33.8	42.9
5. Equilibrium	44.2	39.1	35.1	27.2	21.3	30.3
9. Hygiene	64.3	60.3	60.1	57.1	52.9	61.8
11. Personal unfolding	7.2	6.7	4.4	3.5	3.7	3.6
17. Not to feel one's body	5.9	3.1	3.0	3.1	3.3	1.4
4. Joy of living	14.0	16.6	15.4	18.4	13.7	13.7
6. To know oneself well	10.3	12.3	9.0	9.9	11.2	8.6
8. To be able to face all problems	13.6	12.5	13.8	16.6	13.8	18.4
15. Medicine	18.5	19.1	24.3	21.1	23.5	21.6
7. Take precautions	16.4	17.9	17.0	22.3	24.8	24.2
10. Good morale	7.5	10.7	18.9	24.2	28.4	27.9
12. Work	7.8	10.6	8.8	13.2	16.6	10.9
13. Top of one's form	27.1	26.9	26.2	26.7	32.9	24.5
14. Physical resistance	22.8	21.2	24.5	20.1	21.7	25.4
16. To be lucky	8.1	7.3	7.9	8.6	12.7	9.6
18. Not to be sick	17.3	19.5	27.0	32.8	38.0	28.8
0. Fatalism	20.6	18.5	20.9	19.9	22.5	24.0

(three based on prevention and precaution, three based on psycho-physiological adaptation and social efficiency) draw more choices among the older age groups.

When we come to the six socio-occupational categories which we have retained because of their clear-cut distribution in the social hierarchy (Table IX), the allocation of the themes is a little more complex, though close to certain tendencies according to age.

The first four items in group 1 are clearly dominant among top and middle management (cadres). The last four themes (group 4) and the fatalistic attitude prevail among semi-skilled workers or service personnel; that is to say, among the economically least well-off manual workers.

Among the other eleven themes, four are clearly predominant in top and middle management: *equilibrium*; *hygiene*; *personal unfolding*; *not to feel one's body*.

Three themes are clearly predominant among the manual workers: *good morale*; *work*; *taking precautions*.

The last four themes fluctuate in various ways: *joy of living* and *medicine* are predominant among employees, *to know oneself well* simultaneously among management and semi-skilled workers, finally *to face all problems* among service personnel, but with semi-skilled workers at the same level as employees and top management.

In all, six themes emerge more among the younger age groups and in management: *good living and working conditions*; *leisure*; *to feel well in one's skin*; *equilibrium*; *hygiene*; *personal unfolding*.

Six other themes clearly group together the older age groups and the manual workers: *not to be sick*; *being lucky*; *physical resistance*; *work*; *good morale*; *taking precautions*. Coming rather closer are *fatalism; to face all life's problems*; and *medicine*.

On the other hand, the younger age groups and the manual workers have in common: *to be at the top of one's form*. And common among the older age group and management are: *not to feel one's body* and, close to that, *to know oneself well*.

Comparisons of Results of the Closed and Open Questions

In this last section we propose a brief comparison of the results of the closed questions survey of 11,002 adults undergoing a medical health examination in 1978 with those of the open questions survey of 4,000 adults undergoing the same examination in 1971–74. The methodological comparison having been made in the first part of this paper, we shall now proceed directly to definitions of health, of which there are forty-one in the second survey and eighteen in the first.

We have presented and commented on the results of the open question in our already cited publications in French (d'Houtaud, 1976, 1978) and English (d'Houtaud and Field, 1984).

The Frequency of the Themes in the Open and Closed Questions

Ten themes which were the subject of two closed questions have been taken up again just as they emerged from the research in the open question. These are the ten which appear in Table III under 'B. Health is . . .'. In respect of the answers under 'A. Health comes from . . .', four of these (*hygiene*; *medicine*; *taking precautions*; *work*) have been selected to form a basis for comparison since the remaining four themes under this heading (*luck*; *leisure*; *good living and working conditions*; *physical resistance*) were less easily given exact equivalents in the responses to the open question.

Comparing first the ten themes (see Table III, B), only *to be at the top of one's form* rates an almost identical percentage in both surveys. *Not to be sick* has scarcely changed. On the other hand, in the closed question research, *equilibrium* is halved while *to feel well in one's skin* quadruples; *good morale*, *to be able to face all problems* and *personal unfolding* double, but *joy of living* and *to know oneself well* each lose nearly 3 per cent, and *not to feel one's body* virtually disappears.

Comparing the four comparable themes from the eight to be found in Table III, A, *medicine* keeps the same percentage in the two surveys and *work* is slightly reduced in the closed-question results. On the other hand, *hygiene* shows a 20 per cent increase in the responses to the closed questions, compensated for by *precautions*, which has halved.

Overall, the ranking of the fourteen comparable themes is very different in the closed and open questions. Listing them in respect of each survey in order of significance, one finds *equilibrium, hygiene* and *to be at the top of one's form* among the most significant five in each survey. Among the least significant in both are *to be able to face all problems*, *work*, *personal unfolding* and *not to feel one's body*.

Tables showing details of these comparisons will be found in d'Houtaud (1981).

Comparison of the Results According to Age

Taking account of the ten identically formulated themes in the two surveys:

1. Three themes are common to the younger age group: *top of one's form*; *to feel well in one's skin*; *personal unfolding*.

2. Three themes are common to the older age groups: *good morale*; *to know oneself well*; *facing all problems*.
3. Of the other four themes, *equilibrium* and *joy of living*, which have a bell-shaped distribution in the open-question results, are far ahead in the younger age groups in the closed question. *Not to be sick* and *not to feel one's body*, which predominate in the younger age group in the open question become more significant in the older age groups in the closed questions.

Comparison of the Results According to Socio-occupational Category

The convergences between the two surveys are more obvious from the socio-occupational angle:
1. Four themes are common among management: *to feel well in one's skin*; *equilibrium*; *personal unfolding*; *not to feel one's body*.
2. Three themes are common among manual workers: *not to be sick*; *top of one's form*; *good morale*.
3. Of the other three themes, *to know oneself well*, which has a U-shaped distribution in the closed question, is predominant in the older age groups in the open question. *To be able to face all problems* fluctuates irregularly in both surveys; *joy of living* has a bell-shaped distribution in both cases.

The Correlation Between Age and Socio-occupational Category

In the two surveys:
1. Management and the younger age groups share in common: *to feel well in one's skin* and *personal unfolding*.
2. Manual workers and the oldest age group have in common *good morale*.
3. Manual workers and the youngest age group have in common *to be at the top of one's form*.
4. Two themes fluctuate in an irregular way between age and socio-occupational category: *joy of living* and *to be able to face all problems*.

As for the other four themes appearing in both surveys:
1. Management and young people have *equilibrium* in common only in the closed question.
2. In the open question, manual workers and the oldest age

253

group have *to know oneself well* in common, while in the closed question this is a theme which management and the older age groups share.

3. In the open question, management and the younger age groups have in common *not to feel one's body*, while in the closed question, management and the oldest age group have this in common.

4. In the open question, manual workers and the younger age groups have in common *not to be sick* while in the closed question, manual workers and the older age groups have this in common.

Conclusion: The Path From the Open Questions to the Closed Questions

To look at images of health in the open questions and then study them more systematically in the closed questions constitutes an empirical progression which shows both marked convergences in the results and irreducible differences. As we move along, the differences seem to us to resolve themselves in a preference for the results in the closed questions, not only because of the numerical superiority of the most recent sample but also because of the greater rigour of the second enquiry and despite its more constraining methods (only the terms of the closed questions) with regard to the respondents.

The greatest differences between the two approaches are of course not only concerned with methodology (since the samples are noticeably different, the two main differences being the preponderance of men in the first survey and the absence of farmers and agricultural workers in the second). Nevertheless, since in our closed questions we were not able to take up all the themes found in the responses to the open question, the links between the themes change according to the unequal attractions of the same themes, which vary depending on one constellation or the other.

In any case, the most radical difference comes from the fact that, in the open question, health is only defined according to the immediate or spontaneous evocations of the respondents, whereas, when facing an already formulated series of definitions, the choices are elicited preferably towards this or that theme as a function of more or less conscious attitudes and according to reactions resulting from the location of each theme in the sequence and the theme's own connotation, with reference to those of other themes. This is why *hygiene*, for example, or *to feel well in one's skin*, have assumed such importance in the closed questions, whereas *equilibrium* or *taking precautions* came more readily to the minds of the respondents in the open question.

Essentially, in any case, the variations according to age and socio-occupational categories remain fairly stable and are thus symptomatic of relatively constant sets of attitudes in the way people think about our collective images of health.

In particular, one notes the strong discrimination of the socio-economic parameter which leads to a good scalar structure ranging from the most positive and egocentric definitions which are noticeably predominant among managers, to the most negative and sociocentric definitions which are clearly predominant among manual workers.

The age dimension is shown to be more of a discriminating factor in the closed questions than in the open question. Hence the more marked correlations between the synchronic and diachronic dimensions, managers and young people combining to emerge together at the positive and egocentric pole of the attitudinal grid, with manual workers and the older age groups at the negative and socio-centric pole. This is, however, a group of themes to which correlations of age and socio-economic category do not apply.

We have undertaken other analyses which it is not possible to include in this publication. At the same time it would also be important to examine the psycho-social significance of the major groups of images and the tendencies underlying them; thus the present article will serve as a starting point for further reflection.

13

The next study was undertaken in South Wales at a time when the British Department of Health and Social Security (DHSS) was encouraging the citizenry to accept greater personal responsibility for their health. Would this approach be likely to find echoes in the concepts of illness causation held by the mothers studied? The study is thus a particular contemporary example of Claudine Herzlich and Janine Pierret's analysis in Chapter 4. For the Welsh mothers, the germ theory remains important. However, it apparently lacks the moral component — namely, that personal hygiene and household cleanliness would protect not only oneself but others — which was so prominent from the end of the nineteenth and well into the twentieth century. For these mothers, 'germs' are part of the external and uncontrollable environment. It is interesting that in the midst of a biomedical society, whose healing system Allan Young would undoubtedly describe as 'internalising' (Ch. 7, above), a considerable proportion of the Welsh sample subscribed to notions of aetiology which have to be called 'externalising' and that these include notions borrowed from biomedicine itself.

Although an open-ended method of interviewing was used in this study, it seems likely that these are what Jocelyn Cornwell (1984) would describe as 'public accounts' (see also p. 17, above) rather than those accounts which emerge in private when a particular illness-episode is being discussed among friends and 'off the record'.

This paper contrasts with that of Alphonse d'Houtaud in the previous chapter (whose accounts were also 'public' in the Cornwell sense), because he was asking about health, while these authors were asking about illness causation. It does, however, discuss some implications of the gender order, which Alphonse d'Houtaud does not. Like Caroline Currer's study (Ch. 9, above), the respondents were mothers involved in rearing children. Just as Caroline Currer could not account for the health and illness concepts of her Pathan women without drawing attention to their position in patriarchal Islamic households, so Roisin Pill and Nigel Stott are obliged to take into account the wife–mother role of their respondents. They show, in particular, how the mothers do not always take for themselves the health-protective measures which they believe it right to take on behalf of their children. This is not on account of any carelessness or lack of responsibility but because of a conflict between fulfilling the obligations of the wife–mother role at the same time as fulfilling one's obligations to oneself as a person (and a citizen in DHSS terms).

There is a question to be posed about the Pill–Stott conclusions. They find that only half their sample thought individual behaviour played some part in illness causation; the rest could see only limited personal responsibility. The latter left school earlier and lived in council houses; the former had more education and were buying their own houses. Were these differences a matter of individual responsibility or did they themselves derive from circumstances outside individual control?

Eds.

ROISIN PILL
NIGEL C. H. STOTT

Concepts of Illness Causation and Responsibility: Some Preliminary Data from a Sample of Working-Class Mothers

Introduction

The second half of this century has been associated with an effort to bring the major hospital specialities within reach of the population and a re-structuring of the primary care services to improve teamwork and community care.[1] In 1976 the government launched a consultative document which emphasised the need for a change in *all* sectors of the health service towards a more preventive approach to ill-health as 'curative medicine may be increasingly subject to the law of diminishing returns' (HMSO, 1976: 6). One of the most prominent themes underlying the official thinking in the consultative document was the need for the individual citizen to assume greater responsibility for his own health because 'the greatest potential, and perhaps the greatest problem for preventive medicine, now lies in changing behaviour and attitudes to health' (HMSO, 1976: 95). The public were reminded that it is in everyone's own interests to adopt a healthier style of life, and health professionals were urged to cooperate with the plan which represented a major reorientation of emphasis from the comprehensive provisions offered in the nationalised health service after the Second World War to a situation where the individual may be expected to hold the key to his/her health.

Several authors have been concerned about the motivation and assumptions which underlie a shift of emphasis to individual responsibility for health because the approach focuses so narrowly on

---

1. This paper is a slightly abridged version of the original (Pill and Stott, 1982) which included suggestions concerning the practical implications of the authors' findings. These were omitted here only for reasons of overall length. [Eds.]

those aspects of behaviour that are supposed to be under individual control and makes the assumption that people have the power and facilities to alter their life-style (Crawford, 1977; Davis, 1979; Graham, 1979; Stacey, 1980). It becomes easy to ignore other environmental variables and also to ignore the reality of class and the impact of social inequality and political disruption on health. Therefore, it is implied that lack of change or failure to follow an appropriate life-style must be due to failings in the individual himself, the focus being on his personal characteristics rather than the social situation he is in. This 'victim-blaming ideology', as Crawford graphically calls it, leads to the conclusion that the appropriate therapy for the erring individual is education, persuasion and motivation since he must be either ignorant or does not hold the 'right attitudes'.

What is missing, however, both in the official documents and the criticisms of them, is any discussion of how members of the general public may feel about the onus for illness being shifted onto the individual. The establishment of just what the concept of individual responsibility for health means to various groups in our society would seem to be a necessary first step in assessing how effective official policy on preventive health is likely to be and formulating appropriate strategies for behaviour change.

A person's readiness to accept responsibility for health, defined here as accepting that one may be accountable for falling ill and for maintaining one's health, can be seen as depending partly on his/her view about the aetiology of illness and partly on his/her perceptions of the factors constraining behaviour, both areas about which there is relatively little data for British society. This paper is an attempt to explore the former topic, using data collected from a sample of forty-one working-class mothers on a suburban housing estate. The focus of interest here is the kind of language used in discussing the causes of illness in general and, in particular, the circumstances under which respondents appeared either to make moral judgements or to accept a degree of personal responsibility.

The Study

The data was collected during semi-structured interviews conducted in the women's homes; the strategy followed relied heavily on Brown and Rutter's techniques for conducting interviews, with their emphasis on the elicitation of feelings and emotions (Brown and Rutter, 1966). The aim of this feasibility study was to see whether, by exploring the language and concepts used by respondents in discussing health and illness, it might be possible to develop a tool which would measure the extent to which people saw their day-to-day decisions regarding diet, exercise, habits, and so on, as being choices which will determine their future health. In other words, we hoped eventually to be in a position to develop an instrument which would measure how salient life-style was to our respondents and how relevant they thought it was to future health. Such an index of 'potential health behaviour' has obvious appeal for health educators and the primary care team concerned to evaluate its preventive role.

All the interviews were recorded on tape and later transcribed for analysis, although the original tapes were used in order to code the degree of conviction expressed on a particular theme.

The Sample

The sample consisted of forty-one mothers aged between thirty and thirty-five years, living with their husbands and having two or three children, at least one of whom was between five and eleven years of age. It was drawn from the age/sex register of the main practice serving the estate, which was staffed by members of the Department of General Practice, Welsh National School of Medicine. The women were deliberately selected from what was by far the largest socio-economic group among the practice population — socio-economic group 9, the skilled manual workers — in order to give as homogeneous a group as possible.

The majority had worked since their marriage and, if not actually working at the time of the interview, intended to do so in the future. Seventeen mothers (41.6 per cent) were full-time housewives when interviewed; the remainder were generally in part-time cleaning work or in jobs connected with the various schools of the estate. (Only two were working full-time.) On average, they had been registered with the practice for over six years, while approximately 30 per cent had been coming to the Health Centre for nine years, since the very first days of the estate. The estate itself was situated on the outskirts of Cardiff and contained about 10,000 people in modern, good-quality housing, which is partly council and partly

261

Table 1. Education and housing tenure of sample

	Owner-occupiers 21	Council tenants 20	Total 41
No. who left school at			
15 years of age	8	18	26
16 + years of age	13	2	15
No. with any further			
education or training	8	3	11

private. Thus twenty-one of the respondents in the sample were buying their own houses and twenty were in council houses. The former were significantly more likely to have stayed on at school past the statutory school-leaving age ($\chi^2 = 13.2$, d.f. $= 1$, $P = 0.01$), and they were also more likely to have received some kind of further education or training. Nearly two-thirds of the total sample left school at the minimum age and just over a quarter had further education or training (Table 1). Thus, although at first sight these women were in a very similar social situation since they were the wives of skilled manual workers and lived in the same type of housing with access to the same facilities and had similar family commitments, they differed in both the type of housing tenure and their level of formal education. One of the aims of this paper is to discover whether any of the differences described in this paper can be correlated with these variables. The significance of home owner-ship as contrasted to council tenancy appeared to lie in the possibility that buying a house was an index to a cluster of attitudes with potential relevance for attitudes of responsibility and beliefs about health and illness. Within the same broad socio-economic grouping it was hypothesised that house buyers were more likely to believe in their ability to control their own destiny, the need to plan for the future and postpone immediate gratification. Evidence supporting this view was provided by the Multi-dimensional Health Locus of Control Scales developed by Wallston and his colleagues (Wallston, Wallston and Derellis, 1978), from Rutter's earlier work on Inter-nal–External locus of control (Rutter, 1966). Briefly, these scales measure the extent to which people believe that their health is determined by their own actions (internal control), or by luck, chance or by powerful others — external factors over which they have little control. Using the Mann-Whitney *U*-test, home buyers were significantly more likely than tenants to believe that their own behaviour determined their health (P = 0.001) and less likely to believe in the role of chance (P = 0.02).

Concepts of Causation

It was argued earlier that the respondents' readiness to accept that they were responsible for their health would be ultimately linked with their theories about illness causation. Broadly speaking, the concepts of aetiology can be divided into two main groups: those which place the cause with the afflicted individual and those which place it outside him. In the first group, the individual is regarded as responsible for choices resulting in sickness, either directly or through the action of the supernatural — God, spirits or ancestors. Such beliefs are widespread, not only in preliterate societies such as the Nuer and Zulu, but can also be paralleled to some extent in our own society, since psychoanalytical interpretations of mental disturbance and psychosomatic symptoms lay great stress on the individual's own guilt, aggression and negative projection (Salzberger, 1976). According to the second group of hypotheses interpreting human sickness, the individual is considered fated. No blame can attach to him, anyone else or a super-natural power if sickness is attributed to chance or coincidence. He is also not responsible for his physiological structure and consequent predisposition to fall victim to certain diseases.

It can be seen, therefore, that theories of aetiology which regard the causes of illness as external to the individual do not encourage feelings of responsibility for illness and subsequent guilt. Herzlich, who has argued that such views are typical of her sample of eighty middle-class and professional French men and women (Herzlich, 1973) claims that her respondents, the vast majority of whom lived in Paris, made a fundamental distinction between self as source of health and other as bringer of illness, which found expression in the contrasts drawn between the individual and society, between healthy and unhealthy, and between natural and artificial. For them it was the way of life, especially life in towns, which was accorded a preponderant role in the genesis of illness.

Whatever the importance of mental states to its development, the responsibility for the actual beginning of the illness belongs to the way of life. It is, after all, the way of life which provides the harmful stimulation and

263

causes of nervous tension and anxiety. The individual feels, and affirms himself to be, *infinitely more threatened than guilty* [Herzlich, 1973: 50, emphasis added].

The question we are seeking to answer here is whether the Welsh working-class mothers subscribe to concepts of individual control or external factors when discussing illness causation. We recognise that, within a society, the weight given to interpretations based on one or other group of hypotheses may vary at different periods of time and that different interpretations may well co-exist or be used in different situations, not necessarily being mutually exclusive. Nevertheless, an assessment, albeit crude, of the balance struck between the two main groups of theories in the beliefs of the women interviewed provides a starting point for analysis.

Responses to the straight question 'What do you think are the main reasons for illness?' elicited seventy-three comments from thirty-seven respondents, the remaining four saying that they did not know or 'you can't help it'. The following categories were produced:

1. Environmental factors, e.g. the weather, pollution, pesticides (8)
2. Heredity and family susceptibility (6)
3. Individual susceptibility (4)
4. Germs, bugs, viruses, infection (13)
5. Stress, worry (6)
6. Type of person you are, e.g. more nervous type/unhappy (6)
7. Being 'run down' (10)
8. 'Way of life' (3)
9. Diet (6)
10. Hygiene (4)
11. Neglect, not looking after yourself properly (7)

The first five categories may be regarded, and are so regarded by the respondents, as being factors which are essentially outside individual control, whereas categories 7 to 11 reflect an awareness of the potential of individual behaviour. Category 6 is more ambiguous since allocation to the 'responsible' or 'fated' group of hypotheses depends on whether one believes that individual personality characteristics are inherited and thus immutable or not. This is relevant to readiness to attribute blame (cf. later references to 'more neurotic' types).

The reason most frequently advanced by this group of women

Table 2. Statements in each interview concerning illness causation

	Numbers	%
Mention of 'germs'	178	60
'life-style'	118	40
heredity	101	34
stress	59	20
environmental factors	46	15
individual susceptibility	36	12
Total number of statements	297*	

* The number in each category came to more than the total as many respondents mentioned more than one cause when discussing a condition.

followed the medical model of infectious illness with symptoms being caused by various 'germs, viruses or bugs'. It seems likely that these women were considering a model of short-term acute illness; Field has pointed out that when most people talk of illness they envisage a short-term and definite episode (Field, 1976). This also reflects the actual experiences of this group with young, dependent children who are relatively unlikely, as yet, to have experienced the symptoms of chronic degenerative diseases. For example, practically no spontaneous mention was made of the wearing out of bodily systems or ageing as explanations for illness causation.

Analysis of the responses to a single question on illness causation may be expected to give an oversimplified picture of the women's view of aetiology, because most people operate with multifactoral theories of causality. Therefore, all the transcripts were studied for examples of statements about the causes of illness, each individual being coded according to all aetiological categories she mentioned. However, the overall picture did not alter much (Table 2).

There was evidence of consistency of approach by individuals when the sample was divided into those who only mentioned germs, stress, environment, heredity, and so on (external causes only), and those who also invoked individual behaviour (i.e. recognised the role of individual choice). The latter group were also significantly more likely (χ^2 = 11.29, d.f. = 1, P = 0.001) to mention more life-style factors when discussing the causation of heart attacks and cancer and were less sceptical of those they mentioned. Moreover, when comparing their health today with that of their grandparents' generation, they were more likely to stress the importance of food ('good' food, 'enough' food, 'fresh' food),

Table 3. Aetiological beliefs and housing tenure and education

Nos.	*Those who stressed:* External factor only	Individual behaviour	Total
	21	20	41
House buyers	7	14	21
Council tenants	14	6	20
Left school at 15	16	10	26
Left school at 16+	5	10	15

hard work, and mental attitudes ('being content', 'not trying to keep up with the Joneses'). The others (twenty-one in number and thus approximately half the sample), who only mentioned theories of external causation, tended to lay more stress on better medical services, more cures, new and better medicines, and so on, and also on improved environment and facilities in the home; for example, central heating, inside lavatories. Other important differences between these two groups of women were that those who do mention individual behaviour in aetiology were significantly more likely to be buying their own house ($\chi^2 = 5.51$, d.f. = 1, $P = 0.02$) and also more likely to have had more formal education ($\chi^2 = 5.76$, d.f. = 1, $P = 0.02$). These findings support our early tentative hypotheses about the potential relevance of these variables (Table 3).

It was also noticeable, though difficult to illustrate in a written account, that many of the respondents seemed unsure of themselves and less articulate when discussing aetiological topics. In many of these tapes there was a marked contrast between the pace and firmness of tone in the first part of the interview when the woman was asked to describe her own last episode of illness and her views on doctors — areas in which she was the undoubted expert — and the pace and tone of the second phase. For example, such phrases as 'They say', 'I suppose', 'I don't know' appeared to be indicators of uncertainty, often paralleled by increasing hesitancy, loss of fluency and sometimes a pronounced lowering of the voice. This is perhaps not so surprising since most people usually only attempt to interpret causes of sickness in relation to a specific incident and find it difficult to think about the topic in more general terms. Nevertheless, the data collected illustrate the nature and range of the explanatory models they choose. The following extract is typical of emphasis being placed on factors outside individual control:

(Do you think some people get things more badly than others?)
No, I don't know, I don't think so really. I think it's just sort of how it comes, you know.
(I wonder what you yourself thought were the main reasons for people being ill?)
Well, my ideas . . . I think, as I say like, if it's chickenpox or anything like that it more or less gets passed around and colds could be through what may be not dressed right the same day or the cold weather and rain and all things like this, you know. Then there's something like my little boy with the eczema, and asthma is a thing — well, he hasn't had it from birth but it's something that just occurred like, you know. . . .
(Do you think people sometimes have themselves to blame if they fall sick?)
What do you mean now? You mean with something you can't catch or something you sort of bring on yourself?
(That's two interesting ideas.)
Well, I think something like you bring on yourself, like nerves or anything like that, it's partly down to you I would think — to what sort of person you are. Like I'm a little bit highly strung, you know. I think things like that are due to worries, if you've got worries in the house, worries with your husband, money problems can all bring it on as regards nerves. But as regards the other thing I can't really put that down to anything else except if you pick something up. . . .
(I was interested in what you were saying about people bringing 'nerves' on themselves.)
Well, I don't say bring the whole thing on themselves but a little bit — like I really wish I could be like a sort of one of those persons that takes everything in their stride and calm. You do see people like this and I quite often think I wish I could be like that, but you can't. It's the type of person you are, isn't it really? . . . *(I was wondering whether you felt being healthy is really a matter of luck or if there was anything you could do about it?)*
Oh, I don't think you can do anything about it. *(So, if you've good health that's fine, but if you've got poor health, that's it, you can't do a great deal to alter it?)*
Well, if I did have poor health I mean I would try and do something you know, if I could help myself in any way or the children, but I think it is a little bit down to that, I don't think you can really help it. You know, either you are a healthy person or you're not. You know, as I say, other things you just pick them up just like anybody else. But then that still goes for that really because another person might be in contact with somebody and they might not get anything and another person do. It's just . . . you know.

In marked contrast to this woman were the responses of the following respondent, who had a very clearly articulated philosophy about the healthy life:

(Do you think some people tend to fall ill more easily than others?)
I never get ill, I know it sounds daft, but apart from my periods, which I ignore.[2] But here I think it's all on what you eat — I think we eat the right foods. My children, touch wood, everything goes round, very rare do they get things, very rare.
(You think that's important, do you?)
Oh yes, I think it's all in the diet and fresh air, we've got the caravan, we're always here, there and everywhere. We have one month in the south of France every year, maybe we've got a better chance than most people. You know, you see little kiddies getting a bad chest and things; my neighbour's children all have conjunctivitis, well, it's got to be *something*. You know, you can go over there any time of the day and night and those kids are up. They're not having a start. I've always been very strict about their going to bed.
(What do you think yourself might be the main reason for illness?)
Oh dear — it may be that some people are made that they catch things. I don't know. We're not that sort of family so far. My mother says she had three children and none of us ever had to go to hospital; no one ever had anything awful. There again, the upbringing was very much the same, a good diet — probably too good, my brothers are both fanatic keep-fit bods you know, it's just the way we've been brought up, I think, I really do think it's just total grounding.
(Do you think people sometimes have themselves to blame if they fall ill?)
Not if they catch pneumonia, tonsillitis, polio or something — oh, I don't know maybe if you neglect something. . . . *(Some people would say that being healthy or not is largely a matter of luck and nothing you can do is going to alter it very much. I wonder what your view is?)* No I don't agree. If you're going to get cancer of the breast or something then, yes, that is just something you cross your fingers and hope for, I think, but I think lots of people make far more of what they've got, and perhaps by ignoring diets — I don't think people with very full, happy lives are often as ill as people who really haven't got much else to think about.

Individual Behaviour as Cause of Illness

As mentioned above, twenty women, approximately half the sample, referred to behavioural choices made by the individual when discussing aetiology, and they tended to differ from the others in their level of formal education, housing type and present work situation. Four respondents apparently thought in quite simple instrumental ways about the relationship between behaviour and outcome; for example, if you wash your hair or had a bath and then

2. This respondent had fibroids, resulting in very heavy menstrual losses every two weeks or so and had been advised to have a hysterectomy, but refused to do so. Despite this, she refused to regard this as an illness.

immediately went out, a cold, chill or cough was likely to be the result. Such specific risk-taking, with its very direct link between cause and effect, can be compared with the much less specific links postulated by the majority of those who mentioned lifestyles. The concept of 'resistance' is crucial here. One becomes 'low', 'run down' and thus vulnerable to illness. People who eat the right foods, exercise and do not abuse their bodies are in a much better position to 'fight off' germs effectively.

The notion of accumulated resistance is a flexible view of health and is important since it implies development, a process (cf. Polgar's description of the 'elastic' view of health, in Polgar, 1968). One can *become* more or less resistant; one becomes 'run down'. The implications of holding such concepts are that health is seen as a process, even a balance between the individual and his environment. This theme was clearly stated by a couple of respondents. For example:

Well, if you're low in yourself, you're more susceptible to get illness, you know. It all depends on the state of the body and that. . . .
(*Can we do anything about it, do you think?*)
Well yes, trying to have a good regular diet, you know, a healthy diet, fresh food and, you know, vitamin-wise and protein. . . . Well, I think that general health has got a lot to do with it . . . because I think if the general health breaks down or we don't look after ourselves as we should, the way we eat will bring our immunity down because the body isn't strong enough to cope because we've all got those types of viruses in our body and something motivates them all, you know, triggers it all off and then that is what happens.

In contrast, many did not see behavioural choices as having any bearing on the resistance to disease enjoyed by a particular individual. The term was mentioned in statements about causation, but the contexts clearly showed that resistance was viewed as a relatively immutable personal characteristic. Those women recognised that some people did seem to be more prone to illness than others but interpreted their greater resistance to constitutional or genetic factors:

Looking back at when we were children, there were three of us and we didn't all get the same illnesses — you know, those childhood diseases. I think some people have got a better body resistance than somebody else. I don't really know why — whether it's to do with the blood grouping.

Well, some do pick up things more than others. I think, if the parents are healthy, then the children are.

269

One or two even mentioned the weather as a factor that might affect individual resistance:

(What do you think are the main reasons for illness?)
Well, you just get a low resistance against something. Sometimes I think the atmosphere and that could have a lot to do with it — the way the weather is at the moment. Some people are born resistant to colds and things or you are not.

There are obvious similarities to a term used by several of Herz-lich's respondents; namely, 'reserve of health'. She comments that:

Its particular characteristic lies in its being a capital asset rather than a state. . . . This capital asset has two main aspects: physical robustness or strength, on the one hand, and a certain potential for resistance to attacks, fatigue and illness, on the other. . . . As such, it can have degrees: everyone is not born with the same reserve of health. It may be good, less good or poor, and may also vary according to the kind of life the individual leads; one may build up one's reserve of health or break into it. This capital asset of vitality and defence may increase or dissipate in the course of time, like all capital. [Herzlich, 1973: 56–7]

It is recognition of this last point, we would argue, that distinguishes the two categories within our sample. It is the extent to which people are prepared to admit that their decisions increase the risk of being vulnerable which will influence their readiness to accept notions of 'blame' and 'responsibility', and we go on to examine this proposition in the following section. As Herzlich herself puts it, 'The individual feels guilty for having allowed his health to be impaired or undermined, not for having caught an illness but for having lost his health' (Herzlich, 1973: 50).

To sum up, about half the sample did not refer to the individual's day-to-day lifestyle choices in their discussion about illness causation. Many who did mention life-style choices were unsure and found it difficult to articulate their thoughts on the subject; indeed, they may not have thought about it much before the interview. The majority of the women subscribed to the belief that germs are the main causes of illness, which is, of course, essentially an amoral theory of causality, but they differed when it came to the perennial questions that people in every culture and society have tried to answer; namely, 'Why me?' and 'Why now?' It was noted that those who were prepared to consider that the individual might play some part in becoming sick held a different concept of resistance and health. They saw people falling ill because they had become vulnerable as a result of their own actions and were more likely to view health as a dynamic relationship between the individual and his environment and therefore susceptible to a variety of influences, some of which were under individual control. They also tended to have had more formal education, to be buying their own homes and to be working at the time of the interview when compared with the rest of the group.

Willingness to Accept Blame

So far the emphasis has been on the patterning of the women's theories of causality, and we argued that this will be correlated with readiness to accept the notion that one may be morally accountable for becoming ill. Certainly those who made no mention of the role of the individual behaviour in discussing aetiology reacted rather differently to the question 'Do you think that people sometimes have themselves to blame if they fall ill?' Of the twenty-one who fell into this category, four rejected the idea outright, three said you would be to blame if you did not go to the doctor (early enough), four mentioned that the 'more neurotic types' could be to blame. Nine gave examples of situations where they felt blame could be attributed, but it was striking that these all tended to involve the taking of short-term, very direct risks. For example:

> Well, I mean if they are susceptible to colds and they go out in cold, wet weather or go near someone who has a cold, I presume they are to blame. I wouldn't willingly take my children in to somebody with, you know, something catching . . . and if people cook food that is not properly thawed or things like that, I mean they get tummy bugs and that's their own fault for not looking after . . . .

> Sometimes I think they are to blame — like not letting children sit around in wet clothes and you don't wash your hair and go straight out into the cold and you wrap up.

According to this line of reasoning, sickness can result from one particular action or neglected precaution in contrast to the longer perspective which sees illness resulting from a continuing process of neglect or 'letting oneself get run down'. Only two of the twenty-one whose views on aetiology stressed exogenous factors used these concepts in response to the question about blame.

These themes were much more prominent in the answers of the twenty women who were prepared to give some weight to the role of individual behaviour in causality and, as we have seen, held a more flexible concept of health. Their answers reflected the importance of regimen in their lives. For example:

> Oh, yes, I think it's neglect with what they eat — the convenience foods are so easy but I don't think they do you a lot of good if you have them all the time. And also warmth and what you wear. There again, lack of sleep and, you know, burning the candle at both ends — I think then you are asking for troubles; I think people are only capable of doing so much.

(Fourteen people out of twenty gave similar replies: of the remaining six, one rejected the notion of blame entirely, three were ambivalent and unsure, while one each mentioned being to blame if one did not go to the doctor and/or were the 'more neurotic type'.) Thus there is some empirical support for the proposition that readiness to accept blame varies with the emphasis laid on the role of individual behaviour in the theories of illness causation held by the individual respondent. What is more, the circumstances under which blame is attributed and hence the definitions of responsible behaviour are also correlated with those beliefs.

Taking the sample as a whole, two positive responses can be discerned in relation to the notion that one might be morally accountable for illness. Blame is attributed, firstly, if one does not go to the doctor or delays too long and, secondly, if one puts oneself in a situation of danger or risk through carelessness, stupidity or lack of foresight. It has been argued that, within the second category, there is an important difference between those who see risk-taking in a short-term perspective and those who take a longer view. The former define responsible behaviour in terms of obvious common-sense precautions and, provided these have been met, do not consider themselves to blame for illness. The latter also accept the need for basic precautions but, in addition, tend to see health maintenance as an ongoing task, linked to patterns of daily living and designed to maintain the individual at an optimum level of resistance. It is this interpretation which comes closest to the official criteria of the 'responsible individual'. On the other hand, the frequent and early recourse to the doctor advocated by some of the latter respondents as responsible behaviour may be seen to run counter to the tenor of recent DHSS pronouncements, particularly the exhortations not to consult your GP unnecessarily for minor ailments.

Lay and Official Definitions of Responsibility

'The responsible individual' in official terms is one who avails himself of the various preventive and screening measures offered by the health services, leads a healthy life-style and does not bother his/her doctor unnecessarily with trivia. Since responsible behaviour is defined from the perspective of the service providers, the consumers' point of view and problems are largely ignored. Thus failure to act responsibly is attributed to the individual's ignorance, inappropriate attitudes or personal characteristics; the answer is seen to lie in health education which will both inform and motivate. But, as we have seen for example, beliefs about the value of a healthier life-style and readiness to accept that one may be to blame through not leading one, are intimately linked with much broader general conceptualisations about illness causation and health, and possibly also to one's entire world-view, and they may be highly resistant to change.

It also seems that the current emphasis on the individual improving his health through leading a healthier life-style is not in tune with the most frequently mentioned explanation offered for illness; namely, the germ theory. As Helman points out (1978, and p. 223, above)

> The cardinal attribute of Germs is their externality. . . . They originate outside the individual, but not outside human society. . . . The risk, however slight, of Germ infection appears to be inherent in all relationships but neither party is to blame for the infection. There is no malevolence or *maleficium* involved; that is, the Germ has its own volition and cannot be directly controlled by its host. The victim of a Germ infection is, therefore, blameless.[3]

To the extent that an increasing number of the population invoke the germ model of causation for an increasing number of conditions, there is a potential conflict between lay concepts and those promoted by health professionals/administrators owing to the 'cultural lag' (Illsley *et al.*, 1977). Helman argues that this is in fact

3. As quoted by Pill and Stott, but see p. 222, above.

happening among his younger patients with the result that the amount of personal responsibility felt for illness seems to have declined (certainly for colds and chills) and illness has become more social and dangerous and the process of seeking medical treatment for it is increasingly common. He links the spread of the germ theory in lay models of illness causation with the introduction of antibiotics and the establishment of the National Health Service.

The women in our sample were certainly members of the 'antibiotic generation', and reflected the views noted by Helman. As argued earlier, it was in the different interpretations of the concepts of vulnerability and resistance to disease that the possibility of effective action by the individual was recognised by some respondents. Even so, it is interesting to note that even those who exhibited greatest awareness of the relevance of life-style still said that they stressed the germ theory when explaining illness to their children. The emphasis was laid on the essentially capricious nature of the germ; thus, when children asked why they kept getting ill, or why their sibling/friend did not, the mothers said 'that's just the way it is', 'perhaps it will be his turn next week'. Very few made any link between behaviour and illness, and those who did simply mentioned common-sense precautions such as washing hands to avoid carrying germs, wrapping up warmly and not sitting around in wet clothes. Not one used the opportunity to mention the implications of patterns of daily living for health.

This sample is not atypical if we also consider the data presented by Stacey on the answers given by university students to the question 'Thinking back to the last time you were sick, disabled or hurt, how would you communicate this to a child under five years? (Stacey, 1978). She reports that 'students use the old mechanical model, the old germ theory; many are pragmatic: "It just happened"; it was "just an accident"'. Very few accepted moral responsibility and indeed the number of mentions of morality in the responses has declined annually while a high degree of dependence on health professionals is apparent. This is in sharp contrast with the original study of American undergraduates (Zola, 1975) which Stacey was replicating, where Zola concluded that at nearly every level from getting sick to recovery a moral battle raged. The evidence from the British students and working-class mothers suggests that Helman may well be right in connecting the introduction of free medical care to the entire population with the increased popularity of the germ theory of disease among lay people and the decline in acceptance of personal responsibility for illness.

One of the most cogent criticisms levelled at the DHSS's definition of the responsible individual is that it assumes that everyone has the resources and the autonomy to effect the necessary changes in behaviour and lead healthier lives. Cullen has used an extended diary method of collecting information on the problems of family life in an urban setting and came to the conclusion that typically 'we find very little in the way of perceived flexibility associated with the events of the working day, and thus also very high levels of routinisation' (Cullen, 1979). He comments that for working-class inner London families, the dominance of a strict and choiceless routine was very striking since respondents typically described around 70 per cent of the working day (excluding sleep) as routine and over 90 per cent as characterised by the absence of any real choice. Within the perceived constraints imposed by everyday working life, the individual then has to allocate limited resources of time, money and energy. There was certainly evidence that one or two of the Cardiff sample felt that lack of money was preventing them from providing the food they would like for their families, while others mentioned the problems of getting enough of the right kind of exercise. Such comments immediately bring into focus another implication of the official definition of the 'responsible individual'; namely, the fact that the concept is used without gender and free-floating, apart from any social context. Immediately one looks at particular groups of men and women living in society, the problems become apparent.

For example, let us consider the sample, the situation that these women who combined roles of mothers, housewives and (often) outside workers, were in. A common theme was, 'Of course, I hardly ever go to the doctor' or 'I only go for myself when it is absolutely necessary', contrasted with, 'I always take the children straight away if I'm a bit worried about them'. Such a contrast highlights a possible dilemma faced by mothers who are responsible both for their own health and for the health of their children and husbands. It may be felt that there need be no conflict between the two, but as Graham has cogently shown in a recent study of the experiences of early motherhood, there is a pervasive ideology of maternal sacrifice which results in women placing the health needs of their family above their own (Graham, 1979).

This was certainly paralleled in the present sample. For example, the constraints on adopting the sick role were clearly recognised by three-quarters of the mothers interviewed:

> I would say that when I was single I always had a lot more things wrong
> with me, or I felt I did. You know, but being married, well, I haven't
> really had much wrong with me and I think it's partly down to the fact
> that I haven't got time to worry about anything being wrong. Not only
> that, I think with a family you can't afford to be ill, you know what I
> mean? You think, well you'll be ill after you've cooked the tea. But of
> course if you're very ill you'd have to give up, but I never have — being
> healthy you can sail through everything.

The good mother is one who 'keeps going' and copes with the
multifarious demands that her family make of her. She sees that they
are well fed, warm and do not expose themselves to unnecessary
risks; furthermore, some respondents would stress the importance
of warm, loving relationships within the home and orderly patterns
of daily living. The emphasis is on health as functional capacity and
one is 'really ill' when immobilised for one reason or another.
Otherwise, the responsible mother 'carries on' and it is quite clear
that this is seen as her duty. Moral opprobrium was heaped on those
women who were deemed to be too ready to think they were ill and
to seek the advantages of the sick role when the appropriate behaviour was seen as 'not giving in' and 'fighting it off' or by 'keeping
going and working it off'. Of course, it is possible to argue that these
women are overdramatising their role as linchpins of the family
without whom everything would collapse, but the interview data
shows that the pressures are perceived as very real. These examples
serve to highlight the conflicts which any one individual may face by
virtue of occupying a particular position in the social structure. The
way in which the word 'responsible' is attributed to actions will
depend on the viewpoint and expectations of the people making the
judgement, some behaviours being regarded as more or less obligatory
for certain roles (and appropriately sanctioned), while others are more
negotiable.

In conclusion, at least half of the sample of working-class mothers
held fatalistic views about illness causation and were prepared to
accept the concept of blame only under very restricted circumstances involving direct risk-taking. The remainder were prepared
to recognise that individual behaviour had *some* part to play in
illness causation and were more likely to accept that one was
morally accountable if one neglected oneself and thereby reduced
the level of resistance to illness. This broad dichotomy in the nature

of the health beliefs held appeared to relate to the amount of formal education these women had received; the greater the amount, the nearer these respondents were to official views on effective ways of maintaining health. In our sample, there was also an association between education level and type of house tenure. The decision to buy one's house may be regarded as an indicator of a much broader cluster of attitudes with possible relevance for health behaviour; for example, a willingness to postpone immediate gratification, a belief that one is essentially in control of one's destiny. With a small sample it was impossible to disentangle the relative importance of housing type *versus* education, but it has been shown that with social class held constant, owner occupiers have lower mortality rates than private tenants, and they, in turn, have lower rates than council tenants (cf. DHSS, 1980: 42 and 9, Table 2).

Our data shows that while the women's beliefs about aetiology vary according to their level of education, there were considerable similarities in the ways they talked about the implications of illness and the appropriate behaviour to be followed. This stemmed from their common role as mothers of dependent children. The common themes here echo Herzlich's characterisation of the concept of illness as destructive; for example, individuals insist on their responsibilities, their indispensability, on maintaining behaviour characteristic of health, whatever their objective state of health. It is not difficult to see that such attitudes may conflict with the need to maintain one's level of resistance or 'reserve of health' at an optimum level.

Looking at the sample as a whole, eight (20 per cent) rejected the idea of 'blame' outright or were unsure that it was appropriate; nine (22 per cent) interpreted it in terms of direct risk; sixteen (40 per cent) mentioned neglect and lowered resistance; four (10 per cent) thought one was responsible for one's state of mind, whilst the remaining 4 (10 per cent) interpreted responsible behaviour in terms of failure to make appropriate use of health professionals. Thus there was dissonance between the views expressed by these women and those being promulgated as part of official health education policy, with only a minority appearing to define 'responsible health behaviour' in a similar way to official publications. It is argued that the beliefs held by the others form a reasonably coherent cluster of theories about health, illness and the individual's role which, because of their deep-rooted nature, may be highly resistant to change through the traditional approaches of health education.

14

Most of the extracts in this volume so far have dealt with the way lay people conceptualise health, healing or illness or with how lay conceptualisations relate to professional ones. In this final extract, first written some ten years ago, we have included a piece which focuses upon differences in *medical* conceptualisation. Magdalena Sokolowska from Poland contrasts the conventional curative orientation of the majority of medicine with that of social medicine or public health. The former is orientated entirely towards the individual decisions made and the treatment offered in relation to the clinical needs of the sick person. In contrast, the public health doctor is concerned with groups of people; indeed, with whole mass populations. In this case the interest of the majority may sometimes override those of particular individuals. It is, as she shows, such medical practitioners, interested in improving the health of whole populations, who may be expected to be more interested in understanding the social and psychological aspects of suffering and, one might add, how lay people understand their healthiness and illness.

Two notes of caution should perhaps be struck. The first is that as we have seen in the previous chapter, a concern for whole-population health does not necessarily embrace a collective or group orientation. It has been the whole-population concerns of successive British governments which have led them to encourage individuals to look after their own health and to stress the individual behaviouristic facets of disease inducement. These have been stressed more strongly than those causes of ill health which reside in the environment outside the individual's control. Many such environmental hazards arise from the actions of other human beings outside the control of any one citizen. Their authors may be chemical manufacturers, tobacco, alcohol or armaments manufacturers and advertisers, building and transport engineers and those who employ them. Public health in the sense of collective action towards a healthier environment is a different matter from preventive health policies which are individualistically based and 'victim blaming' (Crawford, 1977).

The second caution derives from the public health need to put the collective above the individual good, something which we all recognise sometimes must happen. However, a careful balance has at all times to be struck, for, as Phil Strong (1979) has pointed out, environmental medicine, involving increased medical policing, could exercise more oppressive control than curative medicine ever has.

The paper was published previously in 1973.   *Eds.*

MAGDALENA SOKOLOWSKA

Two Basic Types of Medical Orientation

Physicians, as well as the entire medical field, are characterised by an orientation which in this paper is called 'individualistic'. It corresponds with the traditional subject of medical interest — the individual organism. Our times are witness to the changes which make it necessary for medicine to widen or even change its traditional subject of interest and to study the individual within his surroundings, or even to shift the major interest to these surroundings. Thus a new orientation is developing. It is called 'group orientation' in this paper.

Individualistic Orientation

The traditional medical approach considers the individual as a singular human organism and, in the more modern approach, it is 'soma' together with 'psyche', or 'psyche' alone in some psychiatric areas. The typical practical procedure, based on this orientation, is clinical treatment. Beyond the traditional-professional aspects, it also comprises elements of psychotherapy which is understood and administered in various ways.

Some Characteristics of Traditional Medical Science and the Education of Doctors[1]

The similarity between medicine and sociology is based on the fact that both of them have the same main subject of interest — the man. But each of them approaches this subject quite differently.

The medical approach is, in fact, individualistic; it is characterised by a preoccupation with the single organism and by a specific approach to disease. The organism constitutes an environment (a

---

1. This section is based on concepts presented by Freidson (1970a).

so-called internal environment, i.e. a habitat for germs) or a body influenced by the characteristics of the environment in which it exists (a so-called external environment). The influence of the environmental characteristics on the organism is a negative one — contagious or traumatic. Positive influence is not examined; it is assumed to exist when negative influences are not found. Examining a positive influence would probably seem quite ridiculous to the majority of physicians. Bodies have their own self-sufficient integrity; they are influenced by the environment but do not function simply because of it. The single organism is the basic unit of analysis and the basic point of reference because its functions are explained by the operation of its body and 'mind'; for example, through physical damage, intellectual performance or motivation. The disease of a patient is, therefore, explained by finding in it the characteristics of a definitive disease.

The traditional medical doctor deals with the problems of particular individuals in his daily activities. He is not interested in statistical units or aggregates nor does he rely on probability. Probability may only help to define the patient as sick or healthy. Individual variability creates a permanent problem of evaluation, even in those areas of knowledge which are characterised by the accumulation of hard facts. This variability results in the necessity of performing a personal examination of every case and the difficulty of doing something simply on the basis of abstract scientific knowledge.

Helping the sick is characterised by the 'ideological' individualism of the physician's opinion of himself and his work. According to this orientation, the solution to the problem of bad or non-ethical work lies in the recruitment of candidates who are better motivated and more capable, and in the improvement of the quality of professional training. Such activities are aimed at changing the quality of individuals and are based on the assumption that pathologies concerned with aiding the sick, are best remedied by treating individuals rather than by treating the environmental aspects of the situation, as though the diseases of mankind are caused by the characteristics of the *individuals giving* the aid rather than by the characteristics of the *environment* in which these individuals are giving aid.

In the process of medical training, two chief values are stressed: (1) the immediate responsibility and (2) the clinical experience. The responsibility — personal and immediate — concerns the physician who works directly with the patient. He is responsible for the patient's life, fate and welfare. The physician is a physician when he is faced with such responsibilities. The clinical experience denotes the real experience in the treatment of patients and diseases. It serves as a substitute for knowledge scientifically verified but can also be used as a justification for the choice of certain procedures in the process of treatment — even those which dismiss scientifically founded methods. It is most probably connected with the fact that making a diagnosis requires the physician to use various senses which can only be developed by being used in immediate practice. The clinical experience emphasises, therefore, the unsuitability of 'book' and scientific knowledge in the face of the practical complexities of individual cases.

The Role of 'Healer of the Individual'

For a large majority of people, the 'real' physician is one who interacts with the patient, diagnoses disease and cures it. The doctor, in general, is not expected to treat the whole world; he is supposed to heal a sick individual. Neither is it expected that the prevention of the causes of disease would be his major area of interest, though some changes in this opinion emerge. The general public thinks that the fundamental obligation of a physician is to combat the results of those causes presented in an individual's getting ill. The physician is the only member of society who is granted the right to cope with disease. He is the only scientific expert in the value of health (Freidson, 1970b), and the only person entitled to make decisions in this sphere. Disease has accompanied man from the beginning of human history and, until now, rendering health has constituted a general symbol of medicine's contribution to the happiness of man. Due to the role of 'healer of the individual', the physician occupies, in all societies, the highest position according to the social scales of occupational prestige. As 'healer', he appears in almost all sociological works on the medical profession. Other roles of the physician are difficult to conceptualise. Among other things, the designation 'healer' is a hindrance.[2]

A scientific healer has far-reaching privileges and power in modern society. Society upholds the authority of the physician. If the physician's diagnosis is believed to be incorrect by the patient, the

2. In Polish, the word 'physician' (*lekarz*) denotes someone who heals (*leczy*). In German the word's for 'physician' (*Arzt*) and 'drug' (*Arznei*) are derived from the same root.

physician's finding is invariably the accepted one. And, if someone feels ill but cannot get a physician's verification, the fact of his illness is not socially approved or accepted. Instead, he might be labelled a malingerer or a loiterer and become a client of a legal institution (Freidson, 1970b). A doctor's statement is highly prestigious in society. It may possibly assure special conditions of recreation and recuperative care, enlarge living space, grant rent and various financial benefits, and promote work, military and prison exemptions. Doctor's rights are constantly increasing as they reach further beyond traditional medical areas. It seems that societies still extend a 'safety-valve', created by themselves and personified in a doctor, because of their uncertainty and insecurity. A doctor's advice is not always obeyed because the species *Homo sapiens* has sold itself to development and progress — conditions which do not always mean health and happiness (Dubos, 1960). The way of progress is inevitably full of bruises and wounds. There must be someone within the society able to care for people professionally.

Salus Aegrotis Suprema Lex

Salus aegrotis suprema lex are those words which constitute the fundamental medical ethical value. From the very beginning of his training, the medical student is taught the first commandment of the medical profession; he must always, under all circumstances, place his patient's interests above all other values. A dedicated doctor is one who is willing to make sacrifices in order to care for a patient.

The indispensable condition for a doctor's satisfaction with his work is his conviction that his behaviour conforms with the principal norm of his profession. Any doubts he may have about this question may result in role-conflict; for example, a doctor working in an industrial or military organisation. The patient, too, must be sure that his welfare is considered by the doctor to be above everything else. Otherwise he cannot fully trust the doctor.

No one knows when he will have need of a doctor. But the fact that a doctor is present in society is reassuring and so is our strong belief that a doctor will do everything to help the sick — the individual himself or the people close to him. When a sociologist becomes ill, he becomes a sick human being who is no longer interested in discussing the norm of individualistic medicine; he needs his doctor and the knowledge that the doctor will help him, and that this is the most important aim of the doctor.

The Welfare of the Dying Man[3]

In olden times death played a central role in man's life. A man suffered from disease and died very solemnly in his home. The whole family felt the proximity of death; every member of the clan took part in this event, which, in view of softening the tragic reality, was defined as an origin and not as the end. Today one still observes magnificent funerals, but, in general, death does not play such an important role. Even the fear of cardiac illness or cancer does not cause one to think of preparing for death but, rather, of avoiding it. Death is regarded almost as a 'technical error', and this topic is not discussed in societies of the twentieth century. It is a theme to be avoided and some people think that it came before sex as a social tabu.

Death becomes distant. More and more often people die in hospitals instead of at home. Man loses the privilege of dying in an environment well known to him, in a circle of assembled relatives, as a focus of their interest and the lord of his destiny. However, well-known surroundings are no longer enough since medicine has progressed so rapidly and much-needed special equipment has been developed. Therefore is it not better to bring the sick person to a hospital and give him the care of a competent professional? Systematic investigations in this area started only a short time ago. They seem to demonstrate that doctors are usually rather unprepared to deal with the needs of a dying patient. Medical schools stress healing and prolongation of life to such a degree that the question of care in the case of inevitable death is almost excluded. Health service personnel, in accordance with their professional aims, and also with the attitudes of the general public, are avoiding the question of death and dying and would like to avoid discussions with the patient and his relatives of the question of imminent death. When efforts aimed at stopping the process of dying fail, doctors lose interest and leave the scene. Death seems to be an outrage to their profession.

How does dying look in the hospital? Nursing personnel sometimes utter their views also. Usually there is no opportunity for them to share such thoughts and opinions, but when the change arises, the dam bursts suddenly.[4]

3. This section is based on concepts presented by O. G. Brim *et al.* (1970).
4. The author teaches sociology to instructors of nursing schools from all over the

285

The Individual and the Doctor's Area of Action

As is known, the human structure is comprised of two components — the biological (the body) and the psychological (the personality). Traditional treatment deals with the biological component and, in the shade of this basic area, with the natural component of the organism's environment. Traditional treatment also consists of the application of natural remedies. These are most suitable for the healing of somatic diseases, but in the last few years thay have also been used successfully in psychiatry.

The systematic knowledge of the psychologic and social personality is not included in the area of professional medical knowledge. However, medical practice is not limited to the treatment of bodily diseases. Many doctors, especially those who work at the 'first line' of interaction with patients (e.g. those in the out-patients' clinics), assume the role of moral advisors, consolers and defenders. Probably the notion of charisma, which is still maintained in one's image of a doctor, contributes to the high prestige of the medical profession in society.

The patients crowding the waiting rooms of general practitioners' offices are undoubtedly in need of the skills and characteristics of the doctor. In the case of many patients, a doctor cannot find any organic background to their disorders. People visit doctors because of different problems — personal, emotional and social. They may be looking for advice related to their psychological states, their marital life, the problem of alcoholism in their family, the difficulties connected with the rearing and educating of children, the problems emanating from bad living conditions, or in the care of old people as well as cripples, the disabled, the chronically ill, and so on.

These questions are not considered to be professional by the majority of doctors; they do not belong to the area of competence of a 'real' physician. Such a physician wants to take care of 'real' patients who are in hospitals and specialised out-patients clinics.

---

country who are enrolled in the two-year extramural graduate course in Warsaw. In one of their required papers they were asked to describe their experiences with death in hospitals. The results of these papers showed that almost all of them had been confronted with this situation and that they still thought about it even though it had sometimes taken place a long time ago. These papers also showed that they are deeply moved by these memories while, at the same time, they seem to consider the conditions of death in a hospital to be something unchangeable, inherent and inevitable in any hospital.

The more 'real' patients, the narrower the specialisation and *vice versa*. The nature of this problem is universal. Could it somehow be solved?

One such solution, theoretical rather than practical and realistic, would be the limitation of the broad scope of psychological and social phenomena which are called 'diseases' at the present time. When any state or behaviour is called 'disease', control over it is overtaken by medicine, i.e. from religion or law, on the premise that physicians are competent in dealing with disease (Freidson, 1970b). Virtually nothing denotes a possible change in this area. Rather, a continually opposite trend is observed. An example can be the contemporary process of transformation of the traditional model of alcoholism into a medical one; namely, that of alcoholic disease. The traditional approach to alcoholism consisted chiefly in condemning and punishing, but disease calls for concern and medical treatment. It takes place in special health institutions, anti-alcoholic out-patient clinics.

Another solution, perhaps more realistic, would involve the changing of control over the various states and disturbances, from the doctors to the other health workers; for instance, the psychologist, the social worker or the nurse. However, some systematic studies existing in this area seem to point out that neither the psychologist nor the social worker can replace the physician (Silver, 1963). It is the opinion of this author that there is only one health worker who could be taken into consideration, namely, the nurse. However, she is not trained, consciously and systematically, to play such a role. Besides, it is unknown to what extent it would diminish the load of the doctor. The above-mentioned study, as well as daily observations, seem to indicate that patients are not, in general, inclined to follow the advice as to who should help them. Most people are not inclined to separate their personal problems from professional-medical ones and so they bring both to the doctor.

Thus, the majority of doctors feel compelled to attend to the individual's medical problems, as well as to problems resulting from his natural and social environment. Therefore, knowledge of the 'bio' type, which is now considered to be synonymous with professional medical knowledge, will have to be supplemented by knowledge of the 'psycho' and 'socio' type.

Rehabilitation Specialists

Rehabilitative medicine quite recently began to make its way in modern medicine. The sphere of rehabilitative activities grows up, its form widens and differentiates and the orientation of the doctors involved is transformed. At the beginning, their action was aimed at rendering physical fitness to the patient; immediately afterwards, it was directed towards the physical and psychological. Now, their aim is the physical, psychological and social.

Until recently, this area was dominated by a psychological way of thinking and approach. The disability of the individual (the individual constitutes an analytical unit in the area of rehabilitation) was regarded as a feature or need of the individual — as something inherent in the individual. The rehabilitation process was not considered to constitute a part of the social system, comprised of the family, the working situation or friends. The failure of rehabilitation was explained psychologically, for instance, by the fact that the disabled person is not adequately prepared for rehabilitative procedures — he resists them because he does not accept himself as a cripple.

Now it is the sociologist who is becoming more essential to the rehabilitation specialists, and sociologists find such specialists easier to work with than 'healing' doctors. Although it is true that both the healer and the rehabilitator are individually orientated, the aim of one is the return to health whereas the aim of the other is the return to society. The success of clinical (medical and psychological) rehabilitation is determined by social norms.

The Doctor as a Psychological Engineer

The prevention and treatment of many contemporary diseases make it necessary for a doctor to persuade the individual to change his style of life. Such changes, however, require a constant effort and it is an apparent collision with the personal freedom of man. The desired changes might involve a restriction of smoking, drinking or overeating, walking instead of driving, refraining from the use of drugs, stopping air and water pollution, and so on.

Actions aimed at convincing the individual that he should change his style of life in order to maintain health is a psychological engineering one; its goal is to accomplish some predicted psychological transformations of the given individual (Podgorecki, 1968).

In the area of individual health and illness, the psychological engineering orientation of a doctor is indispensable. A defined and unique individual suffering from disease or exposed to it, constitutes the specific contents of this area. Notwithstanding the rationalisation of the social life, it seems that there will always be a demand in society for a system acting in the narrow circles of 'face to face' behaviours; a system chiefly aimed at securing the interests of the ill and disabled members of the society; a system guided by the welfare of a given individual and not by the success of social engineering. The social engineer has little to say in this area beyond the fact that he acts in another area and applies other ideological and evaluative criteria to his action.

Group Orientation

As we have seen, individual medical orientation is based on definite scientific premises, ethical values and principles of behaviour. They are so powerful that they are identified with the image of all medicine. This is not quite justified because, for several years, rather imperceptible developments of another orientation have been taking place. It is incomparable to the main orientation — not typical of traditional medical knowledge and professional behaviour.

The Knowledge of Social and Environmental Medicine

In contrast to traditional clinical medicine, traditional social medicine does not examine man as an isolated unit but approaches him as an individuum connected with his environment. The discipline of social medicine is interested in the consequences of this interaction for the individual. The environment in which he is located represents a chiefly natural environment — the holism of physical, chemical and biological problems.

As is known, the environment, to the sociologist, is not a natural *Unwelt*, but a social and cultural reality in which the individual is, simultaneously, an object and a subject. The fact that social medicine regards the environment as natural surroundings whereas sociology considers it to be a social and cultural reality results from the fact that each of these disciplines examines a different reality.[5]

5. These ideas stem from Nuyens (1969).

Both disciplines have one common aspect; namely, the reality concerning the individual. It is to be noticed that this individual has here another character than that found in the mainstream of medicine. Very often it is a defined group of differing size. It numbers thousands or millions of people in some epidemiological studies.

Today social medicine is interested in the significance of social and cultural reality for health and disease. Until recently, knowledge of this area was limited to an indication of the connection between patterns of infection and various forms of human societies. But now, more is at stake, namely, the verification of the role of social and cultural reality as a definite aetiological agent.[6] Today sociologists are more and more often invited to collaborate and more and more of their works are being published in the areas designated by the already popular term 'sociology in medicine'. The process of introducing sociology into the centres of social medicine is progressing in many countries.

Doctors of Public Health

The conceptual apparatus of medicine and the ethical norms of the medical profession concern the individual. The curriculum of medical schools is the same for all students. Everyone becomes socialised for the role of 'healer of the individual' — the only model of a doctor presented to the students. Probably this is one of the main reasons that many doctors resist work in public health; they do not wish to give up their role of 'real' doctor by abandoning the hospital or out-patient clinics. Many candidates for key positions in medical administration accept them only because they are simultaneously granted work in hospitals and assured of specialisation in one of the clinical disciplines.

Thus, the process of changing the fundamentals of thinking — from an individualistic orientation to a group orientation — is very difficult. But this basic change takes place somehow. The number of doctors involved in activities which do not correspond with the name 'healer' is continually increasing. These doctors are defined in various ways: as doctors of public health, social medicine, preventive medicine, social hygiene, and so on.

In only one European country known to this author do social hygienists constitute a strong professional group — the German

6. These ideas stem from Nuyens (1969).

Democratic Republic. This group is a spokesman for all medicine and a decisive factor in the whole area of national health policy. The social hygienists are to be met at all levels of political institutions where the problems of health have been brought by them. These problems become very important and are regarded as one of the fundamental national areas of life and concern.

The curriculum of contemporary medical schools is of little relevance to the role of the public health doctor. He can complete his education only during his professional career, on the graduate level — more or less formal. Some representatives of this group maintain that it becomes increasingly difficult for them to identify with the medical profession. It seems that the starting point for the primary difficulties is the change of approach to the group, regarded not as a mass of sick and disabled people but as a mass of healthy people who are not especially interested in medical problems and who see fewer diseases than those observed by the doctors.

Public health doctors differ from other doctors by the level of decision making and the establishing of priorities. The technical progress in medicine increases the chances for human life, but unavoidable economic restrictions force the doctor to make the dramatic decision of who shall live and who shall die. The 'healers' decide on the life of the given individuals. The public health doctors decide instead on the distribution of general funds assigned for health; for instance, whether they should be used for a few patients or for the building of a hospital for a great number of cardiac patients, for artificial kidneys for two thousand patients with kidney failure or for a care centre for thirty thousand mentally retarded people (which would cost the same), for early detection of cancer, mental health out-patient clinics, and so on.

The case of Professor Lew Davidovitch Landau (Lasagna, 1970) is an example of the great technical possibilities of modern medicine — when it is not financially restricted and organisationally restricted — and also of the typical approach used by healers of the individual. As is known, the genial Soviet physicist was able to survive six years after the car accident which caused his clinical death several times. He never recovered fully but his life was a testimonial to the skills and perseverance of the treating team as well as to the value of the intellect to society.

In the above case, the decision was comparatively simple: the exceptional intellectual abilities of the patient. Other situations are more complicated. The decisions belong to the public health doctors; they are not present at the patient's bed. The healers of the individual cannot make any decision against him.

Conclusions

1. The fundamental dividing line between doctors is determined by the style of their medical orientation. There are two basic styles of medical orientation — the individualistic orientation and the mass orientation, depending upon what constitutes the point of reference, the individual or the group. The individualistic orientation corresponds to the traditional character of medical knowledge; its conceptual apparatus is related to the individual and the fundamental unit of analysis is a singular organism. Mass orientation shifts the point of interest towards the group, changing the fundamentals of the way of thinking and becoming a qualitatively different medicine.

2. A 'typical' doctor is a healer of sick individuals. Such doctors constitute a main body of the medical profession in any society. Nothing indicates that the societal need for the individual healer may decrease (Sokolowska, 1971). Rather, a reverse phenomenon is observed. It results from the growth of the technical–medical possibilities and of achievements and attainments, and one observes an increasing trend towards assigning individual psychological problems to medical doctors. People beset by such problems become their patients. Thus, a doctor's interest in the area of 'psyche' deepens. This interest is presented in the treatment of mental disturbances without perceptible organic background, in the application of psychotherapy to somatic diseases and in the attempt to change behaviour suspected of being harmful to health. In the form of 'health education', doctors attempt to motivate patients to change their habits and adopt recommended behaviour.

As long as the doctor deals with the sphere of the organism, he is a 'biological engineer'. When he enters the sphere of the 'psyche' he becomes a 'psychological engineer'. In this role he is adept as far as the foundations of systematic knowledge and experience are concerned. Until now, his behaviour has been characterised by an individualism based on common sense rather than on scientific knowledge, which is not indifferent to social policy. Thus, a postulate arises — that the behavioural sciences help doctors to rationalise their activities aimed at reaching the progressed psychological effects in given individuals.

3. Doctors thinking in categories of the group, everywhere constitute a minority among doctors. It is not easy to be a doctor of public health, social medicine or social hygiene. The medical school enforces the individualistic ideology and, consequently, strongly influences the students. The doctor is unprepared for a job calling for a group orientation. Above all, he must force himself to overcome the doctor's nature. The problem is that the *salus aegroti* does not always correspond with the *salus societatis*. The public health doctor must give priority to the society. Besides, the name *'lekars'* (healer) is unsuitable for someone who does not heal. Public health is not one more medical speciality among many various specialities. This author thinks that this occupation is new and distinct. It is possible that in the future this occupation will be closer to sociologists, social engineers and social politicians than to medical doctors.

The countries with systems of socialised health service particularly need such an occupation, namely, the new type of 'client' enters the scene there — the global society. Other systems of health care must not consider the needs of such 'collective patient' to the same extent.

CAROLINE CURRER
MEG STACEY

Conclusion

One of our aims in this volume has been to draw attention to the variety of concepts of health and illness that exist, over time and in different locations, as well as to the variations which co-exist in any one time and place. These latter variations are both between and within groups in a society as well as within individuals. Another aim has been to show how different methodological and theoretical approaches lead to different focuses of study and to different conclusions, or at least different emphases in conclusions. Each of the papers contributes to these aims either through the groups or societies it discusses or through its analytic mode. A major theme which has emerged, notwithstanding these differences of approach, is the close association between concepts and the social structure. This theme has been discussed in a number of papers and is implicit in others.

The relationship of concepts of health, illness and healing to a larger cosmology also becomes plain. Mutual inconsistencies in concepts of health and illness in some cases derive from major differences in the assumptions on which cosmologies are based. The cosmologies themselves are in their turn associated with variations in social and economic structures. Unschuld's analysis of changes over time is one example; Seabrook's account of the folk cosmology which was dissolved by later-twentieth-century urban development is another. The Amhari health belief system, poised between externalising and internalising, has resulted, Allan Young tells us, from many thousands of years of conquest by and contact with other peoples and civilisations. In ways like these, in any one society, not only may there be groups of people who differ in the way they conceive of health and illness, but individuals may hold concepts which are mutually inconsistent, not only with each other but also in terms of any one cosmology. Jocelyn Cornwell (1984) showed this most clearly in the differences she demonstrated between the public and private accounts of health which her Bethnal Green informants gave her.

In reading all the accounts, it has become clear that these variations are not random but have certain systematic characteristics. The variations may relate systematically to groups or categories within the society; they relate also to questions of power. In some papers the variations are seen as differences which involve conflict, latent or overt, which some authors draw out (see, for example, Graham and Oakley); others (such as Ablon and Currer) stress differences but do not propose conflict.

So far as systematic variation between groups or categories is concerned, in examples drawn from societies with highly elaborated industries and technologies and with complex divisions of labour, concepts vary not only between the highly trained professional and the untrained client (i.e. between professional and lay persons) but also between broader groups and categories. Thus both Roisin Pill and Nigel Stott, on the one hand, and Alphonse d'Houtaud and Mark Field, on the other, demonstrate variations in concepts of health and illness among respondents from different social categories — the well-to-do and the poor, bosses and workers, house owners and house renters. Conceptual differences may thus be related to life circumstances and to variable command of resources as well as to clusters of attitudes about various aspects of living.

Gilbert Lewis's work indicates how one who is quite powerful in one arena may lack power in another. He has been at pains to describe the Gnau's system of beliefs in their own terms. But at the same time he draws out the profound contrasts between their beliefs and his own, the latter deriving from his training in biomedicine, his assumptions about scientific method and his experience as a medical practitioner. When he was among the Gnau, who knew him as a doctor as well as an anthropologist, Gilbert Lewis was sometimes consulted about a sick person, but he had to behave in the way that they, not he, thought right. Thus he was not allowed to examine a patient, for example, as any biomedic might wish to (Lewis, 1975). The situation was reversed for the pregnant women in Britain discussed by Hilary Graham and Ann Oakley. In this case the women had to bow to the biomedical conceptualisation of the phenomenon of pregnancy, the phenomenon that they themselves were experiencing. The examples are different, however, because nowhere are the women's views accepted as dominant, while in many societies Gilbert Lewis would be able to practice as he was taught to and as he saw fit.

Other papers describe the co-existence of mutually incompatible concepts and behaviour without suggesting that conflict and challenge are necessarily involved. Thus, in Joan Ablon's paper, the conceptual differences leading to the Samoans' different reactions to disaster and pain is reported as leading to a kind of wonderment on the part of those caring for them. This wonderment at difference which characterises Joan Ablon's study is also present in Caroline Currer's. Both also point to the powerlessness of the minority ethnic group described. The notion of a dominant mode belonging to dominant social groups again emerges, although neither writer suggests conflict.

The papers also raise the issue of the transformation of concepts and how this can be explained, and suggest different answers to this key sociological question. Some address the issue at the level of face-to-face interaction, others at the society-wide level. Overall the evidence suggests that to talk only in terms of one dominant mode is insufficient, especially if a wider time span is taken. Jocelyn Cornwell (1984) has shown how lay beliefs have been 'medicalised' over the years. Cecil Helman, in the paper we have reproduced here, suggests that medical practitioners modify their practice and the way they speak about illness and healing towards the folk models held by their patients. He suggests also that the patients may have changed their conceptualisation in consequence of the increased availability of biomedical advice and the greater array of treatments available, specifically effective pharmaceuticals. His patients had apparently moved from a belief system much more like that of Jeremy Seabrook's forebears towards accommodation with biomedicine, although they did not entirely understand biomedicine's concepts in its own terms. Cecil Helman sees both practitioners and patients changing their thought and behaviour at least partly because of changes in social arrangements (the NHS) and of industrial production. In this way the impact of nation-wide changes at the grass roots is indicated.

Other authors address the question of change at a macro-sociological level. Paul Unschuld's analysis suggests that ideas about health and illness change along with changes in overall social structures — indeed, are determined by them — albeit that they have to be worked out within the systems of ideas themselves. Allan Young's analysis tends in the same direction. Claudine Herzlich and Janine Pierret see health concepts as social representations and show how many persist over the centuries, although new concepts are added as time goes on.

More or less latent in all the analyses is a challenge to biomedicine itself, as a system of concepts and as an organised healing mode with its own elaborated division of labour. Some of the papers seem simply to be saying 'There are other ways of thinking about suffering and handling it at the personal and group level than those offered by biomedicine — think on that'. Other writers, speaking from within biomedicine, seem to be saying, 'We have a powerful healing system, but others go about things differently; if we are smart we will take account of their different views'. There are again others who, while acknowledging the great value but also the marked limitations of biomedicine, seem to be suggesting that it should be seen in a wider perspective, reminding us that the practitioners of biomedicine are human beings, creatures of their time and place and with their own interests to pursue. Such authors recognise biomedicine as a mode of healing which has considerable power and has alleviated much suffering in those areas where it is effective, but they issue warnings also, suggesting that it is unwise to go overboard for this way of healing and for its trained practitioners to the exclusion of all others. Caroline Currer's and Joan Ablon's accounts of how suffering was borne by people in their studies suggest ways of handling illness and pain which are beyond biomedical conceptualisation. Overall this message seems to be, 'Let us recognise the value and limitations of biomedicine and ask its practitioners to acknowledge the contribution of the untrained in the recognition and healing of illness and also to consider the contribution made by other healing systems'. Papers included here, such as Meg Stacey's, which seem to carry this message, recognise the conundrum so well exposed in the analysis of theory and practice in relation to asthma analysed by John Gabbay. Having attempted to show how medical knowledge about asthma could be said to be socially constructed, he stresses the difficulties of that process and the even greater difficulties of attempting to go beyond it:

> . . . by focusing on its production and ignoring the continuing process of its acceptance and utilisation, we have not begun to explain the powerful role which medical knowledge has been made to play as a form of intellectual and social practice. To answer such questions is immensely difficult. . . . We have found problems enough in explaining how and why people write books about asthma; to explain how and why people read them is surely a challenge. [1982: 42]

In putting together this volume, we as editors have attempted to indicate some of the complexities of enterprises such as this. We also wish to say that issues of inconsistency and change are not merely of academic interest. It is important to understand not only how health and illness are conceived and by whom, but also to understand what happens when the concepts are made operational, whether by professionals, individuals or governments. Illness and its treatment are neither simple matters of fate nor of capitalism making one sick; the issues are complex. The very knowledge of the concepts of health and illness themselves may be used in a variety of ways to further the interests of individuals or groups, interests which will not necessarily be those of the person who is ill or those whose health is jeopardised by the social arrangements they find themselves in, which individually they are powerless to change. Since any greater knowledge which is acquired may be used for good or ill, we wish also to draw attention to the need for social scientists as much as biomedical scientists to be responsible and vigilant in the application of their knowledge. For our part, we would wish knowledge to be used, not for the aggrandisement of a few but for the alleviation of the suffering of the many.

Bibliography

Ablon, J. (1970) 'The Samoan Funeral in Urban America', *Ethnology* 9:209
(1971a) 'The Social Organisation of an Urban Samoan Community', *Southwest Journal of Anthropology* 27: 75
(1971b) 'Bereavement in a Samoan Community', *British Journal of Medical Psychology* 44: 329
(1973) 'Reactions of Samoan Burn Patients and Families to Severe Burns', *Social Science and Medicine* 7: 167–78
Ackerknecht, E. (1946) 'Natural Diseases and Rational Treatment in Primitive Medicine', *Bulletin of Historical Medicine* 19: 467–97
Adler, A. (1943) 'Neuropsychiatric Complications in Victims of Boston's Cocoanut Grove Disaster', *Journal of the American Medical Association* 123: 1098
Ahern, E. (1975) 'Sacred and Secular Medicine in a Taiwan Village', in A. Kleinman *et al.* (eds.), *Medicine in Chinese Cultures*, Fogarty International Center, NIH, Bethesda, Maryland, pp. 91–114
Aitken Swan, J. (1977) *Fertility Control and the Medical Profession*, London: Croom Helm
Alland, A. (1970) *Adaptation in Cultural Evolution: An Approach to Medical Anthropology*, New York: Columbia University Press
Allendy, R. (1980) *Journal d'un médecin malade*, Paris: Eds. du Piranha
Armstrong, D. (1983) *Political Anatomy of the Body: Medical Knowledge in Britain in the Twentieth Century*, Cambridge: Cambridge University Press
Arney, W. R. (1983) *Power and the Profession of Obstetrics*, Chicago and London: The University of Chicago Press
Aron, J. P. (1969) *Essais d'epistemologie biologique*, Paris: Christian Bourgeois
(1980) *Misérable et glorieuse; la femme du xixᵉ siècle*, Paris: Fayard
Aslam, M. (1979) 'The Practice of Asian Medicine in the United Kingdom and the Role of the Visiting Hakim', *Medicos* 4 (2)
Auge, M. (1975) 'Theórie des pouvoirs et idéologie', Paris: Hermann
Barnes, S. B. (1974) *Scientific Knowledge and Sociological Theory*, London: Routledge and Kegan Paul
Barrett, M. and Roberts, H. (1978) 'Doctors and Their Patients: The Social Control of Women in General Practice', in C. Smart, and B. Smart (eds.), *Women, Sexuality and Social Control*, London: Routledge and Kegan Paul

Basham, A. L. (1978) in *Sonderdruck aus Krankheit, Heilkunst, Heilung*, Verlag Karl Alber, Freiburg

Beck, B. E. F. (1969) 'Colour and Heat in South Indian Ritual', *Man* 4: 553

Beecher, H. K. (1943) 'Resuscitation and Sedation of Patients with Burns which Include the Airway, *Annals of Surgery* 117: 825

Benassar, B. (1969) *Recherches sur les grandes épidémies dans le noid de l'Espagne a la fin dur XVIe siècle*, Paris: SEVPEN ·

Blaxter, M. (1981) *The Health of the Children: A Review of Research on the Place of Health in Cycles of Disadvantage*, London: Heinemann

Blaxter, M. and Patterson, E. (1982) *Mothers and Daughters, A Three-Generational Study of Health Attitudes and Behaviours*, London: Heinemann

Boccaccio (1972) *The Decameron*, Harmondsworth: Penguin Books

Bonnef, L. and M. (n.d.) *Les métiers qui tuent: enquête aupres des syndicats ouvriers sue les maladies professionelles*, Paris: Bibliographie sociale

Boyle, C. M. (1975) 'Differences between Patients' and Doctors' Interpretations of some Common Medical Terms', in C. Cox and A. Mead (eds.), *A Sociology of Medical Practice*, London: Collier Macmillan

Brankaerts, J. (1984) Oral communication to the Nijmegen Conference (Tax, 1984)

Brent CHC (1981) *Black People and the Health Service*, London: Brent CHC

Brim, O. G., Freeman, H. E., Levine, S., Scotch, N. A. (eds.) (1970) *The Dying Patient*, New York: Russell Sage Foundation

Brontë, C. (1969) *Jane Eyre*, Jack Lane and Margaret Smith (eds.), Oxford: Clarendon Press

Brown, G. W. and Harris, T. (1978) *Social Origins of Depression*, London: Tavistock Publications

Brown, G. W. and Rutter, M. (1966) 'The Measurement of Family Activities and Relationships', *Human Relations* 19: 214

Butler, S. (1872) *Erewhon*, London: Trübner

Cannon, I. M. (1943) 'Social Service Activities', *Annals of Surgery* 117: 809

Cartwright, A. (1977) 'Mothers' Experiences of Induction', in *British Medical Journal*, 17 September

Cassell (1964) *Cassell's New German Dictionary*, London: Cassell

Cassell, E. J. (1976) *The Healer's Art: A New Approach to the Doctor–Patient Relationship*, New York: Lippincott

Castiglioni, A. (1947) *A History of Medicine*, New York: A. Knopf

Cawte, J. (1974) *Medicine Is the Law: Studies in Psychiatric Anthropology of Australian Tribal Societies*, University of Hawaii Press

Cay, E. et al. (1975) 'Patient Assessment of the Result of Surgery for Peptic Ulcer', *The Lancet* 1: 29.

Chen, P. C. Y. (1975) 'Medical Systems in Malaysia: Cultural Bases and Differential Use', *Social Science and Medicine* 9: 171

Cobb, S. and Lindemann, E. (1943) 'Neuropsychiatric Observations', *Annals of Surgery* 117: 814

Cochrane, R. (1977) 'Mental Illness in Immigrants to England and Wales: An Analysis of Mental Hospital Admissions', *Social Psychiatry* 12 23–5

Cochrane, R., Hashmi, F. and Stopes-Roe, M. (1977) 'Measuring Psychological Disturbance in Asian Immigrants to Britain', *Social Science and Medicine* 11: 157–64

Coe, R. (1970) *Sociology of Medicine*, New York: McGraw Hill

Cornwell, J. (1984) *Hard Earned Lives*, London: Tavistock Publications

Cotterau, A. (1980) *Le Sublime*, Maspero

Crawford, R. (1977) 'You Are Dangerous to Your Health: The Ideology and Politics of Victim Blaming', *International Journal of Health Services* 7: 663–80

Croizier, R. (1968) *Traditional Medicine in Modern China*, Cambridge Mass.: Harvard University Press

Crystal, D. (1976) 'The diagnosis of Sociolinguistic Problems in Doctor–Patient Interaction', in B. Tanner (ed.), *Language and Communication in Medical Practice*, London: Hodder and Stoughton, p. 49f

Cullen, I. (1979) 'Urban Social Policy and the Problems of Family Life: The use of an extended Diary Method to Inform Decision Analysis', in C. Harris (ed.), *Sociology of the Family*, Sociological Review Monograph no. 28, University of Keele

Currer, C. (1983a) 'The Mental Health of Pathan Mothers in Bradford: A Case Study of Migrant Asian Women', final report to DHSS, June, unpublished

(1983b) 'Pathan Mothers in Bradford', shortened version of the findings, November, unpublished; available from author, University of Warwick.

Currier, R. L. (1966) 'The Hot–Cold Syndrome and Symbolic Balance in Mexican and Spanish American Folk Medicine', *Ethnology* 5: 251

Damon, A. (1975) *Physiological Anthropology*, New York: Oxford University Press

Davis, A. (1979) An Unequivocal Change of Policy: Prevention, Health and Medical Sociology', *Social Science and Medicine* 13a: 129

Davis, A. and Horobin, G. (eds.) (1977) *Medical Encounters: Experience of Illness and Treatment*, London: Croom Helm

Desaive, J-P., Goubert, J-P., Le Roy Ladurie, E., Meyer, J., Muller, O., Peter, J-P. (1972) *Médecins, climat et épidémies à la fin du XVIII siècle*, Paris: La Haye, Mouton

DHSS (1980) *Inequalities in Health*, Report of a Research Working Group

Donnison, J. (1977) *Midwives and Medical Men. A History of Inter-Professional Rivalries and Women's Rights*, London: Heinemann

Douglas, M. (1966) *Purity and Danger: An Analysis of Concepts of Pollution and Taboo*, London: Routledge and Kegan Paul

(1970a) *Purity and Danger: An Analysis of Concepts of Pollution and Taboo*, London: Penguin Books

(1970b) 'The Healing Rite', *Man* 5: 302

(1973) *Natural Symbols: Explorations in Cosmology*, New York: Vintage

Dubos, R. (1960) *Mirages of Health*, London: Allen and Unwin

Dunn, E. (1976) 'Traditional Asian Medicine and Cosmopolitan Medicine as Adaptive Systems', in C. Leslie (ed.), *Asian Medical Systems*, Berkeley: University of Califronia Press, pp. 133–58

Dunnell, K. and Cartwright, A. (1972) *Medicine Takers, Prescribers and Hoarders*, London: Routledge and Kegan Paul

Edelstein, L. (1967) 'The Dietetics of Antiquity: Ancient Medicine', in O. Temkin and C. L. Temkin (eds.), *Selected Papers of L. Edelstein*, Baltimore: Johns Hopkins Press, pp. 303–16

Ehrard, J. (1957) 'La peste et l'idée de contagion', *Annales, Economie, Sociétés, Civilisations*, 12th year, 1: 46–59

Ehrenreich, B. (1974) 'Gender and Objectivity in Medicine', *International Journal of Health Services* 4: 617

Ehrenreich, B. and English, D. (1979) *For Her Own Good: 150 Years of the Experts Advice to Women*, London: Pluto Press

Eisenberg, L. (1976) 'Delineation of Clinical Conditions', in Ciba Foundation Symposium no. 44, *Research and Medical Practice: Their Interaction*, Amsterdam: Elsevier/Exerpta Medica, pp. 3–23

(1977) 'Disease and Illness: Distinctions between Professional and Popular Ideas of Sickness', *Culture, Medicine and Psychiatry*, 1: 9–23

Emerson, J. (1970) 'Behaviour in Private Places: Sustaining Definitions of Reality in Gynaecological Examinations', in H. P. Dreitzel (ed.), *Recent Sociology*, no. 2, New York: Macmillan

Englehardt, H. (1974) 'Explanatory Models in Medicine', *Texas Reports on Biology and Medicine* 32: 225

Evans-Pritchard, E. E. (1956) *Nuer Religion*, London: Oxford University Press

(1965) *Theories of Primitive Religion*, Oxford

Fabrega, H. (1970) 'Dynamics of Medical Practice in a Folk Community', *Milbank Mem. F.Q.* 48:391.

(1973a) *Disease and Social Behaviour*, Cambridge, Mass.: MIT Press

(1973b) *Illness and Shamanistic Curing In Zinancantan: An Ethnomedical Analysis*, Stanford: Stanford University Press

(1975) 'The Need for an Ethnomedical Science', *Science* 189: 969–75

(1976) 'The Function of Medical-Care Systems: A Logical Analysis', in *Perspectives in Biology and Medicine* 20: 108–18

Farge, A. (1977) 'Les artisans malades de leur travail', *Annales, Economies, Sociétiés, Civilisations* 5: 993–1006

Feierman, S. (1979) 'Change in African Therapeutic Systems', *Social Science and Medicine* 13B 277–84

Field, D. (1976) 'The Social Definition of Illness', Ch. 10 in D. Tuckett (ed.), *Introduction to Medical Sociology*, London: Tavistock Publications

Fleury, P. M. (1967) *Maternity Care: Mothers' Experiences of Childbirth*, London: Allen and Unwin

Foster, G. M. (1976) 'Disease Aetiologies in Non-Western Medical Systems', *American Anthropologist* 78: 773–81

Foucault, M. (1961) *Historie de la folie à l'âge classique*, Paris: Plou

(1965) *Madness and Civilization: A History of Insanity in the Age of Reason*, New York: New American Library

(1970) *The Order of Things: An Archaeology of the Human Sciences*, New York: Vintage

Bibliography

(1973) *The Birth of the Clinic: An Archaeology of Medical Perception*, trans. A. M. Sheridan Smith, New York: Vintage, and London: Tavistock Publications
Fox, R. C. (1968) 'Illness', in *International Encyclopaedia of the Social Sciences*, 7:90–5, New York: Free Press/Macmillan
Frank, J. (1974) *Persuasion and Healing*, New York: Schocken
Franz, A. (1909) *Die Kirchlichen Benediktionen im Mittelalter*, Freiburg
Freidson, E. (1970a) *Profession of Medicine: A Study of the Sociology of Applied Knowledge*, New York: Dodd, Mead and Co.
(1970b) *Professional Dominance*, Chicago: Aldine
Friedman, D. (1982) 'Anatomy of Ambiguous Folk Medicine', in T. Vaskilampi and C. P. MacCormack (eds.), *Folk Medicine and Health Culture: Role of Folk Medicine in Modern Health Care*, Kuopio: The University of Kuopio
Gabbay, J. (1982) 'Asthma Attacked? Tactics for the Reconstruction of a Disease Concept', in P. Wright and A. Treacher (eds.), *The Problem of Medical Knowledge: Examining the Social Construction of Medicine*, Edinburgh: Edinburgh University Press
Garrod, L. P. and O'Grady, F. (1968) *Antibiotics and Chemotherapy*, London: Livingstone
Gillie, L. and Gillie, O. (1974) *Sunday Times*, 13 and 20 October
Gillin, J. (1948) 'Magical Fright', *Psychiatry* 2: 387
Ginsberg, M. (1961) 'Essays in Sociology and Social Philosophy,' vol. III, *Evolution and Progress*, London: Heinemann
Goldberg, D. (1978) *Manual of the General Health Questionnaire*, London: NFER-Nelson Publishing Co.
Goldberg, D. P., Cooper, B., Eastwood, M. R., Kedward, H. B. and Shepherd, M. (1970) 'A standardised Psychiatric Interview for Use in Community Surveys', *British Journal of Preventive and Social Medicine*, 24:18–23
Goldthorpe, W. O. and Richman, J. (1974) 'Maternal Attitudes to Unintended Home Confinement', *Practitioner* 212: 845
(1975, 1976) 'The Gynaecological Patient's Knowledge of Her Illness and Treatment', *British Journal of Sexual Medicine*, December 1975 and February 1976
Good, B. (1977) 'The Heart of What's the Matter: Semantics and Illness in Iran', *Culture, Medicine and Psychiatry* 1: 25
Goodfield, G. J. (1960) *The Growth of Scientific Physiology: Physiological Method and the Mechanist–Vitalist Controversy, Illustrated by Problems of Respiration and Animal Heat*, London: Hutchinson
Goodman, L. S. and Gilman, A. (1965) *The Pharmacological Basis of Therapeutics*, New York: Macmillan, and London: Collier-Macmillan
Goubert, J. P. (1977) 'L' art de guérir. Médicine savante et medicine populaire dans la France de 1790', *Annales, Économies, Sociétes, Civilisations*, 32ᵉ année, 5: 908–26
Gould-Martin, K. (1975) 'Medical Systems in a Taiwan Village', in A. Kleinman, *et al.* (eds.), *Medicine in Chinese Cultures*, Fogarty International Center, NIH, Bethesda, Maryland, pp. 115–42
Graham, H. (1976) 'The Social Image of Pregnancy: Pregnancy as Spirit

Possession', *Sociological Review* 24: 291

(1977) 'Women's Attitudes to Conception and Pregnancy', in R. Chester and J. Peel (eds.), *Equalities and Inequalities in Family Life*, London: Academic Press

(1979) 'Prevention and Health: Every Mother's Business: A Comment on Child Health Policies in the 1970s', in C. Harris (ed.), *Sociology of the Family: New Directions for Britain*, Sociological Review Monograph no. 28, University of Keele

(1982) 'Coping: Or How Mothers Are Seen and Not Heard', in S. Friedman and E. Sarah (eds.), *On The Problem of Men*, London: The Women's Press

Griaule, M. (1930) *Le Livre de recettes d'un dabtara abyssin*, Travuz et Memoires de l'Institut d'Ethnologie, no. 38, Université de Paris, Paris

Grmek, M. (1961) 'Arnaud de Villeneuve et la médecine du travail', *Yperman, bulletin de la Société helge de la medicine*, VIII

Haire, D. (1972) *The Cultural Warping of Childbirth*, International Childbirth Education Association News

Hall, T. S. (1969) *Ideas of Life and Matter*, Chicago: University of Chicago Press

Hallowell, I.A. (1963) 'Ojibwa World View and Disease', in I. Gladstone (ed.), *Man's Image in Medicine* and *Anthropology*, International Universities Press, 258–315

Halsband, R. (ed.) (1965) *Complete Letters of Lady Mary Wortley Montagu*, vol. 1, 1708–20, Oxford: Clarendon Press

Hamburg, D. A., Artz, C. P., Reiss, E., Amspacher, W. H. and Chambers, R. E. (1953a) 'Clinical Importance of Emotional Problems in the Care of Patients with Burns', *New England Journal of Medicine* 248: 355

Hamburg, D.A., Hamburg, B. and DeGoza, S. (1953b) 'Adaptive Problems and Mechanisms in Severely Burned Patients', *Psychiatry* 16:1

Hanks, L. M. and Hanks, J. R. (1955) 'Diphtheria Immunization in a Thai Community', in B. D. Paul, (ed.), *Health, Culture and Community*, New York: Russell Sage Foundation

Hannay, D. (1979) *The Symptom Iceberg: A Study in Community Health*, London: Routledge and Kegan Paul

Harman, J. B. et al. (eds.) (1976) *British National Formulary, 1976–78*, London: British Medical Association, 63, 115.

Harnack, A. (1892) 'Medicinisches aus der Ältesten Kirchen geschichte', in *Texte und Untersuchungen zur Geschichte der Altchristlichen Literatur* 8:37–147

Harrison, D. F. N. (1976) 'Nasal Drops, Sprays and Inhalations', *Prescribers Journal* 16: 69–74

Hart, N. (1977) 'Technology and Childbirth: A Dialectical Autobiography', in A. Davis and G. Horobin (eds.), *Medical Encounters: Experience of Illness and Treatment*, London: Croom Helm

Harwood, A. (1971) 'The Hot–Cold Theory of Disease: Implications for Treatment of Puerto Rican Patients', *Journal of the American Medical Association* 216: 1153

Helman, C. G. (1978)'"Feed a Cold, Starve a Fever": Folk Models of Infection in an English Suburban Community, and Their Relation to

Medical Treatment', *Culture, Medicine and Psychiatry* 2: 107–37

Herzlich, C. (1973) *Health and Illness: A Social Psychological Analysis*, London and New York: Academic Press

Herzlich, C. and Pierret, J. (1984) *Malades d'hier, malades d'aujourdhui*, Paris: Payot

—— (1985) 'The Social Construction of the Patient: Patients and Illnesses in Other Ages', *Social Science and Medicine* 20 (2), 145–51

HMSO (1961) *Human Relations and Obstetrics*, Standing Maternity and Midwifery Advisory Committee Document, London

—— (1976) *Prevention and Health: Everybody's Business*, London

Holmes, T. and Rahe, R. (1967) 'The Social Readjustment Rating Scale', *Psychosomatic Research* 11: 213

Horton, R. (1967) 'African Traditional Thought and Western Science', *Africa* 37

—— (1970) 'African Traditional Thought and Western Medicine', in M. Warwick (ed.) (1970) *Witchcraft and Sorcery: Selected Readings*, Harmondsworth: Penguin Books

—— (1971) 'African Traditional Thought and Western Science', in M. F. D Young (1971) *Knowledge and Control*, London, Collier Macmillan

d'Houtaud, A. (1976) 'La représentation de la santé: recherche dans un centre de bilan de santé en Lorraine', *Revue internationale d'Education pour la Santé* 19 (2), 99–118 and 19 (3), 173–88

—— (1978) 'L'image de la santé dans une population lorraine: approche psychosociale des représentations de la santé, *Revue d'Epidémiologie et de Santé publique* 26: 299–320

—— (1981) 'Nouvelles recherches sur les représentations de la santé, *Revue Internationale d'Education pour la Santé* 24 (3), 3–22

d'Houtaud, A. and Field, M. (1984) 'The Image of Health: Variations in Perception by Social Class in a French Population', *Sociology of Health and Illness*, 6 (1), 30–60

Huard, P. and Wong, M. (1968) *Chinese Medicine*, New York: McGraw-Hill

Hughes, C. (1968) 'Ethnomedicine', in *International Encyclopaedia of the Social Sciences*, vol. 10 pp. 87–93, New York: Free Press/Macmillan

Hulka, B. *et al.* (1972) 'Determinants of Physician Utilization', *Medical Care* 10: 300

Illsley, R. (1967) 'The Sociological Study of Reproduction and Its Outcome', in S. A. Richardson and A. F. Guttmacher (eds.), *Childbearing: Its Social and Psychological Aspects*, Baltimore: Williams and Wilkins

Illsley, R. *et al.* (1977) Review paper in *Health and Health Policy: Priorities for Research, Report of an advisory panel to the Research Initiatives Board*, Social Science Research Council

Ingham, J. (1970) 'On Mexican Folk Medicine' *American Anthropologist* 72: 76

d'Irsay, S. (1930) 'Christian Medicine and Science in the Third Century', in *The Journal of Religion*, 10: 515–44

Jansen, G. (1973) *The Doctor–Patient Relationship in an African Tribal Society*, Assen, the Netherlands: Koninklijke van Gorcum

Janzen, J. M. (1978) 'The Comparative Study of Medical Systems as

Changing Social Systems', in *Social Science and Medicine* 12: 121–9
Jaspers, K. (1963) *General Psychopathology*, trans. from the German 7th ed. by J. Hoenig and M. W. Hamilton, Manchester: Manchester University Press
Kafka, F. (1967) *Briefe an Felice*, Frankfurt: Fischer Verlag
Kagan, A. and Levi, L. (1974) 'Health and Environmental-Psychosocial Stimuli: A Review', *Social Science and Medicine* 8: 225
Kaiser, B. L. and Kaiser, I. H. (1974) 'The Challenge of the Women's Movement to American Gynaecology', *American Journal of Obstetrics and Gynaecology*, pp. 652–65
Kane, R. *et al.* (1974) 'Manipulating the Patient: A Comparison of the Effectiveness of Physicians and Chiropractic Care', *Lancet* 1: 1333
Kiritz, S. and Moos, R. (1974) 'Physiological Effects of Social Environments', *Psychosomatic Medicine* 36: 96
Kitzinger, S. (1962) *The Experience of Childbirth*, London: Gollancz
(1972) *The Experience of Childbirth*, Harmondsworth: Penguin Books
(1975) *Some Mothers' Experiences of Induced Labour*, London: National Childbirth Trust
(1979) *Giving Birth: The Parents' Emotions in Childbirth*, 2nd edn, London: Sphere
Kitzinger, S. and Davis, T. A. (eds.) (1978) *The Place of Birth*, Oxford, New York, Toronto: Oxford University Press
Kleinman, A. (1973a) 'Medicine's Symbolic Reality', in *Inquiry* 16: 206–13
(1973b) 'Toward a Comparative Study of Medical Systems: An Integrated Approach to the Study of the Relationship of Medicine to Cultures, *Science, Medicine and Man* 1: 55–65
(1974) 'Cognitive Structures of Traditional Medical Systems', *Ethnomedicine* 3:27
(1975a) 'Social, Cultural and Historical Themes in the Study of Medicine in Chinese Societies: Problems and Prospects for the Comparative Study of Medicine and Psychiatry', in A. Kleinman *et al* (eds.), *Medicine in Chinese Cultures*, Fogarty International Center, NIH, Bethesda, Maryland, pp. 589–657
(1975b) 'Medical and Psychiatric Anthropology and the Study of Traditional Forms of Medicine in Modern Chinese Cultures', *Bulletin of the Institute of Ethnology Academia Sinica* 39: 107
(1975c) 'Explanatory Models in Health Care Relationships', in National Council for International Health, *Health of the Family*, Washington, DC: National Council for International Health, 159–72
(1977) 'Depression, Somatization and the New Cross-cultural Psychiatry', *Social Science and Medicine* 11: 3
(1978a) 'Cultural Construction of Clinical Reality: Comparison of Practitioner–Patient Interactions in Taiwan', in A. Kleinman *et al.* (ed.), *Culture and Healing in Asian Societies*, Cambridge, Mass.: Schenkman
(1978b) 'Concepts and a Model for the Comparison of Medical Systems as Cultural Systems', *Social Science and Medicine* 12 85–93
Kleinman, A., Eisenberg, L. and Good, B. (1978) 'Culture, Illness and Care: Clinical Lessons from Anthropological and Cross-cultural Research', *Annals of Internal Medicine* 88: 251

Kleinman, A. and Sung, L. H. (1976) 'Why Indigenous Practitioners Successfully Heal: Follow-up Studies of Indigenous Healers in Taiwan', paper presented at the Medical Anthropology Workshop on 'The Healing Process', Michigan State University, April 1976, to be published in the Workshop's proceedings

Knight, L. (1978) 'Protect Their Minds Too', *Mind Out* 31: 12–14

Kunstadter, P. (1975) 'The Comparative Anthropological Study of Medical Systems in Society', in A. Kleinman *et al.* (ed.), *Medicine in Chinese Cultures*, Fogarty International Center, NIH, Bethesda, Maryland, 683–96

Langner, T. S. (1962) 'A Twenty-Two Item Screening Score of Psychiatric Symptoms Indicating Impairment', *Journal of Health and Social Behavior* 3: 269

Lasagna, Luis (1970) 'Physician's Behavior Toward the Dying Patient', in O. G. Brim *et al.* (eds.), *The Dying Patient* New York: Russell Sage Foundation

Lazare, A. *et al.* (1975) 'The Customer Approach to Patienthood', *Archs. Gen. Psych* 32: 553

Lebrun, F. (1995) *Les hommes et la mort en Anjou au XVIIe et XVIIIe siècles*, Paris: Flammarion

Leslie, C. (ed.) (1974) 'The Modernization of Asian Medical Systems', in J. Poggie and R. Lynch (eds.), *Rethinking Modernization: Anthropological Perspectives*, Westport, Connecticut: Greenwood Press

   (ed.) (1976) *Asian Medical Systems*, Berkeley: University of California Press

L'Esperance, J. (1977) 'Doctors and Women in Nineteenth-Century Society: Sexuality and Role', in J. Woodward and D. Richards (eds.), *Health Care and Popular Medicine in Nineteenth-Century England: Essays in The Social History of Medicine*, London: Croom Helm

L'Estoile (1958) *Journal de l'Estoile pour le règne de Henri IV*, Tome II, A. Martin (ed.), Paris: Gallimard

Levine, D. (1972) *Wax and Gold: Tradition and Innovation in Ethiopian Culture*, Chicago: University of Chicago Press

Levitt, R. (1976) *The Reorganised National Health Service*, London: Croom Helm

Lewis, G. (1975) *Knowledge of Illness in a Sepik Society*, London: The Athlone Press

   (1976) 'A View of Sickness in New Guinea', in J. B. Loudon (ed.), *Social Anthropology and Medicine*, London: Academic Press

   (1980) *Day of Shining Red*, Cambridge: Cambridge University Press

Lewis, I. M. (1971) *Ecstatic Religion: An Anthropological Study of Spirit Possession and Shamanism*, London: Penguin Books

Lewis, S. R., Goolishian, H. A., Wolf, C. W., Lynch, J. B. and Blocker, T. G. J. (1963) 'Psychological Studies in Burn Patients', *Plastic and Reconstructive Surgery* 31: 323

Lindemann, E. (1944) 'Symptomatology and Management of Acute Grief', *American Journal of Psychiatry* 101: 141

Lipowski, Z. J. (1973) 'Psychosomatic Medicine in a Changing Society', *Comprehensive Psychiatry* 14: 203

Littlewood, R. and Lipsedge, M. (1982) *Aliens and Alienists: Ethnic Minorities and Psychiatry*, Harmondsworth: Penguin Books

Long, R. T. and Cope, O. (1961) 'Emotional Problems of Burned Children', *New England Journal of Medicine* 264: 1121

MacCormack, C. (1982) 'Traditional Medicine, Folk Medicine and Alternative Medicine', in T. Vaskilampi and C. P. MacCormack (eds.), *Folk Medicine and Health Culture: Role of Folk Medicine in Modern Health Care*, Proceedings of the Nordic Research Symposium 27–8 August 1981, Kuopio, Finland, Kuopio: The University of Kuopio

Macintyre, S. (1976) 'Who Wants Babies? The Social Construction of Instincts', in D. Barker and S. Allen (eds.), *Sexual Divisions and Society: Process and Change*, London: Tavistock Publications

—— (1976) 'Obstetric Routines in Antenatal Care', paper given at the British Sociological Association Medical Sociology Conference, York

Marsh, G. and Kaim-Caudle, P. (1976) *Team Care in General Practice*, London: Croom Helm

Mauss, M. (1950) 'Les techniques du corps', in M. Mauss *Sociologie et Anthropologie*, Paris: Presses Universitaires de France

McCorkle, T. (1961) 'Chiropractic: A Deviant Theory of Treatment in Contemporary Western Culture', *Human Organisation*: 20: 20

McKinlay, J. (1973) 'Social Networks, Lay Consultation and Help-Seeking Behavior, *Social Forces* 51: 275–92

Mead, M. and Newton, N. (1967) 'Cultural Patterning of Perinatal Behavior', in S. Richardson and A. Guttmacher (eds.), *Childbearing: Its Social and Psychological Aspects*, Baltimore: Williams and Wilkins

Messing, S. (1968) Interdigitation of Mystical and Physical Healing in Ethiopia: Toward a Theory of Medical Anthropology', *Behavioral Science Notes* 3: 87

Middleton, J. (1960) *Lugbara Religion*, Oxford: Oxford University Press

Miller, E. J. and Gwynne, G. V. (1972) *A Life Apart: A Pilot Study of Residential Institutions for the Physically Handicapped and the Young Chronic Sick*, London: Tavistock

Mitchell, W. E. (1977) 'Changing Others: The Anthropological Study of Therapeutic Systems', *Medical Anthropology Newsletter* 8 (3), 15–19

Mnecke, M. A. (1976) 'Health Care systems as Socialising Agents: Childbearing the North Thai and Western Ways', *Social Science and Medicine* 10: 377–83

Montaigne, M. de (1603) *The Essays*, trans. John Florio, Scolar Press facsimile, Menston: The Scolar Press, 1969

Morrell, D. C. (1971) 'Expressions of Morbidity in General Practice', *British Medical Journal* 2: 454

—— (1972) 'Symptom Interpretation in General Practice', *Journal of the Royal College of General Practitioners* 22: 297–309

Murphy, J. M. (1964) 'Psychotherapeutic Aspects of Shamanism on St Lawrence Island, Alaska', in A. Kiev (ed.), *Magic, Faith and Healing*, New York: Free Press

Nathanson, C. A. (1975) 'Illness and the Feminine Role', *Social Science and Medicine* 9: 57

—— (1977) 'Sex, Illness and Medical Care', *Social Science and Medicine* 11 (1),

13–25

Nott, P. N. and Cutts, S. (1982) Validation of the 30-Item General Health Questionnaire in Post-partum Women, *Psychological Medicine* 12: 409–13

Nuyens, Y. (1969) *Sociologie en gezondheidsborg (Sociology and Health Care)*, Antwerp, Netherlands: Boekhandel

Oakley, A. (1975) 'The Trap of Medicalised Motherhood', *New Society* 34: 639

— (1976) 'Wisewoman and Medicine Man: Changes in the Management of Childbirth', in J. Mitchell and A. Oakley (eds.), *The Rights and Wrongs of Women*, Harmondsworth: Penguin Books

— (1977) 'Cross Cultural Practice', in T. Chard and M. Richards (eds.), *Benefits and Hazards of the New Obstetrics*, London: Heinemann

— (1979) *Becoming a Mother*, Oxford: Martin Robertson

— (1980) *Women Confined: Towards a Sociology of Childbirth*, Oxford: Martin Robertson

— (1984) *The Captured Womb: A History of Pregnant Women*, New York: Basil Blackwell

Obeyesekere, G. (1976) 'The Impact of Ayurvedic Ideas on the Culture and the Individual in Sri Lanka', in C. Leslie (ed.), *Asian Medical Systems*, Berkeley and Los Angeles: University of California Press, pp. 201–26

O'Brien, M. (1977) 'Home and Hospital: A Comparison of the Experiences of Mothers Having Home and Hospital Confinements', paper given at the Second Seminar on Human Relations and Obstetric Practice, 30 July [1977] University of Warwick

Ollstein, R. N., Symonds, F. C. and Crikelair, G. F. (1968) 'Current Concepts of Burn Injury', *New York Journal of Medicine* 68: 1708

Papanek, H. (1973) Purdah: Separate Worlds and Symbolic Shelter, *Comparative Studies in Society and History* 15: 289–325

Parekh, B. (1974) 'The Spectre of Self-Consciousness', in B. Parekh (ed.), *Colour, Culture and Consciousness*, London: Allen and Unwin

Pearson, M. (1983) 'The Politics of Ethnic Minority Health Studies', *Radical Community Medicine* 16 (Winter), 34–44

Peter, J. P. (1971) 'Les mots et les objets de la maladie', *Revue Historique*, 499

Phillips, A. and Rakusen, R. (eds.) (1978) *Our Bodies Ourselves: A Health Book by and for Women*, British Edition of the Boston Women's Health Book Collective volume, Harmondsworth: Penguin Books

Pill, R. and Stott, N. (1982) 'Concepts of Illness Causation and Responsibility: Some Preliminary Data from a Sample of Working-Class Mothers', *Social Science and Medicine* 16: 43–52

Platonov, K. I. (1959) *The Word as a Physiological and Therapeutic Factor*, Moscow: Foreign Language Publication House

Podgorecki, A. (1968) 'Affecting Individual and the Social Group' (in Polish) *Studia Socjologiczne*, pp. 3–4

Polgar, S. (1968) 'Health', in the *International Encyclopaedia of the Social Sciences*, New York: Macmillan and Free Press

Pollock, K. (1984) *Mind and Matter: A Study of Conceptions of Health and Illness Among Three Groups of English Families with Particular Refer-*

ence to *Multiple Sclerosis, Schizophrenia and 'Nervous Breakdown'*, PhD thesis, Cambridge

Powles, J. (1973) 'On the Limitations of Modern Medicine', *Science Medicine and Man* 1 (1), 1–30

Rack, P. (1982) *Race, Culture and Mental Disorder*, London: Tavistock Publications

Rathbone, B. (1973) *Focus on New Mothers: A Study of Antenatal Classes*, Royal College of Nursing

Reberioux, M. (1980) 'L'ouvrière', in J. P. Aron (ed.), *Misérable et glorieuse: la femme au XIXe siècle*, Paris: Fayard, pp. 59–78

Rich, A. (1977) *Of Woman Born: Motherhood as Experience and Institution*, London: Virago

Richards, M. (1974) 'The One-Day-Old Deprived Child', *New Scientist*, 2 March, 820–2

Riese, W. (1950) *La Pensée Causale en médicine*, Paris: PUF

Riethe, P. (1974) *Hildegard von Bingen*, Salzburg: Otto Muller Verlag

Roche, D. (1981) *Le Peuple de Paris: essai sur la culture populaire au XVIIIe siècle*, Paris: Aubier-Montaigne (transl. as (1986) *The People of Paris: an Essay in Popular Culture in the 18th century*, Leamington Spa: Berg)

Rosen, G. (1977a) 'Wirtschafts- und Sozialpolitik in der Entwicklung des öffentlichen Gesundheitswesens', in E. Lesky (ed.), *Sozial-Medizin Darmstadt*, 26–61

(1977b) 'Merkantlismus und Gesundheitspolitik im Franzosischen Denken des 18 Jahrhunderts', in E. Lesky (ed.), *Social-Medizin Darmstadt*, 62–93

Rousseau, J. J. (1967) 'Les Confessions oeuvres complètes', *Edition de la Pléiade* 1: 247

Royal College of Obstetricians and Gynaecologists (1975) *The Management of Labour*, Proceedings of the Third Study Group

Rubel, A. J. (1964) 'The Epidemiology of a Folk Illness: Susto in Hispanic America', *Ethnology* 3: 268

Rutter, J. B. (1966) 'Generalised Expectations for Internal versus External Control of Reinforcement', *Psychological Monograph* 50 (1)

Ruzek, S. B. (1978) *The Women's Health Movement: Feminist Alternatives to Medical Control*, New York: Praeger.

Saifullah-Khan, V. (1976) 'Purdah in the British Situation', in D. Barker and S. Allen (eds.), *Dependence and Exploitation in Work and Marriage*, London: Longmans

Salzberger, R. C. (1976) 'Cancer: Assumptions and Reality Concerning Ignorance and Fear', in J. B. Loudon (ed.), *Social Anthropology and Medicine*, ASA Monograph 13, London: Academic Press

Scheff, T. J. (1963) 'Decision Rules, Types of Error and Their Consequences in Medical Diagnosis', *Behavioral Science* 8: 97–105

Schmale, A. *et al.* (1970) 'Current Concepts of Psychosomatic Medicine', in O. Hill (ed.), *Modern Trends in Psychosomatic Medicine*, New York: Appleton-Century-Crofts

Schofield, J. (1981) 'Behind the Veil: The Mental Health of Asian Women in Britain', *Health Visitor* 54 (April, May, June)

Schwartz, L. R. (1969) 'The Hierarchy of Resort in Curative Practice', *Journal of Health and Social Behavior* 10

Scully, D. and Bart, P. (1972–73) 'A Funny Thing Happened on the Way to the Orifice: Women in Gynaecology Textbooks', *American Journal of Sociology* 78 (4), 1045

Seabrook, J. (1973) *The Unprivileged: A Hundred Years of Family Life and Tradition in a Working-Class Street*, Harmondsworth, Penguin Books

Seijas, M. (1973) 'An Approach to the Study of the Medical Aspects of Culture', *Current Anthropology* 14: 544

Selassie, T. B. (1971) 'An Ethiopian Medical Text-Book Written by Gerzazmac Gabrawald Aragahan Daga Damot', *Journal of Ethiopian Studies* 9: 95

Sharma, U. M. (1980) 'Purdah and Public Space', in A. de Souza (ed.), *Women in Contemporary India and South Asia*, Manohar

Sigerest, H. E. (1943) *Civilization and Disease*, Chicago and London: University of Chicago Press

(1951) *A History of Medicine*, New York: Oxford University Press

Silver, G. A. (1963) *Family Medical Care*, London: Oxford University Press

Singer, C. (1926) 'The Historical Relations of Religion and Science', in J. Needham (ed.), *Religion and Reality*, London

Sokolowska, M. (1971) 'The Societal Need for a Personal Doctor', paper prepared for the Fourth World Conference on Medical Education

(1973) 'Two Basic Types of Medical Orientation', *Social Science and Medicine* 7: 807–15

et al. (1975) 'The Sociology of Health of Polish Society: Trends and Current State of Research', in M. Archer (ed.), 'Problems of Current Sociological Research', *Current Sociology* 23

Sontag, S. (1979) *Illness as Metaphor*, New York: Random House

Snow, L. (1974) 'Folk Medical Beliefs and Their Implications for Care of Patients', *Annals of Internal Medicine* 81: 82

Stacey, M. (1978) 'Sociological Concepts of Health and Disease and Critiques of Such Concepts', paper given at SSRC Sheffield Symposium.

(1980) 'Realities for Change in Child Health Care: Existing Patterns and Future Possibilities', *British Medical Journal* 280: 1512

(1982) 'Changing Public and Domestic Domains', unpub. set of diagrams, mimeo, University of Warwick

(forthcoming) *The Sociology of Health and Healing*, London: Allen and Unwin

Stimson, G. and Webb B. (1975) *Going to See the Doctor: The Consultation Process in General Practice*, London: Routledge and Kegan Paul

Stoller Shaw, N. (1974) *Forced Labor: Maternity Care in the United States*, New York: Pergamon Press

Strelcyn, S. (1975) 'Un magicien grecen Ethiopie, *Journal Asiatique* 234: 175

Strong, P. (1979) 'Sociological Imperialism and the Profession of Medicine: A Critical Examination of the Thesis of Medical Imperialism', *Social Science and Medicine* 13A: 199–215

Sudhoff, K. (1907–78) 'Phillip Begardi und sein Index Sanitatis', in *Archiv für Geschichte der Medizin* 1: 102–21

Sydenham, T. (1676) 'Medical Observations Concerning the History and Cure of Acute Diseases', 3rd ed., in *The Works of Thomas Sydenham*, trans. R. G. Latham, vol. 1, The Sydenham Society, 1848

Tambiah, S. J. (1968) 'The Ideology of Merit and Social Correlates of Buddhism in a Thai Village', in E. R. Leach (ed.), *Dialectic in Practical Religion*, Cambridge Papers in Social Anthropology, no. 5, Cambridge: Cambridge University Press

(1973) 'Form and Meaning of Magical Acts: A Point of View', in R. Horton and R. Finnegan (eds.), *Modes of Thought: Essays on Thinking in Western and non-Western Societies*, London: Faber and Faber

Tax, B. (ed.) (1984) 'Proceedings of Workshop on Lay Culture and Illness Behaviour', Nijmegen: University of Nijmegen, mimeo

Teichner, W. (1968) 'Interaction of Behavioural and Physiological Stress Reactions', *Psychological Review* 75: 271

Thomas, K. (1970) 'The Relevance of Social Anthropology to the Historical Study of English Witchcraft', in M. Douglas (ed.), *Witchcraft Confessions and Accusations*, London: Tavistock Publications

(1971) *Religion and the Decline of Magic*, New York: Scribners

Thomas, L. (1977) 'Medicine in America', *TV Guide*, December, 25–6

Trempé, R. (1981) 'Les Luttes des ouvriers mineurs français pour la création des caisses de retraits au XIX siècle', Colloque Developpement et effets sociaux des politiques de la vieillesse dans les pays industrialises, Paris, July 1981

Turner, V. (1964) 'An Ndembu Doctor in Practice', in A. Kiev (ed.) *Magic, Faith and Healing*, London: The Free Press of Glencoe, Collier-Macmillan

(1966) 'Colour Classification in Ndembu Ritual: A Problem in Primitive Classification', in M. Banton (ed.), *Anthropological Approaches to the Study of Religion*, Association of Social Anthropologists Monograph no. 3, London: Tavistock Publications

(1967a) *The Forest of Symbols*, Ithaca: Cornell University Press

(1967b) *The Ritual Process*, Chicago: Aldine

(1968) *The Drums of Affliction: A Study of Religious Processes among the Ndembu of Zambia*, London: Oxford University Press

Tylor, E. B. (1873) *Primitive Culture; Researchers into the Development of Mythology, Philosophy, Religion, Language, Art and Custom*, London: John Murray

Valentin, M. (1978) *Travail des hommes et savants oubliés: histoire de la médecine du travail de la sécurité et l'ergonomie*, Paris: Docis

Waddington, I. (1985) *The Medical Profession in the Industrial Revolution*, London: Gill and Macmillan

Wadsworth, M. E. J., Butterfield, W. J. H. and Blaney, R. (1971) *Health and Sickness the Choice of Treatment*, London: Tavistock Publications

Wallston, K., Wallston, B. S. and Derellis, R. (1978) 'Development of the Multidimensional Health Locus of Control (MHLC) Scales', *Health Education Monograph* 6:2

Weisz, A. E. (1967) 'Psychotherapeutic Support of Burned Patients', *Mod-*

313

ern Treatment, 4: 1291

Werner, H. and Kaplan, B. (1967) *Symbol Formation*, New York: Wiley

White, A. D. (1897) *A History of the Warfare of Science with Theology*, New York: Appleton

Wilkes, E. (1974) 'The Treatment of Cough in General Practice', *Prescribers Journal* 14: 98–103

Williams, R. G. A. (1983) 'Concepts of Health: An Analysis of Lay Logic', *Sociology* 17 (2) 183–205

Wilson, A. (1978) *Finding a Voice*, London: Virago

Wollheim, R. (1971) *Sigmund Freud*, New York: Viking

WHO (1975) *Schizophrenia: A Multinational Study*, WHO Public Health Paper, no. 63, Geneva

— (1979) *Schizophrenia: An International Follow-Up Study*, New York, Chichester, Brisbane, Toronto

Young, A. (1975a) 'Why Amhara Get *Kureynya*: Sickness and Possession in an Ethiopian *Zar* Cult', *American Ethnologist* 2: 567

— (1975b) 'Magic as a Quasi Profession: The Organisation of Magic and Magical Healing in Ethiopia', *Ethnology* 14: 245

— (1976a) 'Some Implications of Medical Belief and Practices for Social Anthropology', *American Anthropologist* 78: 5–24

— (1976b) 'Internalizing and Externalizing Medical Belief Systems: An Ethiopian Example', *Social Science and Medicine* 10 (3–4), 147–56

Young, J. Z. (1971) *An Introduction to the Study of Man*, New York: Oxford University Press

Zola, I. K. (1972a) 'The Concept of Trouble and Sources of Medical Assistance', *Social Science and Medicine* 6: 673

— (1972b) 'Studying the Decision to See a Doctor', in Z. J. Lipowski (ed.), *Advances in Psychosomatic Medicine* 8: 216

— (1975) 'Medicine as an Institution of Social Control', in C. Cox and A. Mead (eds.), *A Sociology of Medical Practice*, London: Collier-Macmillan

About the Contributors

Joan Ablon, PhD, is Professor and Chairperson of the Medical Anthropology Program in the Departments of Epidemiology and International Health and Psychiatry at the University of California in San Francisco.

Caroline Currer, PhD, is an Associate Fellow in the Department of Sociology, University of Warwick.

Mark G. Field, PhD, is a Professor in the Department of Sociology at Boston University; Fellow in the Russian Research Center and Lecturer in the School of Public Health at Harvard University; and Assistant Sociologist, Department of Psychiatry, Massachusetts General Hospital, Boston.

Hilary Graham, PhD, is Head of the Department of Applied Social Studies at Lanchester Polytechnic.

Cecil G. Helman, MBChB, Dip. Soc. Anthrop., is Lecturer in General Practice at the Middlesex Hospital Medical School and Honorary Research Fellow in the Department of Anthropology, University College, London.

Claudine Herzlich, PhD, is Director de Recherches at CNRS, Centre d'Etude des Mouvements Sociaux, Paris.

Alphonse d'Houtaud PhD, is researcher at the 'Institut National de la Santé et de la Recherche, Médical', Nancy, France; and Director of the 'Cellule de Sociologie et d'Economie de la Santé', Faculté de Mécine de l'Université de Nancy. I.

Arthur Kleinman, MD, PhD, is Professor in the Departments of Anthropology at Harvard University, and Psychiatry at Harvard Medical School.

Gilbert Lewis, BM, MRCP, PhD, is Lecturer in the Department of Social Anthropology at the University of Cambridge.

Ann Oakley, PhD, is Deputy Director of the Thomas Coram Research Unit of the University of London's Institute of Education.

Janine Pierret, PhD, is Chargée de Recherches at CNRS, Centre de Recherdie sur le Bien-Etre, Paris.

Roisin Pill, PhD, is Senior Research Fellow in the Department of General Practice at the University of Wales College of Medicine.

Jeremy Seabrook, BA, is a journalist and writer.

Magdalena Sokolowska, PhD, is Professor at the Institute of Philosophy and Sociology in Warsaw.

Meg Stacey, B. Sc. (Econ.), is Professor of Sociology at the University of Warwick.

Nigel Stott, FRCP, MRCGP, is Senior Lecturer in the Department of General Practice at the University of Wales College of Medicine.

Paul U. Unschuld, PhD, MD, habil., PhD habil., MPH, is Professor in the Institute for the History of Medicine of Munich University.

Allan Young, PhD, is an Associate Professor at the Department of Anthropology, Cape Western Reserve University, Cleveland, Ohio.

Index

Author

Index

Subject

Index